INTIMATE ASSOCIATIONS:
THE LAW AND CULTURE OF AMERICAN FAMILIES

The rise in divorce, cohabitation, single parenthood, and same-sex partnerships, along with an increase in surrogacy, adoption, and assisted reproductive technologies, have led to many and diverse configurations of families, or intimate associations. J. Herbie DiFonzo, a law professor, and Ruth C. Stern, an attorney and social worker, chart these trends over the past several decades and investigate their social, legal, and economic implications.

The fluidity of modern families may give adults more personal choices, but, DiFonzo and Stern argue, it comes at the price of economic stability and social well-being. Drawing on a wealth of social science data, they show that, by a number of measures, children of married parents fare better than children in a household formed by cohabiting adults. This is not to condemn nontraditional families but, rather, to point out that society and, particularly, the law do not yet adequately provide for the needs of such families. DiFonzo and Stern applaud the ways in which courts and legislatures are beginning to replace rigid concepts of marriage and parenthood with the more flexible concept of "functional" family roles. In the conclusion, they call for a legal system that can adapt to the continually changing reality of family life.

J. Herbie DiFonzo is Professor of Law at the Maurice A. Deane School of Law at Hofstra University. Before devoting himself to teaching, he practiced law for 20 years. He is the author of *Beneath the Fault Line: The Popular and Legal Culture of Divorce in Twentieth-Century America*.

Ruth C. Stern is an attorney and social worker. She has worked with families in crisis and represented parents and children in numerous family court proceedings.

Intimate Associations

THE LAW AND CULTURE OF AMERICAN FAMILIES

J. Herbie DiFonzo and
Ruth C. Stern

THE UNIVERSITY OF MICHIGAN PRESS
ANN ARBOR

Copyright © by the University of Michigan 2013
All rights reserved

This book may not be reproduced, in whole or in part, including illustrations, in any form (beyond that copying permitted by Sections 107 and 108 of the U.S. Copyright Law and except by reviewers for the public press), without written permission from the publisher.

Published in the United States of America by
The University of Michigan Press
Manufactured in the United States of America
♾ Printed on acid-free paper

2016 2015 2014 2013   4 3 2 1

A CIP catalog record for this book is available from the British Library.

Library of Congress Cataloging-in-Publication Data

DiFonzo, J. Herbie.
    Intimate associations : the law and culture of American families / J. Herbie DiFonzo, Ruth C. Stern.
      pages   cm
    Includes index.
    ISBN 978-0-472-11730-7 (hardback) — ISBN 978-0-472-03538-0 (paper) — ISBN 978-0-472-02942-6 (e-book)
    1. Domestic relations—United States.   2. Human reproductive technology—Law and legislation—United States.   3. Family policy—United States.   I. Stern, Ruth C., 1953–   II. Title.
    KF505.D54   2013
    346.7301'5—dc23
                                                                      2013025444

CONTENTS

	Acknowledgments	vii
	Introduction	1
CHAPTER 1.	American Marriages Yesterday	9
CHAPTER 2.	How Marriage Became Optional: Cohabitation, Gay Marriage, and the Continuing Role of Gender	24
CHAPTER 3.	Luxury Goods: The Well-Being of Families	43
CHAPTER 4.	The Children of *Baby M*: Alternative Reproductive Technologies and the Remaking of Contemporary Families	64
CHAPTER 5.	Parenthood in the 21st Century: The Evolving Functional Norms	85
CHAPTER 6.	Unsafe Havens, Unplanned Children, and Future Generations	109
CHAPTER 7.	The Uses of the Law for Contemporary Families	128
	Conclusion: Echoes in a Canyon	148
	Notes	151
	Index	227

ACKNOWLEDGMENTS

We wrote this book to appeal to a broad range of readers, and our blend of legal and social science analysis reflects the capacious dimensions of the issues involving American families. We want to thank Patricia Kasting, law librarian extraordinaire at Hofstra University's School of Law, who cheerfully and quickly provided everything we requested and who often sent us helpful material we did not even know existed. Hofstra's School of Law and its then dean, Nora Demleitner, provided Herbie with a sabbatical and with summer grants for the research. Thanks also go to Andrew Schepard for sharing his insightful views on all aspects of family law, as well as to Herbie's research assistants in the course of this project: Danielle Passano, Angela Burton, Lauren Krisa, Ashley Lane, and Elisa Rosenthal.

Portions of chapter 1 have appeared in *The Winding Road from Form to Function: A Brief History of Contemporary Marriage*, 21 J. AM. ACAD. MATRIMONIAL L. 1 (2008). An earlier version of chapter 2 appeared in *How Marriage Became Optional: Cohabitation, Gender, and the Emerging Functional Norms*, 8 RUTGERS J.L. & PUB. POL'Y 521 (2011). Finally, parts of chapters 4 and 5 have appeared in *The Children of Baby M.*, 39 CAPITAL U. L. REV. 345 (2011), and in *Breaking the Mold and Picking Up the Pieces: Rights of Parenthood and Parentage in Nontraditional Families*, 51 FAM. CT. REV. 104 (2013).

Introduction

The early 1960s was our last chance to take a snapshot of what we believed to be the typical American family: husband, wife, and their two or more children. By the end of the decade, the composition would begin to blur with bodies in motion—spouses splitting up and often remarrying, children transported from one household to another, the coming and going of stepparents and stepsiblings. As we progressed toward the end of the century, the family photo looked even more unfamiliar—featuring same-sex couples, many with children; single and married individuals with offspring created by reproductive technology; and cohabiting couples either moving toward marriage or spinning away from each other in fluid, unstable arrangements trailing children. By the 21st century, the family portrait would never again depict a single, recognizable entity. Instead, it had morphed into a veritable gallery of unconventional relationships.

Family structures have crumbled in places and arisen renewed in others. Marriage has declined in relevance, pushed aside by intimate relationships that are less stable and permanent, chiefly cohabitation. At the same time, the fight to formalize same-sex unions reaffirms the worth and allure of commitment and constancy. Children are born both inside and outside of marriage, with vastly different consequences. Nonmarital births are frequently mistimed or unintended, with ties between parents often fragile and ephemeral. Children of these unions, much like children of divorce, risk poverty, dislocation, and the strain of adjusting to reconstituted family arrangements. Relations with stepparents and stepsiblings are too often fleeting, not always harmonious, and likely to be legally ambiguous.

Other would-be parents are creating offspring with the help of sperm and egg donors and surrogate child bearers. Not only are these children planned, prized, and paid for, but they are sometimes fought over by the various participants who brought them into being. Nontraditional families, whether born of technology or nonmarital partnerships, present new complexities in the apportioning of parental rights and responsibilities. Old presumptions of paternity and even maternity no longer apply, and biological ties are no longer strictly determinative.

To keep pace with cultural change, family law is shifting its focus from biological to functional norms. Today, in the resolution of legal disputes in blended and upended families, nature is beginning to yield to nurture. Thus, biological parents who have not taken a significant role in raising their children are losing court battles to adults with no genetic tie but with an actual, established parent-child bond. Regardless of marital status, sexual preference, or biological relationship, what matters most is whether the adult has functioned as a parent in the child's life.

Questions arise as to whether the rights and benefits of marriage should be shared among the less formal unions. In terms of their stability, security, and durability, all intimate associations are not created equal. Still, the law must take these families as it finds them, awarding parental status, custody, support, and visitation in furtherance of their welfare and survival. To do otherwise would be to earmark legal remedies based solely on outmoded notions of what families should look like. But to accord equal rights and privileges to all domestic unions, regardless of form, ignores the different levels of commitment that go into building them. Married individuals entrust their futures to each other in ways that most cohabiting couples do not. Whether by choice, economic constraints, or both, the decision to cohabit and bear children out of wedlock sidesteps long-term bonding and responsibility. Formally committed partners evince at least the intent to take care of each other through good times and bad. By contrast, those in informal arrangements that are less stable are more apt to place their families at risk of becoming public charges. In this light, rewarding uncommitted couples with the same legal, social, and governmental benefits allocated to married partners seems illogical and unwarranted. At what point, however, do nontraditional families so closely mirror conventional unions in the ties that bind and in their devotion to children that marital status ceases to be the deciding factor in shaping social or legal outcomes?

Riddles such as these abound in contemporary family issues. At times, in our current century's domestic life, legal and social realities seem to beg a formal introduction to each other. In this book, we trace the parallel developments in law and culture that have reconfigured America's families. In both law and culture, however, a critical tension has emerged. Families are now viewed as intimate associations, free of the restraints of traditional marriage. But in reconstituting the family, these informal unions have proved less capable at accomplishing its central task: creating a stable, long-lasting framework for domestic happiness and child rearing. Cohabitation is far more popular and far less permanent than marriage, with adverse consequences to the parties and to their offspring. At the same time, a legal system that pretends that the majority of domestic unions are exceptions to marriage is engaged in wishful and harmful rationalization. Neither law nor culture can afford to elevate the erstwhile at the expense of actual families.

One of our principal objectives is to reframe family law so that it properly addresses the way 21st-century American families constitute themselves and live out their lives. Our current system reflects an outdated set of rules privileging marriage and biological connection to children. The trends toward cohabitation and de facto parenthood are strong and getting stronger, and we propose that the formal legal system be adjusted to reflect the actual shape of today's families. At the same time, it is critical to point out that the looser and less-established forms of American families are not conducive to family stability or children's welfare. The social science research on these points is overwhelming: nonmarital unions are not as healthy and long-lasting as marital ones, and children do not benefit from the parade of partners that often characterizes cohabitating relationships.

Across the country, a crazy-quilt pattern of legal norms now governs the resolution of family disputes. We argue that greater coherence is sorely needed, but we do not want to claim too much on this score: the relationship between legal and social change is far from linear. Neither law nor society is "in charge" of the process of transformation; indeed, it is sometimes difficult to discern which is the driver and which the driven. The legal system often tracks social change, although it provides a rather distorted mirror of social reality when it finally arrives at a statutory or judicial pronouncement on a particular issue. At the same time, law often has a pedagogical value, and so the regularization of legal norms we propose should have a positive impact, at least in steering society toward a consensus on the true scope and substance of today's family law issues. All too often, as this book documents, the legal system has frustrated the intent of those who created a particular family, by resolving the contest according to legal norms to which the family did not subscribe at the outset.

The current dilemmas of family life have their visible roots in recent history, and we begin this book with an exploration of American families in the latter half of the 20th century. In chapter 1, "American Marriages Yesterday," we note the aspects that have dramatically changed as well as those that have stubbornly resisted adaptation. The 1950s marriage was not at all traditional, and under its veneer of domestic tranquility, the seeds of major cultural disaffections were germinating. These would come to full flower in the decades that followed. That the ideal of marriage was subject to negotiation may be seen in the era's two-sided view of conjugal bliss. Marriage was wildly popular, yet divorce came to be much more widely accepted, even in the teeth of a formal divorce regime that required proof of fault. Indeed, the steep rise in divorce rates began in the decade before no-fault divorce. This simultaneous idealization of marriage and rejection of its lifelong premise establishes a theme that will characterize much of our contemporary attitude toward family life. We still look to marriage as a noble venture, even while many of us entrust our families to arrangements that are far less stable.

Chapter 2, "How Marriage Became Optional: Cohabitation, Gay Marriage, and the Continuing Role of Gender," relates how the bedrock institution of marriage dissolved. Through much of the 20th century, family life was subject to common-law rules that regarded marriage as the sine qua non of family formation. But in the last half century, the legal regime governing domestic institutions has yielded a considerable amount of power from the state to the people it used to regulate. American culture has become a hothouse for domestic experimentation, and family law has struggled to retain coherence and control. The era that gave birth to the baby boomers could not have imagined de facto parents, adoption by same-sex couples, the universal availability of effective contraception, or the enhanced status and independence of women. Nor could the *Leave It to Beaver* generation have foreseen that unmarried adults and their dependents would one day comprise a majority of households. These developments reflect a pragmatic approach to marriage and its alternatives, as well as a distinct shift in legal norms from form to function.

Domestic life in America has never been simple: the major cultural forces that dissolved the primacy of marriage need to be measured alongside the current movement to legalize same-sex marriage. Gender also continues its dominant role in our relationships, no matter what shape our intimate associations take. Ironically, as Americans have frequently chosen alternatives to marriage, they have retained the *ideal* of marriage. But cohabitation is not a fair exchange for marriage. Despite the near ubiquity of cohabiting unions, they often arise by happenstance and are sustained, if at all, by inertia and ambivalence. Unless they are formed as a prelude to marriage and unless this objective is realized in a reasonable amount of time, cohabiting relationships drift toward dissolution. Some long-term cohabitants do marry. But the traits and habits that drew them to live out of wedlock do not serve them well in alliances that are more cohesive and mutually reinforcing.

What might serve these relationships better is the subject of chapter 3, "Luxury Goods: The Well-Being of Families." It turns out that the recipe is both simple and yet more elusive by the day. Two live-in parents, a stable home, and a quantum of economic security—these were once both the premise and promise of marriage. But the social and economic forces that combined to make marriage optional have taken their toll on family well-being. In a withering economy and a job market that increasingly favors the educated, many couples are ill prepared for total, long-lasting commitment. Unstable partnerships provoke even more emotional and financial insecurity, sweeping children along in their wake. Marriage, meanwhile, which is demonstrably better for the health and welfare of families, has become the province of the well educated and well heeled. In a previous era, many of today's working- and middle-class cohabiters might have married. But a sense of financial inadequacy proves a powerful inhibitor, especially in a culture grown more and more materialistic. Cohabiting couples might ponder the option of marriage, but they put it off until the day when they can show they have economically arrived—by procuring savings, a mortgage, or the means for a lavish wedding. Marriage assumes a near-iconic status, and cohabitants resemble new age cargo cultists, scanning the horizon for the ship that will bring them wealth and happiness.

Chapter 4, "The Children of *Baby M*: Alternative Reproductive Technologies and the Remaking of Contemporary Families," begins with a discussion of the seminal 1988 *Baby M* case and explores the reproductive demographics of the succeeding decades. Despite the fears expressed in *Baby M*, the empirical evidence has failed to find that surrogacy and assisted reproductive technology (ART) convert women into childbearing machines and children into commodities. These reproductive practices are a reality for millions, and courts and lawmakers must come to terms with them.

But technology always develops faster than law, and in the reproductive area, neither statutes nor court decisions have kept pace with the rapid transformation of parentage. A market in surrogacy has emerged, and parenthood is now achievable by many who would have been biologically or socially excluded in the past. Marriage, sex, and reproduction have become independent variables in the family equation: none is necessarily linked to the others. The spreading use of ART has pushed the legal system away from the domains of biology and into a more functional approach. Caution is nonetheless essential. We have learned that solid maternal bonding is less dependent on genetic or gestational relationships than on a strong desire for parenthood. However, the children of ART require greater attention and sensitivity to their need to know more about their parentage. Chapter 4 takes a close look at participants in this brave new family world—the gestational surrogates, the donors of genetic material, and the children conceived through ART.

What about the parents? Chapter 5, "Parenthood in the 21st Century: The Evolving Functional Norms," considers the fact that children are increasingly born into families started by adult partners who bear little resemblance to the married heterosexual dyad at the heart of the common law. Neither a marital frame nor a biological one adequately fits these new families. If family law is to encompass the new mainstream of American domestic units, it needs to expand its scope and modify its terminology. Contemporary families have arranged themselves along a wide arc of designs, and their pathways of emotional and financial interdependence are more telling as guides to their structure than are blood relationship or marital status. But when these families face a significant conflict, they turn to a legal system often oblivious of their existence or unwilling to accept their validity as a family. Some courts are recognizing that the legal markers of parenthood have undergone metamorphosis. But many others insist on applying outdated legal tools intended for a family built exclusively on biology or adoption. Legislatures are even slower to expand the legal discourse to include modern families. In light of the inapplicability—or, in some cases, sheer absence—of statutory guidance for resolving these new parentage issues, many courts are forced to craft equitable remedies in order to properly allocate parental rights and obligations.

What happens when a court must decide parenthood in a family consisting of two lesbian partners and the biological child of one of them, when the birth of that child was planned by both women and the child was raised jointly by both as full coequal parents? Chapter 5 tells the story of Julia,

Melissa, and Jacob, an actual North Carolina case illustrating the problematic parameters of parenthood today for many unmarried same-sex couples. And what happens when an unmarried heterosexual couple constructs a family through ART? The story of Cindy, Charles, and the triplets in chapter 5 details the unfortunate battle over parentage in a contemporary Tennessee case. Together, these two accounts from the parenthood frontier reveal the need to incorporate functional parenthood into our system of family law.

The fluidity of American living arrangements creates novel, little-anticipated avenues for redefining parent-child relationships. Cohabitation, the dramatic increase in the number of stepfamilies, the spread of assisted reproductive technology and gestational surrogacy, and the increase in same-sex couples raising children have all contributed to the many-hued palette that currently etches American family life. But these innovations come at a cost. In chapter 6, "Unsafe Havens, Unplanned Children, and Future Generations," we discuss how social change is not always progressive but sometimes reactive and counterproductive. As an increasingly caustic economy eats away at employment opportunities for the working and middle classes, America's families are fast becoming either rich or poor. Unplanned births out of wedlock exacerbate financial and relationship instability. What is worse, today's families are so socially, educationally, and economically imperiled that their vulnerabilities will likely permeate the next generation. Stable families may readily be found among the educated and affluent; but the friable nature of domestic unions among the less educated and the poor grinds away at the ideal of families as safe harbors. The disappearance of the middle class not only is creating an income polarity but threatens to divide America's privileged from the rest of society by access to family well-being. Yet marriage offers no magic cure for these social ills. Shoehorning cohabiting, casual, or "stay-over" couples into matrimony will not retrofit their pairings into stable conjugal unions. A one-size definition of marriage no longer accommodates the multiple varieties of families our culture has generated.

Chapter 7, "The Uses of the Law for Contemporary Families," examines how our current legal system helps, hurts, or ignores today's nontraditional families. By means of a hypothetical from a popular television series, we demonstrate how individuals in unconventional relationships can make use of current legal remedies. But because judicial and statutory solutions are often inadequate or inconsistently applied across the states, nontraditional families must be proactive in protecting their interests. For cohabiting couples, as well as for single, same-sex, and unmarried parents, executing powers of attorney, specific contracts, and documents of backup guardianship can help preserve and clarify their parental and property rights.

We also explore the separate spheres of courts and legislatures in the development of family law. Although judges and lawmakers have been known to work in concert, they sometimes appear to inhabit parallel universes. Legislatures are slow-moving, contemplative bodies that concern themselves with broad issues of social policy. Courts, by contrast, are preoccupied with gritty, day-to-day realities and are more in touch with actual living families. In this sense, judges—more so than lawmakers—have the practical experience and insight to develop and apply legal remedies to emerging family forms. The result, however, especially in light of added input on the national, state, and local levels, is a stew of legal possibilities, with ingredients that vary widely across jurisdictions.

To a certain extent, the law has been responsive to social and cultural transformations, designing marital alternatives to fit our various domestic lifestyles. But there are limits to the law's ability to influence the quality of family relationships. It can set minimum standards for parenting, but it cannot, for example, induce an absent father to assume a significant financial and emotional role in the life of his child. In conclusion, having earlier compared the benefits of marriage with relationships that are less formal, we note the difficulty of fairly apportioning rights and privileges among competing nontraditional arrangements. Marriage may be outnumbered by newer domestic alternatives, but it remains superior in its access to legal and governmental benefits.

Reconfiguring the law to more accurately reflect contemporary families is an ongoing obligation, not a once-and-done project. In our current era, economic hardship and family fragility have made social change less exhilarating and more worrisome. Despite some ill omens and adversities, Americans continue to take pride and sustenance in their families. The myriad ways in which we form intimate and parent-child relationships reveals resilience and determination, even a sense of adventure. But freedom from traditional strictures also leads to loss of coherence and continuity. What do these innovations mean for posterity? Each generation bestows its accumulated wealth, wisdom, customs, and beliefs on the next. Civilizations depend on these linkages. In the next century, our legacy may well be judged by the kind of families we built in this one.

CHAPTER 1

American Marriages Yesterday

American marriage has been characterized as shifting from "rigid, work-centered, custom regulated, with well-defined roles for husband, wife, and children" to "flexible, pleasure-centered, co-operatively regulated, with loosely defined roles for husband, wife, and children." The accuracy of this comparison between conjugal unions past and present may be debated, although the distinction it draws seems defensible on the whole. It might startle the reader, however, that the quoted contrast appeared in a 1955 college sociology text entitled *Making the Most of Marriage*.[1] The author, noted sociologist Paul H. Landis, celebrated the pliable, fun-loving marriage of the 1950s by measuring it against its stern and static predecessor from the early 20th century. Each era's domestic arrangements should never be seen as the best of all possible unions. Beware the Panglossian paradigm, for the family is always "in transition."[2]

The 21st-century American family was not born yesterday, but its promise and perils can best be viewed by taking one half-century step back. We thus begin this book by exploring family life two generations ago and tracing the major legal and cultural alterations since then (as well as the family's unchanging characteristics). The American marriage of the 1950s provided both the appearance of household stability and the roots of later cultural upheavals. Marriage reigned supreme in the era's domestic pantheon. But the insurgency of ever-more-popular divorce soon followed and represented a major cultural reassessment of marriage. The startling fact is that the steep rise in the divorce rate was not triggered by the passage of no-fault laws, which still lay in the future. Marriage may have been undone by its popularity, by its seeming assurance that it could be all things to all people, all comfort, all security, all the time. Yet, oddly, even today, when marriage has lost its substance for many Americans, it has not lost its luster, even for those who choose to live in unmarried relationships.

The 1950s marriage was not at all traditional. On the contrary, family life in that era was the first thoroughgoing effort to fulfill everyone's personal needs through "an energized and expressive personal life."[3] The apparent tranquility of the 1950s marriage, along with its pursuit of domestic perfection and culture of familial bliss, constituted a reaction to the turbulence that surrounded family life during World War II and in the immediate postwar years. In fact, as the fear of Nazis mutated into dread of a Red mushroom cloud, marriages in the Cold War era became models of family engineering, providing shelter against the omnipresent uncertainty of the world beyond the hearth.[4] Marriage was wildly popular in this era. Paul Landis confidently asserted the cultural norm that "through a wise marriage . . . one can be most fully assured of an enduring love in adulthood."[5] Among all relationships, marriage was viewed as the fullest, closest, and most complete.[6] By 1954, more than 70 percent of males over the age of 14 and 67 percent of females above that age were married.[7]

Cold War Families

With amazing cohesiveness, mid-20th-century Americans subscribed to a rarefied vision of the nuclear family and bent their lives, hopes, and energies to achieve it.[8] Never before or since has there been such concerted pursuit of domestic perfection. A tailor-made target for the iconoclasm that followed, the period lasted little more than a decade before falling prey to the individualism that it had sought to suppress. In historical terms, the 1950s was not the eternal domestic mainstay portrayed endlessly on today's televised reruns. Americans often view the 1950s through the screen of television, whose popularity skyrocketed in those years and whose principal sit-com characters, such as Ozzie and Harriet Nelson (*The Adventures of Ozzie and Harriet*), Ward and June Cleaver (*Leave It to Beaver*), and Jim and Margaret Anderson (*Father Knows Best*), came to be seen, along with their children, as icons of middle-class family life.[9] Those years generated a standard of perceived bonhomie that preoccupies us to this day.[10] Succeeding generations have chosen to embrace the nuclear family, modify it, or reject it outright. They have tried to redefine and reinvent it. But the departure point for their analyses and explorations, the yardstick by which alternatives are measured, is often still that one ideal. For a brief historical moment, Americans truly believed they had definitively solved the riddle of marriage.[11]

The years during and immediately following the end of World War II had not been conducive to marital stability.[12] Millions of returning GIs, many of them absent husbands and absent fathers, found that they had to "elbow their way back into their families."[13] Their reassertion of domestic authority often met with the resistance of their wives and children. Further, these men had to readjust to the workplace, find jobs, resume careers, or take on years of schooling under the generous terms of the GI Bill. Working women were displaced by returning soldiers and the closing of munitions plants and were forced by the millions to leave the factory and return home.[14] Faced with a severe housing shortage, young families moved in with friends and relatives, fraying tempers and straining relationships. By 1946, a surging divorce rate was claiming one in three marriages.[15]

Within a short time, however, a buoyant prosperity engendered a celebratory mind-set in those who had weathered nearly two decades of economic depression and war.[16] Sixty percent of Americans attained a middle-class standard of living by the mid-1950s. In the postwar economic glow, the nuclear family was transforming itself into a "secure oasis."[17] Just as communism and the threat of atomic annihilation could, in the parlance of the day, be "contained," each home became the safest of havens, where potential social threats were neutralized.[18] Secure in their homes and surrounded by children, Americans defied "doomsday predictions," determined to act on their dreams and not their fears.[19] With its seemingly endless supply of ranch-style houses and consumer goods, the United States bestowed on its citizens the ultimate in liberty and privacy rights, the "freedom to pursue the good life at home."[20] When U.S. vice president Richard Nixon and Soviet premier Nikita Khrushchev engaged in their famous Kitchen Debate in 1959, the two Cold War rivals focused not on forms of government or deployment of missiles but on the relative merits of American and Soviet appliances, such as washing machines, TVs, and electric ranges.[21]

It was assumed that those who came of age during and after World War II would get married sooner or later. Indeed, they turned out to be the "most marrying generation on record."[22] The century-high peak was reached in 1960, when 68 percent of the population 14 years of age or older was married.[23] All but 5 percent of Americans who reached adulthood in the 1950s eventually exchanged marital vows.[24] The fertility rate, at 3.8 children per woman, was no less stunning.[25] Americans began marrying at younger ages and had more children more quickly after marriage than the previous generation. Because of the accelerated pace of childbearing, many young mothers likely had two or more children in diapers at once.[26] A previous generation might have turned to extended family members for help. In the 1950s, however, the nuclear family reveled in its self-sufficiency, substituting "marital solidarity" for the broader ties of kinship.[27] For many families, the flight to the suburbs signified emancipation from ethnicity and family tradition.[28] Except for emergencies, parents and relatives were expected to refrain from interfering, and social consensus deemed the "isolated conjugal unit" the fitting and desired center of the American family.[29]

What sociologist Talcott Parsons referred to in 1965 as the "normal American family"[30] had distinct internal and external dimensions. From within, the family could be viewed as a heterosexual pair determined to raise their biological children within a lifelong marriage.[31] Gender roles were clear: the husband functioned as the family leader and provider, while the wife served as the mother and "expressive guide."[32] Externally, the household operated as an autonomous unit, beyond the authority of the extended family. The emergence of the solitary nuclear family was seen as "the end point of changes in families that had been occurring for several hundred years."[33]

The deviance of 1950s family patterns from those of earlier eras points up several anomalies. Within the decade, birth control technologies rapidly advanced,[34] yet the U.S. rate of childbearing approached the high rate experienced in India.[35] One of America's largest increases in women's employment occurred in the 1950s, yet women had received greater percentages of doctoral and master's degrees in the 1930s.[36] Rather than following a line of social and political progression, postwar marriage was a "throwback to the Victorian cult of domesticity with its polarized sex roles and almost religious reverence for home and hearth."[37] The white middle class established norms that ultimately shaped the social, political, and economic lives of all Americans.[38] Those who failed to conform were at risk of becoming "marginalized, stigmatized, and disadvantaged as a result."[39] Adaptation, not resistance or political activism, was the ruling wisdom of the day.[40]

Husbands and wives generally performed their culturally delineated roles as breadwinners and homemakers, respectively.[41] Even though Betty Friedan's *The Feminine Mystique* reached for an indefensible metaphor in describing the American home in this era as a "comfortable concentration camp,"[42] her insistence on the troublesome nature of the transitions in family and gender roles rang true. Women and men were not born to their roles; they struggled to find the balance that would support both their needs as individuals and the needs of the family. As historian Jessica Weiss phrased it, the transitional marital pattern of these years could be characterized as "contested egalitarianism."[43] Women pushed the boundaries of gender, even if not as forcefully as their daughters would a generation later. The inaccurate vision of the 1950s as a docile decade hid an ongoing gender adjustment within marriage.[44]

Many young wives worked in the labor force to support their families while their husbands finished their education subsidized by the GI Bill. Their paychecks thus helped finance their families' ascent to suburbia. Even after starting families, many women continued to work outside the home.[45] In 1950, 33.9 percent of women aged 16 or older were in the labor force; their rate of employment steadily increased to 37.7 percent in 1960, 43.3 percent in 1970, 51.5 percent in 1980, and 57.5 percent in 1990.[46] Thus, even at the height of the "decade of domesticity," over a third of all women worked outside the home. The pattern of female employment outside the home that prevailed until 1970 resulted in lower rates for women aged 25 to 34 than those for women aged 16 to 24, since women generally left the labor force when they married or had their first child.[47] The employment rate rose as women reached age 35 to 44 and rose even higher for those aged 45 to 54, because many women returned to work after bearing and rearing their children.[48] Overall, the rate of married female workers increased steadily during these decades. In 1950, almost one-quarter of married women (24.8 percent) were in the labor force.[49] The rate of married female employment increased to 31.9 percent in 1960, 40.5 percent in 1970, 49.9 percent in 1980, and 58.4 percent in 1990. By the beginning of the 21st century, 61.1 percent of married women worked for pay.[50]

In this "era of the expert,"[51] postwar Americans relied on Benjamin Spock's *Baby and Child Care* and Norman Vincent Peale's *The Power of Positive Thinking* as formulas for success.[52] The profession of marriage counseling, which began in the 1930s, developed into the practice of family therapy and became established and respected in the 1950s.[53] There was, apparently, some need for therapeutic intervention in marriage. The dual idealization of married women as scintillating sex objects while wholly absorbed in nurturing their young drove thousands of them "to therapists, tranquilizers, or alcohol when they actually tried to live up to it."[54] Men, too, felt entrapped within the role of "good-provider,"[55] stressed and confined in competitive, increasingly bureaucratic environments.[56] Both men and women looked to the psychologists to label and explain their feelings and to help them adapt.[57] A "distinctly apolitical" strategy, reliance on this type of expertise served to bolster the political consensus by blaming personal weakness rather than flawed institutions for marital dissatisfaction.[58] As couples "sealed the psychological boundaries around the family, they also sealed their fates within it."[59] That these relatively fragile structures were burdened by high expectations was not an immediate cause for alarm in the 1950s.[60] Outside the safety and security of domesticity lurked dangerous emotional, financial, and social hardships.[61] For a while, even a bad marriage was better than the drastic, evil measure of divorce.[62]

Setting the Boundaries

Just after World War II, a Gallup poll showed that 35 percent of Americans favored stricter divorce laws, that 31 percent believed in the status quo, and that only 9 percent supported liberalized measures.[63] Marital unions formed in the postwar decade achieved a notable degree of stability. This cohort of Americans was, in fact, the only group in the last hundred years "to show a substantial, sustained shortfall in their lifetime levels of divorce."[64] Divorce grounds were quite limited, and formal dissolution required proof of marital fault.[65] Marriage licensing laws examined the fitness of marital candidates and excluded "certain types of mental defectives"[66] as well as those with venereal disease.[67] In order to prevent hurried elopements, many states instituted waiting periods, usually from one to five days, before granting marriage license applications.[68] Common-law marriage—legal sanctioning of an informal marriage after the passage of several years—frustrated state efforts to promote formal marriage, and by the early 1950s, only 18 states continued to recognize it.[69] Those states retained common-law marriage in order to "regularize unions which the parties were otherwise free to abandon at will and to prevent the bastardization of children."[70] Both culturally and legally, the preference for marriage was abundantly clear.[71]

But marriage was not open to everyone. In 1952, more than half the states had laws prohibiting marriage between whites and those of other races.[72] Most commonly, whites and blacks were forbidden to marry, although whites in various states were forbidden from taking Indians, Chinese, Japanese, mulattoes, Malays, or Mongolians to the altar.[73] The ban on interracial marriage was extremely popular. In a 1958 Gallup poll, only 4 percent of Americans said they approved of marriages between whites and nonwhites.[74] Cultural and legal change came slowly. Although approval of interracial unions gradually increased over the next few decades, at least half of Americans disapproved of black-white marriages as late as 1983.[75] In the late 1940s, a white woman and a black man brought suit against the state of California for denying them a marriage license.[76] The California Supreme Court struck down the state's mixed-race marriage ban on the equal protection grounds of the 14th Amendment.[77] Following this "signal precedent,"[78] nearly half of the remaining states with interracial marriage prohibitions decided to abolish them.[79] In contrast to the considerable number of states that disapproved of interracial unions in this period, only a few considered habitual criminals, drug addicts, and chronic alcoholics as undesirable marriage partners.[80] Same-sex marriage, of course, was not even contemplated.[81]

The genders were not equal in marriage. By extending 19th-century legal constructs of husband and wife into the postwar era, states ensured the survival of a number of traditions. Thus, husbands were still entitled to manage the family resources and choose the location of the family domicile.[82] Wives were entitled to support but had no power to allocate marital resources.[83] The rule that courts could order husbands to pay support to wives but never wives to husbands reflected society's stringent gender assumptions. A trial court in 1967 rejecting a husband's request for temporary alimony clearly expressed its discomfiture with his "unnatural" challenge to the accepted rationale.

> A husband who looks to his wife for support is placed in an unnatural relationship. Traditionally, the husband is the breadwinner and provides for the family. Indeed, the law contemplates that a husband . . . shall support himself out of his property or by his labor. Any award of alimony made in a matrimonial action is merely the enforcement of a common law liability of a husband to support his wife.[84]

Domestic violence remained hidden behind the couple's front door.[85] A wife who was physically attacked by her husband might seek criminal sanctions, but the legal system rarely treated these crimes seriously, and the law forbade the battered wife from testifying against her abusive husband, thus hamstringing the prosecution in any event.[86] Moreover, most states refused to allow a victimized wife to sue her husband for damages in a tort action.[87] Since the wife's consent to marriage was deemed an irrevocable consent to sex with her husband at any time—indeed, this was viewed as a "male marital sexual right"[88]—marital rape could never be defined as unlawful and was thus not deemed a criminal act.[89]

A double standard was broadly observed in 1950s marriage law and culture. For example, New York's restrictive laws did not allow divorce on the ground of cruelty but did permit judicial separations on that ground.[90] In such actions, courts held that isolated acts of brutality by a husband against his wife did not amount to cruel and inhuman treatment[91] but that a single violent act committed by a wife against her husband constituted sufficient wrongdoing on her part to deny her both a separation and maintenance (spousal support).[92] The courts' double standard in decreeing the consequences of marital cruelty flowed from the era's "[j]udicial blindness to the faults of men and indifference to the difficulties faced by women."[93] As long as a wife appeared able to cohabit and coexist with her husband, courts would deny her a separation.[94] Since 1920, New York courts had enforced a policy of keeping husband and wife together,[95] and the burden of accommodating to a troubled marriage "fell largely on wives."[96]

That wives in troubled marriages had limited options became clear in *McGuire v. McGuire*,[97] a 1953 decision of the Nebraska Supreme Court that has achieved "a paradigmatic stature in American family law."[98] The decision "mobilized the language of marital privacy,"[99] as it held that intact marriages, even deeply disturbed ones, were virtually insulated from legal intervention. Lydia McGuire was a hardworking farmwife whose husband, Charles, although fairly wealthy, deprived her of all but the most basic necessities. Mr. McGuire paid for groceries directly and had not given his wife any money at all for years. Their 1929 Model A Ford coupe was equipped with a faulty heater, and their home lacked indoor plumbing as well as a reliable furnace. Mrs. McGuire was permitted to make only local telephone calls, and she had to pay for out-of-state visits to her adult children with money she earned raising chickens.[100] Desiring neither a divorce nor a separation, she entreated the court to "compel her rich husband to make her life a little less bleak."[101] Overturning the trial court's ruling in her favor, the state supreme court held that a family's living standards were of concern to the household but not to the courts and that even a court of equity should not interfere where the husband and wife were living together.[102] A separated or divorced wife might petition for support, but Lydia McGuire faced the unenviable choice of bowing to her husband's superior property rights or leaving the marriage.[103]

What is the significance of the McGuire case? On one level, it propounded the still-valid rule that courts will not lightly intrude into an intact marriage.[104] But was this marriage truly intact? Lydia's petition described her husband as "a very headstrong man" and averred that she was "afraid of what might happen to her personally" when he was served with suit papers.[105] Lydia asked for and was granted a temporary restraining order against Charles,[106] but the state supreme court noted that she made no attempt to prove her allegations, and it found her decision to continue living with her husband irreconcilable with her accusations.[107] At bottom, the court entered a legal judgment about the sharp boundary between the state and the family, although the borderland between these two institutions was about to become a far more contested terrain.[108]

Occasionally, a court would soften its stance on the husband's prerogatives and introduce a note of realism into its reasoning. As a rule, for example, the husband had the right to choose the family's place of domicile.[109] It was the wife's duty "to go with her husband to the home which he had provided."[110] If the wife refused to accompany her husband, she was deemed to have abandoned him.[111] In *Eftimiou v. Eftimiou*, a husband and wife each sought a judgment of separation based on abandonment by the other.[112] Despite his ownership of a dozen homes, the husband insisted on the couple's residing in a rat-infested cellar with no toilet and no hot water.[113] When his wife declined to accept these conditions, Mr. Eftimiou asserted that "she would be required to live in a sewer" if he so chose.[114] The court disagreed, determining that a husband could not arbitrarily select the marital domicile but "must exercise his right in a reasonable manner with due respect for his wife's health, welfare, comfort and peace of mind."[115] As the court granted a judgment of separation in favor of the wife and dismissed the husband's counterclaim, it remarked on the changing mores: "[T]he assault on the citadel of the husband's supremacy is proceeding in these days apace, so that today the wife is no longer in complete subjugation to the dictates of her husband."[116]

In another case, a wife who attended college and intended to pursue medical studies was deemed "a very ambitious lady" and failed to evoke similar judicial solicitude.[117] Because she had neglected to keep Jewish dietary laws in the home and had paid less attention to her daughter than her husband thought appropriate, she was found to have constructively abandoned her husband and to have breached her duty to the child.[118] The court's reliance on gender norms for its ruling was explicit: "The father has a right to expect the mother to give the child that which is necessary for her development and good, as it is his duty to provide the means to effectuate that, both materially and in cooperation spiritually."[119]

The Symbiosis of Marriage and Divorce

Americans have always believed in a "fundamental right to marry, and marry, and marry."[120] In a 1930 essay entitled "Romantic Divorce," Katharine Fullerton Gerould noted "the American habit of acting promptly on our marital dissatisfactions," a trait she traced to "our seeing marriage as an intensely personal and an intensely romantic affair."[121] She thus identified the tension implicit in the exaltation of marriage: if the wedded state is to be blissful, we must keep trying at it until we have achieved success. Gerould also made plain the consequences of this connubial ideology: "As long as personal happiness is made the only desideratum in marriage, the divorce courts will be full."[122]

Romantic marriage thus depended on trouble-free divorce, which was theoretically unavailable in the 1950s and 1960s. Indeed, in the world limned by appellate court opinions, divorce came at the end of bitter litigation in which "innocent" spouses established serious marital "fault" in an adversary proceeding against their erring partners, whereupon the state "punished" the "guilty" spouses by evicting them from the marriage by issuing a divorce decree. In 1955, the Tennessee Supreme Court forcefully articulated this universal set of legal norms.

> Divorce in this state is not a matter to be worked out for the mutual accommodation of the parties in whatever manner they may desire, or in whatever manner the Court may deem to be fair and just under the circumstances. It is conceived as a remedy for the innocent against the guilty. The unfortunate person against whom a divorce is granted may suffer not only the severance of his or her marital relations, but also the deprivation of those rights, such as alimony, which arise out of the marital relation. These provisions thus are intended to further the policy of rewarding the innocent and punishing the guilty.[123]

But while appellate courts were ponderously recapitulating the formal canon of guilt and innocence, social reality was twisting the legal process into a caricature. By the 1950s, divorce had become precisely "a matter to be worked out for the mutual accommodation of the parties in whatever manner they may desire."[124] The drive to escape bad marriages pushed American couples to pinnacles of legal invention, and divorce courts followed their lead. Of the three most prevalent divorce grounds—adultery, desertion, and cruelty—marital cruelty became the "dazzling success stor[y] of family law,"[125] because its plasticity rapidly allowed it to outpace adultery and desertion as the favored vehicle for dissolution. In the 1860s, cruelty had accounted for only one-eighth of all decrees; by 1922, it had emerged as the most popular ground.[126] In 1950, divorces and annulments premised on cruelty accounted for 58.7 percent of the total; desertion had slipped to 17.6 percent, and adultery registered merely 2.7 percent.[127]

What constituted cruelty? As a divorce ground, cruelty originally branded the respondent a violent offender against social mores.[128] It was the domestic relations analog to a criminal prosecution for assault and battery. The Iowa Code, for example, described a husband's cruelty sufficient to warrant divorce as "such inhuman treatment as to endanger the life of his wife."[129] But long before the no-fault divorce revolution of the 1970s, cruelty had transformed into an expedient way for an unhappy couple to opt out of an unworkable marriage.[130] Far from restricting divorce, the fault system operated as a moral charade, fooling no one but staying in place for want of a cultural alternative. Noted judge and divorce reformer Paul W. Alexander well understood the paradox, observing that "the trouble with guilt as a criterion" is that it "virtually assures mutual consent as a ground for divorce."[131] The pliant cruelty standard rarely foreclosed any divorce, so long as the parties agreed on the legal fable concocted for court presentation.[132] Renowned family law professor Homer H. Clark Jr. pilloried the ancien régime of divorce, which "permits the parties to obtain divorces by consent, but subjects them to [the] humiliation, hypocrisy, sometimes perjury, and needless hostility of having to testify to one of the prescribed grounds."[133] In short, American culture was recognizing a direct, if difficult, truth: when a marriage becomes a prison, no laws can keep the spousal inmates from breaking out. The quest for happy marriages required ready divorce.

Divorces are a product of our cultural assumptions about marriage.[134] Even in the domestic apogee of the 1950s and 1960s, the American legal system was universally acknowledged a failure at limiting divorce.[135] Indeed, a culture tolerant of divorce lived side by side with one espousing marriage. Charlton Ogburn, vice-chair and counsel for the American Bar Association's Interprofessional Commission of Marriage and Divorce Laws, expressed his dismay in 1950 that the public "remained rather apathetic in the face of the disturbing character of the divorce evil: the increasing number of divorces and the laxity of the courts in hearing and granting divorces, especially in undefended cases often based on fraud and collusion in violation of the statutes."[136] But Ogburn had a poor grasp of the zeitgeist. The public did not loudly tout divorce, but it certainly abided it as the remedy for a failed marriage and as the only way to reenter the happiness sweepstakes. Social researcher Maxine B. Virtue's 1956 observation that the "present cultural mores generally disapprove of the spouse who does not cooperate when asked for a divorce"[137] more accurately captured the flavor of a culture that understood the need for flexibility in negotiating and renegotiating the ideal of marriage.

Did No-Fault Divorce Change Marriage?

In considering which cultural and legal developments have had the greatest impact on marriage in the past half century, the dramatic rise in divorce rates in the wake of the passage of no-fault divorce laws has often taken center stage. But a closer look at the divorce statistics shows that notion to be misleading. In 1960, the divorce rate stood at its postwar low of 2.2 divorces per thousand of the population.[138] The rate of divorce then began a dramatic climb in the 1960s, the decade before no-fault divorce, reaching 3.5 divorces per thousand of the population in 1970.[139] The divorce rate thus rose 59 percent during the 1960s. This spectacular and unprecedented rise during peacetime[140] occurred in the face of largely unchanged divorce laws requiring proof of fault.[141]

In 1971, the year after California's no-fault divorce statute—the first modern no-fault law—went into effect, the national divorce rate stood at 3.7 divorces per thousand of the population, then climbed through the decade until it reached the 1980 rate of 5.2.[142] This increase of 41 percent was quite substantial, of course, but it also represented a dramatic slowing of the divorce rate during the first no-fault divorce decade.[143] The divorce rate peaked at 5.3 divorces per thousand of the population in 1981, after most of the country had experienced no-fault divorce for several years. The rate then slowly but regularly declined, reaching 3.4 divorces per thousand in 2009.[144] In sum, during the first four decades of no-fault divorce, the divorce rate rose sharply (although not as steeply as in the decade before no-fault divorce) and then fell gradually as it returned to the rate experienced before no-fault divorce began.[145]

No-fault divorce laws were promulgated in the 1970s in a major effort to retard the rise in divorce, not to liberate couples willy-nilly from their conjugal obligations.[146] No-fault divorce was intended to reduce acrimony, improve the chances of reconciliation, and reduce the divorce rate. The reforms were "designed to transform divorce litigation from an adversarial tempest to an amiable teacup."[147] They failed. But what ensued owed more to the law of unintended consequences than to any blueprint to destroy marriage, as critics have often mistakenly contended. By effectively replacing a fault standard with one of "irreconcilable differences"[148] or its equivalent, "irretrievable breakdown,"[149] no-fault divorce statutes engineered a nationwide overhaul in the process of obtaining a divorce. By 1985, all 50 states had adopted some version of no-fault divorce.[150] Over two-thirds of the states enacted a provision of the "irreconcilable differences" type, either adding it to their menu of dissolution options or wiping the slate clean of all fault-based divorce grounds. The remaining states provided a no-fault divorce ground to be established by couples living separate and apart for a relatively brief time.[151]

The operating principles of the regime governing marital dissolution in the 1950s and 1960s had formally required proof of fault grounds but operationally allowed for mutual consent.[152] Couples who wanted to divorce generally found a way to do so, no matter what the formal grounds demanded. No-fault divorce in the 1970s was revolutionary not because it did away with fault but because it eliminated the need for the couple to agree on the terms of their marital dissolution. No-fault divorce meant unilateral divorce.[153]

The legal system everywhere officially exchanged the culpability theory of divorce for one of marital breakdown. But irreconcilable differences turned out to be unjusticiable: there is no way for a court to adjudicate one spouse's claim that marital differences are irremediable. The "virtually universal understanding [came to be] that the breakdown of a marriage is irretrievable if one spouse says it is."[154] The elimination of the need for spousal consent changed the dynamics of divorce—and of marriage.

What happened to marriage in the age of no-fault? The metamorphosis of divorce into an act of self-actualization was but one component in an emerging ethos featuring "personal autonomy with respect to intimate life choices."[155] Robert T. Michael attributed the divorce rate rise beginning in the 1960s not to the liberalization of divorce laws but to several other factors, including the diffusion of contraceptive techniques and the increase in women's income during this period, which reduced their financial dependence on their husbands.[156] That marriage had lost its preeminence both culturally and legally became evident a generation ago. Comparing national surveys done in 1957 and 1976, Joseph Veroff and his colleagues reported that the most dramatic of the changes in those two decades came in the "increased tolerance of people who reject marriage as a way of life."[157] The dislodgment of a formal culpability analysis in divorce cases was accompanied by cultural rifts in American society that left the individual "suspended in glorious, but terrifying, isolation."[158] We have moved from companionate conjugality to a "post-companionate marriage" whose raison d'être is personal fulfillment.[159] No-fault divorce appeared to foster "autonomous individualism" to the detriment of familial relationships.[160] With divorce at the ready, marriage no longer appeared to require continual tending. "Love," as the posters advertising the wildly popular 1970 movie *Love Story* endlessly repeated, "means never having to say you're sorry."[161]

Conclusion: And So the Bonds of Marriage Weakened

Although the 1950s was a transient, aberrational period in the history of marriage, it invented the modern form of the nuclear family. Americans of the era believed that the answer to the conundrums of family life was to champion marriage for all and unreservedly. Succeeding generations have taken a range of stances toward the nuclear family, from veneration to condemnation. But their measuring rod is that same wedded ideal.

Marriage remains popular, both as a personal goal and as a perceived societal foundation. However, the preeminent role of marriage in our society is gone. Unmarried couples and their dependents now compose a majority of families. As a society, Americans continue to buff the ideal of marriage while they rebuff its relevance to their own intimate associations, as they set up their families on a far less secure footing. Yet the legal system treats the unmarried (and their children) as exceptions to the rule, deviations from a standard that is statistically less and less prevalent. This reluctance to make family law reflect the reality of family life leads to substantial problems when families turn to the courts to resolve conflicts and learn that the legal system is grounded in outdated norms.

The succeeding chapters will argue that families should be adjudged by functional standards. When issues such as family dissolution, parentage, or child custody come to the courts for resolution, judges should be guided by principles derived from the family structure created and implemented by the parties themselves. This turn to functional models and away from formal legal standards is already evident in parts of our family law system. But it is currently implemented in an irregular, piecemeal, and unprincipled way by many courts. These controversial functional norms are best suited to fairly serve America's increasingly diverse families.

CHAPTER 2

How Marriage Became Optional

Cohabitation, Gay Marriage, and the Continuing Role of Gender

In 1953, sociologist Ray E. Baber confidently asserted that marriage's greatest appeal lay in its "opportunity . . . for constant and complete companionship with the person most loved, with the full sanction of society."[1] Another mid-20th-century text maintained that marriage had been seen for ages as the "natural state" for adults.[2] In the middle of the 20th century, almost half (48.9 percent) of all women were wed by age 20, and 8 out of 10 (80.4 percent) were married by age 25.[3] In 1960, two-thirds (68 percent) of all Americans in their 20s were married.[4] But by 2008, just over one-quarter (26 percent) of 20-somethings were wed.[5] According to the Census Bureau's American Community Survey, families headed by married couples constituted only 49.7 percent of all households in 2009.[6] The Census Bureau reported in 2012 that 102 million Americans 18 and older were unmarried, a group comprising 44.1 percent of all U.S. residents in that age-group.[7] Marriage has now become optional, one choice among many ways to form a family.[8]

Children's living arrangements have also undergone substantial change. In the past generation, the percentage of children in the United States who live with two married parents has markedly declined. In 1971, 83 percent of children under the age of 18 lived with two married parents, while only 66 percent did so in 2010.[9] According to the Census Bureau estimates for 2012, of the 73.8 million children in the United States, 50.3 million lived with two parents, while 20.9 million lived with only one parent.[10] Further, 2.1 million children lived with other relatives, while over 495,000 lived with nonrelatives only.[11]

The half century that followed the 1960s has virtually ended the stigma associated with illegitimacy and single parenthood.[12] It also significantly enhanced the status of women, thus increasing the potential for their economic self-sufficiency.[13] These seismic social changes have fundamentally altered our conceptions of what makes a family. Historian Nancy Cott has observed that this present transitional period can be characterized by the "disestablishment" of marriage, since the state no longer effectively supports a single model of marriage and family life.[14]

Marriage may have lost its mainstream cultural primacy, but it has now controversially become a goal for many same-sex couples. The increase in the reported number and visibility of these couples has been striking, paralleling the rise in the growth and acceptance of unorthodox family arrangements. The 2010 U.S. Census reported that same-sex households increased by 80 percent in the last ten years, from 358,390 to 646,464. That number includes 131,729 households headed by same-sex married couples, along with 514,735 households headed by same-sex unmarried partners. Among all those families, 31 percent of couples who identified as spouses and 14 percent of unmarried partners are raising children.[15]

Although same-sex couples have clearly not achieved equality either culturally or legally, they have made tremendous strides in gaining acceptance in the past few years.[16] Research data indicates that the percentage of Americans who favor allowing gays to adopt children rose steadily from 38 percent in 1999 to 46 percent in 2006 to 53 percent in 2009.[17] A 2009 Gallup poll reported that 73 percent believe that same-sex couples should be entitled to inheritance rights, while 67 percent say that gay and lesbian domestic partners should have access to health insurance and other employee benefits.[18] By a large margin, Americans oppose the denial of federal benefits to spouses in same-sex marriages.[19] The repeal of the "Don't Ask, Don't Tell" policy in 2010 reversed a policy that had allowed gays to serve in the military only if they kept quiet about their sexual orientation.[20]

The American family now encompasses a collection of diverse domestic arrangements—at times fragile and at time vigorous—that include single parents with children, blended families, cohabiting heterosexual couples, lesbian and gay partners (married or not), and multigenerational families, in addition to heterosexual married couples.[21] Consider these data points from seven recent years, each markedly at odds with the predominant view of family life in the 20th century:

- In 2007, almost 3 in 10 (28 percent) of the unmarried women who gave birth were living with a cohabiting partner.[22]
- In 2008, more than 4 out of every 10 births (41 percent) were to unmarried women,[23] and more than 6 out of 10 (61 percent) of the women with a birth in the past year were in the labor force.[24]
- In 2009, the Census Bureau reported that 32.3 million Americans lived alone. They comprised 28 percent of all households, up from 17 percent in 1970.[25]
- In 2010, Illinois became the 11th state to pass a "civil union" law; the Illinois measure is the first in the nation to allow unrelated same-sex or opposite-sex couples to share "the same legal obligations, responsibilities, protections, and benefits" as married couples.[26]
- In 2011, a Gallup poll reported the first time that a majority of Americans supported legalizing gay marriage.[27]
- In 2012, a paper presented at the annual meeting of the Population Association of America reported that the proportion of men and women who had never been married by age 35 stood at 14 percent of men and 11 percent of women. By contrast, in 1980 only 6 percent of men and women in that age cohort had never been married.[28]
- In 2013, the Census Bureau reported an all-time high median age at first marriage, 28.6 years for men and 26.6 years for women.[29]

Although our society still exhibits a "cultural ambivalence about families not based on genetic ties,"[30] social acceptance of a wider range of family forms has markedly increased. This multiplicity of family structures signifies that marriage has moved from the required curriculum for creating a family to an elective means. How did this happen, and where is the American family headed, in both cultural and legal terms? This chapter explores three interrelated facets of the current conjugal divide: the displacement of marriage as the central family-building institution, the contrasting drive of many same-sex couples to take the field abandoned in droves by millions of their heterosexual counterparts, and how pervasively gender continues as a key component of modern American couples.

How Did Marriage Lose Its Primacy?

Americans have a paradoxical relationship to marriage. Most Americans, even if they reject the institution entirely or defer their entry into it, still hold up marriage as the ideal. In a 2006 Gallup poll, 91 percent in a national sample reported that they were either married or planned to be so someday.[31] Only 4 percent had definitely ruled out marriage.[32] The ideal of marriage still serves as the pedestal for intimate partnership. National poll results from 2009 reflected strong support for marriage as the exclusive moral framework for sexual relationships and bearing children.[33] Ninety-two percent expressed the belief that an affair between married persons is morally wrong; 45 percent deemed having a baby outside marriage to be immoral; 40 percent also condemned sex between unmarried women and men; and, a generation after the no-fault divorce revolution, 30 percent voiced their opinion that divorce is morally wrong.[34] Marriages also score high marks in satisfaction. Almost two-thirds of respondents who graded their own marriages in a 2006 survey gave their unions an A.[35]

Yet the bonds of marriage are unmistakably weaker today. No-fault divorce may not have caused the demise of marriage as the mainstay for domestic partnership, but it served as a significant cultural marker. Our culture is simply too diverse, too variable, and increasingly too atomistic to support the traditional framework of lifelong marriage. Mary Ann Glendon's quip that Americans believe in a "fundamental right to marry, and marry, and marry" exposes the unstable foundation of serial monogamy.[36] While individual couples can hew to a marriage commitment (and millions do), their faith and actions are sustained primarily by themselves and by the support structures they draft into service, not by universal social norms.[37]

The end of marriage's primacy does not, of course, mean that Americans hold *families* in any less regard. The report of a 2010 nationwide survey by the Pew Research Center began by noting the "emphatic margins" by which "the public does not see marriage as the only path to family formation."[38] The report summarized key findings on the American public's views of what constitutes a family.

> Fully 86% say a single parent and child constitute a family; nearly as many (80%) say an unmarried couple living together with a child is a family; and 63% say a gay or lesbian couple raising a child is a family. The presence of children clearly matters in these definitions. If a cohabiting couple has no children, a majority of the public says they are not a family. Marriage matters, too. If a childless couple is married, 88% consider them to be a family.[39]

No matter what family type one belongs to, the members of that family generally see it in very positive terms. Over three-quarters (76 percent) of Americans in 2010 claimed that their own family is the most important part of their life.[40] Seventy-five percent were "very satisfied" with their family life, and more (85 percent) affirmed that the family they live in now is either as close as (45 percent) or closer than (40 percent) the family in which they grew up.[41]

Consider families with children born through assisted reproductive technology (ART). In this area, the pace of cultural change has vividly quickened. Donor insemination efforts in the 1950s and 1960s were "viewed with such horror" that state legislators introduced bills to ban the procedure.[42] But by the end of the 20th century, almost three-quarters of the states had adopted laws facilitating artificial insemination procedures by declaring the consenting husband of the sperm recipient to be the legal father. The development of in vitro fertilization in the 1970s similarly was initially met with revulsion, then was tolerated, and is now both widespread and deemed unremarkable.[43]

ART has vastly increased in complexity and efficacy in the last few years, facilitating births to untold numbers of infertile heterosexual couples, gay and lesbian partners, and single parents.[44] A child created through ART "might have a genetic mother, a genetic father, any number of social/intended parents, and a gestational mother."[45] At the same time, the rise in the number of gestational surrogates—women who bear the genetic children of others—has created another generation of familial and legal dilemmas for our society. Seen as a whole, collaborative reproduction is reconceiving the family by "making a biological distinction between gestation and genetics in determining parentage" as well as by considering "intentionality in defining the family."[46] American society has moved past the freedom to have sex without reproduction and now considers the choice to reproduce without sex.[47]

The last 60 years have seen divorce rates peak and recede. But a far more telling cultural signpost is the plunge in the rates for both marriages and births over the same period. As table 1 shows, the divorce rate rose in the late 1960s, crested in 1980, and has since receded. The present divorce rate has now dipped slightly below the level just before no-fault divorce began in the 1970s. By contrast, the marriage rate wobbled within the range of 8.5 to 10.6 percent during the first three decades following 1955. It then began a pronounced decline, from 9.8 percent in 1990 to 6.8 percent in 2009. The birth rate has tracked the marriage downturn, dropping steadily from a 1955 high of 25 percent to a 2009 low of 13.6 percent, a reduction of nearly 46 percent.

The decline in the marriage rate is more than matched by the rise in the percentage of children born outside marriage. Between 1940 and 1955, the percentage of births to unmarried women slowly grew from 3.8 to 4.5 percent of all births.[48] It then began a sharp climb, and over 40 percent of all births in 2008 were to unmarried women, as shown in table 2. Not surprisingly, the trend for the percentage of children living in families formed by marriage follows the same downward pattern as the trajectory of marriages, as seen in table 3.

Americans are clearly dethroning marriage from its place as the primary adult relationship. Millions of couples now cohabit instead of marrying. But the demographics do not tell the entire story. The next section explores the ramifications of the displacement of marriage and suggests that cohabitation is not always a rejection of marriage; it often represents a frustrated yearning for marriage.

TABLE 1. Births, Marriages, and Divorces, 1950–2009 (rate per 1,000 population)

Year	Births	Marriages	Divorces
1950	24.1	11.1	2.6
1955	25.0	9.3	2.3
1960	23.7	8.5	2.2
1965	19.4	9.3	2.5
1970	18.4	10.6	3.5
1975	14.6	10.0	4.8
1980	15.9	10.6	5.2
1985	15.8	10.1	5.0
1990	16.7	9.8	4.7
1995	14.6	8.9	4.4
2000	14.4	8.3	4.1
2005	14.0	7.7	3.7
2009	13.6	6.8	3.4

Source: U.S. CENSUS BUREAU, STATISTICAL ABSTRACT OF THE UNITED STATES: 2007 63 tbl.76 (2007), available at http://www.census.gov/prod/2006pubs/07statab/vitstat.pdf (providing table data for the years 1950–2000); CTRS. FOR DISEASE CONTROL & PREVENTION, U.S. DEP'T OF HEALTH AND HUMAN SERVS., 56 NATIONAL VITAL STATISTICS REPORTS, BIRTHS, MARRIAGES, DIVORCES, AND DEATHS: PROVISIONAL DATA FOR MARCH 2007 1 tbl.A (Oct. 30, 2007), http://www.cdc.gov/nchs/data/nvsr/nvsr56/nvsr56_04.pdf (providing table data for the year 2005, statistics measured by 12-month period ending in March); CTRS. FOR DISEASE CONTROL & PREVENTION, U.S. DEP'T OF HEALTH AND HUMAN SERVS., 58 NATIONAL VITAL STATISTICS REPORTS, BIRTHS, MARRIAGES, DIVORCES, AND DEATHS: PROVISIONAL DATA FOR AUGUST 2009 1 tbl.A (May 10, 2010), http://www.cdc.gov/nchs/data/nvsr/nvsr58/nvsr58_18.pdf (providing table data for the year 2009, statistics measured by 12-month period ending in August).

TABLE 2. Unmarried Childbearing, 1960–2008

Year	Birth Rate per 1,000 Unmarried Women 15–44 years	Percentage of all Births to Unmarried Women
1960	21.6	5.3
1965	23.4	7.7
1970	26.4	10.7
1975	24.5	14.3
1980	29.4	18.4
1985	32.8	22.0
1990	43.8	26.6
1995	44.3	32.2
2000	44.1	33.2
2008	52.5	40.6

Source: U.S. CENSUS BUREAU, STATISTICAL ABSTRACT OF THE UNITED STATES: 2007 (providing table data for years 1960-85); Table 85. Births to Unmarried Women by Race, Hispanic Origin, and Age of Mother: 1990 to 2006, U.S. CENSUS BUREAU, http://www.census.gov/compendia/statab/2010/tables/10s0085.pdf (last visited May 15, 2011); Table 86, Births to Teens and Unmarried Mothers and Births with Low Birth Weight by Race and Hispanic Origin: 1990 to 2007, U.S. CENSUS BUREAU, http://www.census.gov/compendia/statab/2010/tables/10s0086.pdf (last visited May 15, 2011); National Vital Statistics Reports, Births: Final Data for 2008, CTRS. FOR DISEASE CONTROL, 90 tbl.15 (Dec. 2010), http://www.cdc.gov/nchs/data/nvsr/nvsr59/nvsr59_01.pdf.

TABLE 3. Marriage and Children-in-Marriage Statistics, 1970–2000

	1970	1980	1990	2000
Percentage of Adults Married	71.7	65.5	61.9	59.5
Percentage of First Marriages Intact	73.3	67.7	62.5	58.5
Percentage of Births to Married Parents	89.3	81.6	72.0	66.8
Percentage of Children Living with Own Married Parents	68.7	64.0	60.8	59.7
Percentage of Children Living with Two Married Parents	85.2	76.7	72.5	68.1

Source: DAVID BLANKENHORN, THE FUTURE OF MARRIAGE 218 tbl.1 (2007) (data drawn from U.S. Census Bureau statistics).

Cohabitation: Marriage's Alternative or Its Prequel?

Marriage is in decline, but cohabitation rates are soaring. Defined as a man and woman living together in a nonmarital sexual relationship, cohabitation rivals marriage as a means to create a family. It has not, however, dislodged the ideal of marriage in the public mind. The marital state is still very desirable, and most people do participate in it at some point.[49] For some, living together is an exploratory prelude to marriage. Others view it as the only readily available alternative to remaining single. For still others, cohabitation is a waiting room for better times that may or may not arrive. Examining the motivations and characteristics of today's cohabitants presents strong evidence of the evolving social trends in intimate association, since cohabitation has become the norm as both the first form of intimate union and the prevalent one after divorce.[50]

From 1987 to 2002, the percentage of women aged 35 to 39 who had ever cohabited doubled, from 30 to 61 percent.[51] More than half of all marriages occurring between 1990 and 1994 were preceded by cohabitation, a jump of 40 percent as compared to marriages entered into between 1965 and 1974.[52] Approximately 65 percent of marital unions between men and women occurring after 1995 were preceded by cohabitation.[53] Many young adults require an interval of premarital cohabitation in order to assess their compatibility. From their perspective, "marrying without living together first seems quite foolish."[54] Some of these couples have no immediate wedding plans but have discussed marriage prior to moving in together. Although, they have chosen to cohabit for the present moment rather than marry, they "may believe there should be the potential of marriage as a criterion for cohabitation."[55]

Marriage and cohabitation are not competing choices. Rather, the "decision-making calculus"[56] centers on whether to live together or stay single, that is, to live alone with one's parents or with roommates. Since the baby boom era, men and women have been marrying at increasingly later ages. As noted earlier, the median age for first marriage is 28.6 years for men and 26.6 years for women.[57] But while marriage is being postponed, cohabitation has risen to the task of filling in the gap, offsetting and compensating for the vastly slower pace of today's wedding marches. In a 2010 survey by the Pew Research Center, nearly two-thirds (64 percent) of those who have cohabited reported that they considered this living arrangement "a step toward marriage."[58]

Marriage is a "highly valued, even if an elusive, goal."[59] Ironically, our reasons for deferring it attest to the extraordinarily high esteem in which we hold it. Many cohabiting couples will delay marriage until they can demonstrate a certain worthiness of it. To seriously consider marrying, cohabiting couples require a sense of financial security and stability, such as sufficient savings to buy a house or to afford a church wedding and reception. For working-class and lower middle-class young couples, "marriage signifies the achievement of an enhanced financial status."[60] Mere decades ago, these young adults would very likely have married with expectations of having to weather financial hardships, particularly in their first years together. As cultural pressure to marry has receded, cohabitation has become normative, and marriage is increasingly disassociated from childbearing. Matrimony has been reimagined as a symbol of personal and financial attainment. This view fosters the belief that weddings should be delayed until one's individual and economic goals have been met, "however defined and unattainable they may be for some social groups."[61]

The connection between economic stability and one's marital or cohabitation status is "dramatically stratified by race and ethnicity."[62] A greater percentage of whites than blacks and Hispanics are currently married, and across all races, men and women with a bachelor's or higher degree are more likely to wed than those without a high school or general equivalency diploma.[63] The proportion of those who cohabit is highest among those with no high school or general equivalency diploma.[64] Educational achievement often serves "as a proxy for social class,"[65] and cohabitants have lower incomes and higher poverty rates than married couples.[66] Termed a "poor man's" marriage,[67] cohabitation may function as an "adaptive family strategy"[68] or as an "alternative to marriage for those with serious economic difficulties."[69] Cohabitations are, generally, short-term arrangements, half of them ending in marriage and half of them dissolving.[70] More than 50 percent of first cohabitations are expected to transition to marriage within three years, a probability higher for whites than for blacks and Hispanics.[71] Not surprisingly, those who choose living together as a "stepping stone to marriage"[72] are more likely to seek a more permanent union. Furthermore, there is a greater likelihood that men and women with less education will cohabit.[73]

In the United States, about one-third of all births occur outside of marriage.[74] Between the early 1980s and early 1990s, the proportion of births to cohabiting women increased at a considerably higher rate than births to single mothers living without partners.[75] In addition, nonmarital stepfamilies are formed when a custodial parent, generally the mother, joins a cohabiting relationship. American stepfamilies are now as likely to be built on cohabitation as on marriage.[76] Approximately 40 percent of all children will spend some time in a cohabiting household before the age of 16.[77] Compared to white children, black and Hispanic children are overrepresented in cohabiting families.[78] They are also at greater risk for instability: "Overall, 15% of children born to cohabiting parents experience the end of their parents' unions by age one, half by age five and two-thirds by age ten."[79] Academically and behaviorally, children of cohabiting households fare less well than their counterparts in marital families.[80] Further, they are nearly as likely to experience poverty as children in single-mother households and are substantially more likely to be poor than children in married families.[81]

Research by Manning and Smock reveals just how fluid cohabiting arrangements are. In the absence of a formal wedding ceremony, it is difficult to pinpoint the "defining moment"[82] marking the beginning of a relationship. Most often, these arrangements are formed gradually and less deliberately than marriage—as in the case of a girlfriend residing with her parents who spends increasing amounts of time at her boyfriend's home, for example, or a man who arrived for a first date at a woman's house and "just never went home."[83] At times, cohabitants "straddle two living quarters at the same time,"[84] reluctant to deny themselves "somewhere to land"[85] if the cohabiting relationship breaks up. While it is often assumed that married couples will move into homes of their own, more than 37 percent of cohabiting couples in Manning and Smock's study sample were living with roommates, parents, or other relatives at some point in their relationship.[86] The lack of a universally recognizable term to refer to one's cohabiting partner can render social introductions awkward and embarrassing. This absence of commonly understood language to describe cohabiting partnerships is "[o]ne signal that cohabitation is not fully institutionalized."[87]

Premarital cohabitation appears to be associated with instability during marriage and earlier divorce. The probability that a woman's marriage will last at least ten years is lower for those who cohabit before marriage (60 percent) than for those who do not (66 percent).[88] One possible explanation is that cohabitants who later marry are a self-selected group whose personal attributes and attitudes toward marriage reduce the likelihood of marital stability.[89] Moreover, having raised the economic threshold for marriage, we have transformed it into a "luxury good"[90] as well as a social ideal. Our exalted view of marriage helps fuel the retreat from the institution with the urge to avoid such commitment until we can be certain to meet our expectations.[91] Ultimately, this brand of idealism raises the bar not only for the decision to marry but also for the decision to stay married.[92]

The decision to marry is still kept beyond the reach of most same-sex couples in the United States. We now turn to a segment of the population whose struggle to enter the marital institution vividly contrasts with the larger society's ambivalence about marriage.

Gays In and Out of Marriage

That a majority of Americans in 2011 supported legalizing same-sex marriage constituted an extraordinary turnaround in only a few years. Two-thirds of Americans opposed same-sex marriage in 1996, with only 27 percent in favor. By 2004, support had risen to 42 percent, and it stayed within a few percentage points of that level until 2011, when it jumped from 44 to 53 percent. Our attitudes toward gay marriage are strongly aligned with our age cohort. Only 39 percent of those aged over 55 favor allowing gays to marry. Among those aged 35 to 54, support grows to 53 percent. But seven in ten Americans aged 18 to 34 agree that gays should have access to marriage.[93] This level of support is consistent with earlier survey findings that youthful Americans are far more inclined than their elders to have a positive view of cohabitation, same-sex marriage, and interracial marriage.[94]

The broad movement to provide same-sex couples with the same degree of formal recognition as other couples began in the 1990s. Legal recognition was first afforded via civil unions and domestic partnerships, which accorded gay unions some or even all the benefits and burdens of marriage but denied same-sex couples access to marriage itself.[95] Massachusetts became the first state to authorize gay marriage in 2004.[96] As of 2013, same-sex marriages are authorized in twelve more states (California, Connecticut, Delaware, Iowa, Maine, Maryland, Minnesota, New Hampshire, New York, Rhode Island, Vermont, and Washington) and the District of Columbia.[97] Unsurprisingly, the five states with the highest percentage of same-sex couples who self-identified as spouses are all jurisdictions in which same-sex couples can marry: Massachusetts (44 percent), Vermont (35 percent), Connecticut (34 percent), Iowa (34 percent), and New Hampshire (31 percent).[98]

But the opposition to the legal validation of same-sex unions mounted quickly and remains potent. In 1996, Congress passed the Defense of Marriage Act (DOMA), which defined marriage for federal purposes as "only a legal union between one man and one woman as husband and wife," and provided that no state was required to recognize a same-sex marriage authorized by any other state.[99] The Federal Marriage Amendment, proposing to change the U.S. Constitution to limit marriage to heterosexual couples, was introduced in Congress several times in the past decade but has never passed. As of June 2013, 29 states have amended their constitutions to prohibit same-sex marriage, and an additional 6 states have statutory language adopting the restrictive language.[100]

At present, the nation's marriage map reveals that same-sex unions are banned in two-thirds of American jurisdictions. As one-sided as this may appear, the mobile character of American society makes this conflict even worse for same-sex couples. Gay spouses considering relocating to another state for reasons of employment, health, or family considerations must first ascertain whether their marriage will be legally acknowledged in their new home state, as well as in every state through which they travel. If one of them suffers a catastrophic injury, will a hospital allow the other spouse to make the vital decisions of a spouse or even to sit with the injured spouse in the intensive care unit? If they have children, will the nonbiological parent have his or her parental rights denied by schools or health care providers? If the couple decides to formally end their relationship, will they be allowed to divorce?

Most gay couples are denied several important options available to all opposite-sex partners. Individuals involved in an intimate relationship decide when or if to live together and whether or not to marry. If they marry and later relocate, they assume that their marriage will be recognized everywhere. Most gay couples have a far more limited set of options. They may live together only as a cohabiting couple, no matter what their intentions as to the status or permanence of their relationship. As a nonmarried couple, they will—in most jurisdictions—be denied access to programs and services provided under the legal umbrella of marital benefits.[101]

If a gay married couple moves to a state with a mini-DOMA provision, the spouses will find that their marriage has disappeared The state will not recognize them as a married couple in any way, thus rendering inapplicable a bevy of state legal benefits and obligations. Should they seek to end their marriage, they will find the courthouse door blocked to them. Same-sex marriages may only be dissolved in the few states that have authorized these marriages and in a small additional number of states that apply the traditional rules of comity to respect marriages created in sister states.[102] A married same-sex couple that establishes a new home in another state may thus encounter an obstacle that most could never foresee and that, historically, almost no married couples have ever encountered when they have sought to dissolve their unions.

Divorce means many things to a marriage, perhaps most prominently providing closure. Every married American who desires it may readily obtain a no-fault dissolution to his or her marriage. In most of the nation, however, same-sex married partners seeking to wind up their affairs are refused access to divorce. These spouses are, in a word, "wedlocked."[103] They are denied the right to terminate their union, to resolve their financial obligation to each other, and to essay a psychological finis to their marriage.[104] If they have children, the legal system will generally make it much more difficult for the couple to determine and allocate their parenting rights. While adoption orders from other states are conclusive under the Constitution's full faith and credit clause, the same-sex married couple will not be able to rely on the otherwise universal presumption that a child born during the marriage is the child of both spouses.[105]

The determination of the large majority of states not to recognize these marriages contains an ironic twist: even though these states abhor same-sex marital unions, they will not participate in dissolving them.[106] Were they legally to dissolve these marriages, they would have to acknowledge that these unions were lawful, which they will not do. A recent Texas case illustrates the harsh results this policy imposes on the parties.[107] Two men, J.B. and H.B., were married in Massachusetts in 2006 and relocated to Texas in 2008. In the following year, J.B. filed an uncontested petition for a no-fault divorce. The Texas attorney general intervened in the suit, insisting that the court lacked the authority to divorce a same-sex couple. The Texas Court of Appeals agreed, rejecting J.B.'s argument that "a divorce case does not recognize or give effect to a same-sex marriage formed in another jurisdiction."[108] In Texas, both a state statute and constitutional provision limit marriage to a heterosexual couple. The appellate court considered the endeavor to grant a divorce in a same-sex marriage as absurd as the attempt to administer the estate of a living person. Only the dead have an estate, and the view in Texas is that only heterosexuals have dead marriages deserving of legal internment.

What became of the marriage of J.B. and H.B.? The couple had moved to Texas when J.B. was transferred there and had accumulated community property and the type of enmeshed financial arrangement that characterizes most marriages. Those matters are now left in limbo, since the state has refused to allow the parties to settle them in a divorce. The parties remain married in Massachusetts and were never legally married according to Texas. Nor can they be divorced elsewhere, because states generally require that at least one party to a marriage be domiciled in that state in order to process a divorce. As long as J.B. and H.B. live in Texas, they can never be divorced.

The transformation in the number and status of nonmarital intimate associations, whether straight or gay, has been phenomenal. But the power balance *within* our domestic unions, whether married or not, continues—among heterosexual couples—to pivot around gender. The next section considers differentials between opposite-sex intimate partners and finds that gender still plays a major—if slowly fading—role. Same-sex couples, by comparison, have demonstrated far greater partner equality in their day-to-day undertakings.

How Gender Matters in Heterosexual Unions and Why Same-Sex Partnerships Are Different

"[H]usbands were economic providers, disciplinarians, and the heads of families, while wives were nurturers, caretakers, and subservient to their husbands"[109]—thus gender roles were defined in mid-20th-century marriages. Social changes beginning in the 1970s worked the gears of the legal system to erase laws that required and reinforced gender roles.[110] The economic impact of a marital partner's gender has in some ways been inverted. Marriage generally enhanced the financial status of wives a few decades ago; it currently provides an economic boon for men.[111] In the 1960s, "the typical man did not gain another breadwinner in his household when he married. Today, he does—giving his household increased earning power that most unmarried men do not enjoy."[112]

The prevailing norm has shifted away from a breadwinner/bread maker marriage.[113] But it has not shifted far. A generation after women achieved formal legal equality with men, "the vast majority of different-sex marriages still follow to some extent traditional gender roles."[114] Movement toward gender equity in this area has not eliminated the fact that even when women are employed outside the home, they continue to perform the majority of the homemaking and caretaking duties. For heterosexual couples, gender still plays a slightly diminished but still determinant role.[115]

Many family law scholars have pointed to changes in gender norms as a significant feature of the "family law revolution."[116] Indeed, the partnership model of marriage has consequences for divorce law, resulting in a presumption of equal allocation of assets and liabilities upon marital dissolution.[117] This vision of equality has also led to the elimination of gender-based rules in alimony, child custody, property management, and estate oversight.[118]

But the reality on the ground, in the home and at the office, during marriage and after divorce, has changed much more slowly than the legal parameters. The former breadwinners now spend a bit less time earning the bread and do a bit more around the house and with the children. The former bread makers now bring in a substantial portion of the family's bread but continue to do most of the child care and housework. Dual-earner couples became the norm in the late 20th century. By 1977, 66 percent of all married or partnered couples were dual-earner couples. In 2008, that percentage had risen to 80 percent.[119] But gendered norms remain pervasive, often buttressed by marketplace differentiation, reinforced by intentional discrimination by employers.[120] In 1970, the annual earnings of women who were in the workforce full-time were 59.4 percent of what their male counterparts earned. By 2007, the median annual earnings ratio had climbed to 77.8 percent. But the pace of narrowing the gap has stalled and even slipped back since then.[121] The gender wage disparity not only lasts throughout the employment life cycle but worsens over time. One study showed that due to lower work hours and time off for child rearing, employed women in their prime earning years earned only 38 percent of men's income.[122]

Moreover, as the U.S. Bureau of Labor Statistics noted, women and men "tend to work in different managerial and professional occupations."[123] In 2007, while 43 percent of male professionals worked in the high-paying computer and engineering fields, only 9 percent of female professionals were so employed. Professional women were more likely to work in the education and health care occupations. These lower-paying fields employed 67 percent of female professionals but only 30 percent of their male counterparts.[124] Even more strikingly, in 2004, the average annual earnings for men who did not complete their high school education was more than the average for women with a college degree, $36,021 versus $35,338; and the average for women with graduate degrees was only slightly more than the average for men with only a high school diploma, $41,995 versus $40,822.[125] As the Institute for Women's Policy Research summarized the data in 2012, "Male-dominated occupations tend to pay more than female-dominated occupations at similar skill levels, particularly at higher levels of educational attainment."[126]

At home, gender norms continue to regulate the division of labor between parents, which resembles that of previous generations. Mothers are more likely than fathers to work part-time or take a leave from employment.[127] The presence of children in the home also negatively affects women's wages more than men's, since women frequently devote more time and effort than men to family responsibilities.[128] Because of the paucity of subsidized care options for children and elderly relatives, women often have to provide the care themselves. In the typical couple, the woman earns considerably less than her male partner, and the decision to sacrifice her earnings in order to provide the needed family care makes economic sense.[129] As the primary wage earner, the man is in the labor force earlier and more continuously than his female partner, thus securing a higher and a more consistent income stream for the family. Also, since higher-income jobs are often accompanied by more-generous fringe benefits, the man's employment may already supply important benefits, such as health insurance.[130]

Multiplied a millionfold, these results will perpetuate gender stratification in employment and wide disparities in income over time.[131] For example, of college students who graduated in 1992–93, 23 percent of mothers were out of the workforce a decade later, and another 17 percent were employed part-time.[132] By contrast, less than 2 percent of fathers were out of the workforce, with an equally minuscule percentage working part-time.[133] Tellingly, in 2009, the United States had an estimated 5.1 million "stay-at-home" mothers but only 158,000 "stay-at-home" fathers.[134]

Personal choices intertwine with economic choices and consequences, but they are still firmly rooted in gender. In the middle of the 20th century, a man's "thrift and industry" were matched against a woman's "domestic skills,"[135] but their differences were perceived as shrinking. Yet gender largely determined the cultural roles for spouses. A woman in the Eisenhower era needed to accommodate more to marriage than did a man.

> The man goes to shop or office after marriage the same as he did before, and even though he comes home to his own home instead of his parental home or a rooming house, he still comes home as before to someone who provides for his needs in food and rest.[136]

A married woman in the 1950s labor force needed to satisfy the needs of her husband and children as well as those of her boss. She thus faced "the heavy strain of double work."[137] Women in that era could join the labor force but could never leave their domestic employ. In the evocative words of historian Jessica Weiss, "A woman walked up the aisle a bride and back down it a housewife, whether or not she continued to work or study."[138]

Much has changed in the succeeding half century, but much has not. As historian Hendrik Hartog reminds us, marriage has always "meant a dyadic relationship between two unequally situated individuals."[139] The socioeconomic gap between motherhood and fatherhood is still "particularly stark,"[140] and parental obligations "continue to be assigned on the basis of gender."[141] Even when both parents are employed, the social mores continue to induce a woman to undertake the lioness's share in child care and housework, resulting in the unequal division of labor famously described by Arlie Hochschild and Anne Machung as "the second shift."[142]

Hochschild and Machung concluded in 1989 that the gendered tasks of marriage generate an extra month of work per year for women in chores related to home and children.[143] A decade later, a review of research concluded that although men and women now believed that domestic tasks should be shared, "[o]n average, women perform two or three times as much housework as men."[144] That the gender-driven assumptions behind this 21st-century division of labor have been deeply internalized may be seen by the study's finding that "the vast majority of men, as well as most women," consider it fair that women perform twice or thrice as much housework as men.[145]

The sexes are slowly heading toward equal sharing of child rearing and household work—very slowly.[146] Between 1965 and 2003, women doubled and men tripled the amount of time they spent involved in child care.[147] These trends track those of much of the Western industrial world. Data covering this same period for 20 industrialized countries show an overall increase in men's proportional contribution to family work (including housework, child care, and shopping), from less than one-fifth in 1965 to more than one-third by 2003.[148] A 2005 study by the University of Michigan's Institute for Social Research confirmed this emerging trend toward domestic convergence, comparing the average amount of housework done by women and by men in 1976 and 2005. Women's domestic labor decreased from 26 to 17 hours per week.[149] The time men spent on household tasks increased from 6 to 13 hours per week.[150] But a 2010 study from the University of California, Los Angeles, found that mothers still spend an average of 27 percent of their time on housework, compared to 18 percent of fathers' time.[151]

Not only has the actual convergence of gender roles been elusive, but many consider it both unachievable *and* undesired.[152] The percentage of employees who agree (strongly or somewhat) that it is better for the family if "the man earns the money and the woman takes care of the home and children" has indeed dropped substantially over the past thirty years—from 64 percent in 1977 to 41 percent in 2008.[153] But that statistic means that two of five adults in the paid workforce still subscribe to so-called traditional gender roles. Among employees 28 years of age and younger in 2008, over a third (35 percent) believed that a women's place is in the home.[154] Motherhood continues to require "substantial economic and personal sacrifices," while fatherhood "appears to engender a 'wage premium.'"[155] Men spend more time at work after the birth of their children, while women do the reverse.[156] Given the stress levels of the multitasking family, parenting has been aptly limned as "Two people. Three full-time jobs,"[157] and even as we head into the second decade of the 21st century, two of those three jobs are held by a woman.

Cohabiting heterosexual couples generally observe fewer traditional gender roles and work out a more egalitarian division of household labor than their married counterparts.[158] While cohabiting men do a similar amount of housework as married men, cohabiting women perform less housework than married women (although women in all heterosexual couples do more work than their partners).[159] Research also has found that couples that cohabit before marriage tend toward greater equality in sharing postnuptial housework, consistent with the notion that these couples "bring more egalitarian expectations and experiences to their subsequent marriages."[160] But this dynamic of equal sharing has spawned a set of consequences that are less desirable. Cohabiters who adhere to traditional sex roles are more likely to marry or have long-lasting relationships, while couples who are more egalitarian "are at increased risk of relationship separation."[161] The significant linkage between a cohabiting couple's intent to marry and social stability is explored in chapter 3.

While gender continues to dictate, to a significant extent, the role division within heterosexual couples, research on same-sex partners has found a greater uniformity in this area. Research on same-sex couples over the past few decades has shown that these unions "are more egalitarian in division of housework and finances" than heterosexual couples.[162] A 2005 study reported these findings about female partners:

> Married heterosexual women were more likely to report that their partner paid for items in general, including rent/mortgage, utilities, groceries, the women's own clothing, major household appliances, entertainment and eating out, and

the women's personal spending money. Lesbians in civil unions and those not in civil unions tended to report sharing finances more equally. Conversely, married heterosexual women reported doing more of the household tasks than their partners did, including doing the dishes, cooking the evening meal, vacuuming the carpets, doing the laundry, cleaning the bathroom, doing the grocery shopping, ironing, and taking the children to their activities and appointments. Married heterosexual women reported that their partner more often took out the trash, took care of the lawn, fixed drinks for company, and drove the car when the couple was going somewhere in town together. Again, lesbians in civil unions and those not in civil unions were more likely to report sharing these household activities more equitably.[163]

Findings such as these hold true for gay male couples as well.[164] That these are all same-sex couples eliminates the possibility of a traditional gender hierarchy and suggests the possibility of a more equal allocation of roles and tasks, what one study called "degendered parenting."[165] Indeed, it is rare in these couples for one partner to play a "male" role and the other a "female" role.[166] Moreover, majorities of gay and lesbian couples report an equal sharing of power in the relationship. These evenhanded relationships are characteristic of both childless and child-rearing same-sex couples.[167]

The perspective of gender helps refocus the key issue of family policy into one encompassing all types of family composition. In the following chapter, we briefly consider gender in the context of how marriage has evolved over the last few centuries. We also discuss how the apportioning of gender roles within marriage and cohabitation produces two very different types of intimate associations. Our primary focus, however, will be on the characteristics and components of well-functioning families. Stable, successful domestic arrangements are not simply a matter of form. The ability of today's families to adapt and survive amid an increasingly unforgiving economy determines their own well-being as well as that of the generations of families to follow.

CHAPTER 3

Luxury Goods

The Well-Being of Families

There is no secret to constructing well-functioning families. The prime components are two live-in parents, stability, and a measure of economic security. Those of us lucky enough to be born in the baby boom had a fair shot at these blessings. Though never quite as idyllic as pictured, the era seemed to be tinged with gold even before it had passed. If Louis XV's ghost had risen up to warn us of the coming deluge, we could not have been more surprised. The 1960s arrived, the floodgates burst, and change came rushing in.

Fifty years on, marriage is but one selection on the menu of intimate relationships. Its value, however, like any increasingly rare commodity, has risen and been reaffirmed. We use the term *well-being* to denote a family's ability to take care of its members dependably and predictably and to help them flourish physically, emotionally, and materially. Compared to other close associations, marriage has a greater capacity to enrich, enhance, and even extend the lives of its participants. In promoting healthy, well-adjusted families, low-conflict wedded unions have a clear advantage over single or cohabiting parents. When marriage became optional, family well-being became more elusive.

As the poet said, "This too shall pass." Family has never been a static institution, and it has undergone conceptual and structural revisions over time. Many of these alterations have been based in culture, but even the liveliest zeitgeist has its pecuniary side. In the present era, economics functions, perhaps as much or more than culture, as the great enabler and inhibitor of marriage. Working-age couples of low to moderate education have watched their middle-class aspirations vanish in recession and a progressively specialized job market. While they shun or postpone long-term commitment, better-educated couples with sunnier financial prospects are drawn to it and profit by it. In a country that prides itself on democratic access to achievement, family well-being is increasingly apportioned by social and economic class.

Over the last few decades, families have grown fluid, restless, and fragile. It is projected that only half of America's children will live continuously with both of their biological parents before reaching adulthood.[1] Childbearing among married women has declined, while four in ten births in 2007 occurred outside of marriage.[2] A single mother is as likely to cohabit with as to wed the father of her child,[3] although legalizing such unions does not guarantee they will endure. Marriage founded on out-of-wedlock birth tends to be plagued with conflict, a path to instability rather than permanence.[4] Cohabitation is producing its own baby boom, with more nonmarital births occurring within these relationships than to single mothers living alone.[5] Cohabitation rates are also high among the divorced. Since many of them already have children when they enter these arrangements, they form stepfamilies.[6] Children of these newly minted cohabiting and stepfamily relationships undergo significant and sometimes intolerable adjustment.

Divorce, single parenthood, and cohabitation have all been linked to poorer outcomes for children. Social scientists are quick to caution that associations do not necessarily imply cause and effect. But the associations are hard to ignore, especially those between family diversity, rising levels of child poverty, and stagnation in educational attainment.[7] According to Barbara Whitehead, family diversity "in the form of increasing numbers of single parents and stepparent families does not strengthen the social fabric."[8] Instead, it "dramatically weakens and undermines society, placing new burdens on schools, courts, prisons, and the welfare system."[9] Others insist that what is important is not whether a family form comports with a particular model but how well it functions in providing nurturance, love, and care.[10] Still, as current research shows, durable marriages continue to be the most reliable wellsprings of sound families.

Before we pronounce a wholesale indictment of family diversity, however, we should know that marriage, in and of itself, is no cure-all. Aiming the proverbial shotgun at single, divorced, and cohabiting parents and herding them into matrimony will not ensure their future success and happiness. For a number of cultural, economic, and psychological reasons, present-day couples are wary of binding themselves to long-term family commitments. Many will postpone or opt out of marriage because they feel deficient in the personal, financial, and educational resources that will give their unions the best fighting chance. Economic and emotional uncertainty induces a kind of fear and trembling as to deep, permanent commitments. Marriage is still desirable, but for many, it has become an abstraction rather than a tangible objective. The more we idealize marriage and the more we condition its existence on preconceived goals, the further it recedes from the realm of our perceived possibilities. People are not so much rejecting marriage as a life choice as they are deeming themselves unworthy of it.

In chapter 2, we noted that raising the economic bar to matrimony has transformed it into a "luxury good." Marriage has also been termed "the gold-standard for relationships and the best context for raising children."[11] Such material-world metaphors are no accident. Stable marriage, which has increasingly become the province of the relatively affluent and well educated, has been described as "the most highly valued form of family life in America, the most prestigious way to live your life."[12] It has taken perhaps thousands of years for the marital state to reach this pinnacle as the optimal breeding ground for self-fulfillment and high-achieving progeny. Historian Stephanie Coontz wonders whether marriage as an institution can withstand the weight of such lofty and "unprecedented" expectations.[13] Marriage will likely survive, because there will always be those who desire and accept nothing less. For others, marriage attracts yet repels, because they view it as either inaccessible to them or good for other people perhaps but not for them. If marriage is the price of stability and well-being, a fair number of American families are going without.

Coming Apart at the Center

In the mid-1960s, Daniel Patrick Moynihan sounded an alarm about the cycle of poverty afflicting black families. Already burdened by a legacy of slavery and ongoing discrimination, these families, argued Moynihan, were further plagued by dysfunction from within.[14] A "tangle of pathology," woven by the proliferation of female-headed households and the diminished social role of black males, all but assured perpetual poverty for generations of black children.[15] Moynihan's call for a national effort to rebuild the structure of black families fell on outraged ears. Liberals decried Moynihan's seemingly racist assertions, his characterization of black households as pathological, and his penchant for "blaming the victim."[16] Even before it was widely distributed, Moynihan's report "had been consigned to the netherworld of the politically incorrect, where it would remain for decades."[17]

Revisited today, Moynihan's principal argument is still pertinent and quite sound: "Whenever males in any population subgroup lack widespread access to reliable jobs, decent earnings, and key forms of socially rewarded status, single parenthood will increase, with negative side effects on women and children."[18] What Moynihan did not foresee was how these social and economic stresses would creep upward and outward, across class as well as racial boundaries. Poor and working-class whites, increasingly subject to chronic joblessness and decreased earnings, have incurred rates of single parenthood previously seen only among blacks.[19] A "deepening marital divide," cautions the National Marriage Project, threatens to fracture America along class lines, favoring the most educated of all races.[20]

The social mobility of a community's citizens is heavily dependent on the economic health of its neighborhoods. A recent analysis of over a hundred large and medium-sized U.S. metropolitan areas revealed growing disparities in the distribution of wealth.[21] The number of Americans living in middle-income neighborhoods has significantly declined, from 65 percent in 1970 to 44 percent in 2009.[22] During that same period, the number of Americans living at the extremes of affluence or poverty doubled. By 2007, nearly a third of American neighborhoods were either rich or poor.[23] Income segregation, the concentration of either wealth or disadvantage in our neighborhoods, produces hugely unequal opportunities. A jurisdiction's tax base determines the quality of its schools, social institutions, and public resources. As the rich become more isolated within their enclaves, poor communities are left with lower-quality schools and support systems and less access to educated, financially stable neighbors who might serve as role models.[24] Middle-income neighborhoods, meanwhile, are being eaten away at both ends, a casualty of the ever-increasing economic divide.

The "moderately educated middle," which includes those with high school diplomas and perhaps some college but no four-year degree, comprises 58 percent of the population.[25] Traditional family values were once firmly anchored here, in America's center. Now, middle-class respectability appears to be migrating north, to the upper echelons.[26] For the affluent and educated, especially those with children, divorce is becoming unfashionable.[27] Of the most educated Americans, only 11 percent have divorced within 10 years, while the dissolution rate for the moderately and least educated hovers at 37 percent.[28] Formerly, affluent and middle-income Americans were equally likely to enjoy happy, intact marriages. Now more prone to cohabit than marry, with 44 percent of its children born outside of marriage, America's center looks more like the nation's lower, rather than upper, classes.[29] In the heartland, divorce has grown as common among rural Americans as among their urban cousins.[30] Moreover, nonmarital births have risen in pastoral enclaves like Sioux County, Iowa, where "custody cases involving unmarried people used to be so rare that the court did not even have a category for them."[31]

In middle America, women are surpassing men in employment, education, and self-sufficiency, altering their expectations of lifelong commitments. For women who find themselves in unequal partnerships, divorce can be liberating. Affluent couples in "peer marriages," however, depend on joint economic contributions and prosper accordingly.[32] From their wealthier, more secure perspectives, "it's not seen as liberating to divorce. It's scary."[33] Family stability and its attendant financial and emotional benefits is less and less evenly distributed across households of diverse economic background. If the dire warnings of the National Marriage Project are valid, America is sliding toward a "separate-and-unequal family regime."[34]

Middle America's "retreat from marriage"[35] is disturbing, not least because we wonder if we should have seen it coming. Throughout its history, marriage has mirrored the prevailing cultural and economic inclinations of its time. This sensitivity to social change and apparent malleability may account for marriage's survival, at least thus far. The less traditional family forms may challenge it or even try to banish it to a particular stratum of society. But we would be hard pressed to imagine a future entirely without it.

How Marriage Has and Has Not Changed

The term *family* did not acquire its emotive, nesting connotations until fairly recently. In preindustrial times, it referred to kinship or lineage. The marital residence, along with its inhabitants, was more commonly known as a household, composed of husband, wife, children, and servants. Households functioned as economic units of production—for food, clothing, and whatever else its members and surrounding villagers required.[36] Villages, in turn, depended on "the networks of mutual aid and communal accountability"[37] of their farmers and landholders. One's choice of marriage partner carried great social and economic consequences for the community. Villagers were pressured to "choose mates and in-laws who pull their own weight in communal enterprises."³⁸ The potential impact of marriage in terms of the village welfare was far too great for villagers to consider marriage "to be a couple's own private business."³⁹

With the dawn of the market economy, the village way of life and its customs no longer predominated. The young could work for wages, accumulate their own assets, and, within limits, marry whom they chose. The 18th-century Enlightenment gave rise to new ideas of individual rights and freedoms, of institutions and relationships founded on justice and reason rather than absolutism. Marriage grew more secular and private, driven by the pursuit of love and happiness rather than status or financial gain. Wives and mothers became revered and sentimentalized, romantic ideals flourished, and "the new norms of love-based intimate marriage"⁴⁰ began to spread throughout Europe and America.

While pedestals were being built for wives and mothers, children, especially the less privileged ones, had to wait for their defining moment. Nineteenth-century agrarian and working-class families valued children for their labor. With industrialization, the move from farm to city, and the growth of the urban middle class, children "were increasingly sheltered from the world of work."⁴¹ Transformed from "objects of utility into objects of sentiment,"⁴² children came to be seen as beings in need of guidance, protection, and education, and childhood lengthened.

With the lengthening of childhood, infant mortality declined, and women needed to be pregnant far less often. As adult life expectancies rose, "wives and husbands could choose to spend several years together before having children and could expect many more after they were finished raising them."⁴³ As husbands and wives spent more time together, there was more opportunity for "companionship and personal growth."⁴⁴ Acknowledging that wives and husbands could bond over shared interests was a somewhat novel development in marital relations. Each half of the dyad had long been known to be essential to the other but had rarely been openly or even privately regarded as equal.

Gender roles and the division of labor have always been ubiquitous in married life. Stephanie Coontz described the ways in which a typical farming couple shared the work of the farm before the machine age.

> In addition to plowing, [the husband] spread manure, dug peat for fuel, and harvested crops by hand, swinging heavy sickles or scythes. He threshed the grain, turned the hay, and sometimes hired himself out to work in the fields of

larger landowners. His wife milked the cows, made butter and cheese, fed the chickens and ducks, cleaned and carded wool, prepared flax (a process that involved fifteen steps), brewed beer, and carried water. Women also took surplus produce to market, washed their clothes in the village stream, and had their grain pounded at the mill. Both men and women helped with the harvest, gleaned the fields, and collected firewood. Women, like men, hired themselves out as agricultural laborers.[45]

The labor of wives, however backbreaking, did not alter the husband's status as absolute ruler in preindustrial households. The 19th-century rise of the urban middle class did, however, produce a "peculiar compromise between egalitarian and patriarchal views of marriage."[46] Women and men began to be seen as having unique sets of skills, abilities, and inclinations, as being "so completely different in their natures that they could not be compared as superior or inferior."[47] Husbands pursued wage earnings outside of the home, while wives engaged in domesticity. In their different spheres, each made vital contributions to the welfare and survival of the household. During this period, the more modern notions of family began to emerge. The "household was transformed into Home Sweet Home"[48] and now aspired to be a patch of heaven on earth as well as "a nest for the young."[49] By the 1950s, the breadwinner-homemaker model appeared permanent and inviolable, "a crowning achievement that was likely to remain the dominant family form for as long as industrial society survived."[50]

Visions of the perfect union fail to stay fixed, because our expectations of marriage continue to evolve. In the 1920s, feminism, socialism, and a growing fascination with human sexuality forced a reevaluation of marital contentment. The divorce rate doubled between 1880 and the late 1920s. Formerly, a wife or husband seeking divorce might have alleged cruelty or a breakdown in fulfilling the marital role of provider or housekeeper. Increasingly, however, couples sought an end to marriages perceived as lacking in "love, companionship, and emotional intimacy."[51] To the rebellious post–World War I generation, 19th-century separate spheres and sexual repressiveness hindered the formation of close personal attachments. Cultivating deep sexual and emotional intimacy "was seen as the best hope for stability in marriage."[52]

Twentieth-century sociologist Ernest Burgess characterized unions based on love, friendship, and common interest as "companionate marriage."[53] He termed this relationship the prime source of emotional and social support in most people's lives. As the nuclear family became more insulated from "kin, nonrelatives and the rest of society, spouses became more reliant on each other for companionship, assistance and affection."[54] Unlike institutional marriage, with its emphasis on social rules and conformity, companionate marriage encouraged self-expression and personal satisfaction.

Companionate marriage was enjoying its finest hour by the mid-20th century. But it was not long before the rift between the real and the ideal began to show. By pitching intimacy and self-fulfillment as marital raison d'êtres, women's magazines of the late 1950s and early 1960s became unwittingly subversive. In fact, "[i]t was by reading about what marriage *ought* to be that many women saw what their own marriages weren't."[55] Men and women began to feel trapped and alienated in their respective roles as breadwinner and homemaker. No longer needing to grow their own food and make their own clothing, wives had become "consumers rather than producers."[56] They discovered that by going out to work, they could resume "the productive role they had always had, but they did it this time by bringing home a paycheck."[57] In recent decades, women's earnings have grown faster than men's, and by 2007, wives' educational credentials had begun to exceed those of their husbands. The burgeoning economic independence of women has helped to change the course of intimate associations. "[N]ever before in history," observed Stephanie Coontz, "have so many women been capable of supporting themselves and their children without a husband."[58]

More so than in the past, today's Americans are likely to divorce, cohabit, marry late, or pass up marriage altogether. Among those aged 30 to 44, 60 percent were married in 2007, compared to 84 percent in 1970. Decline in marriage rates is steepest among the less educated, with a gap of 16 percentage points between college graduates and those with a high school diploma. Experts assure us that the vast majority of Americans do eventually marry, perhaps as many as 90 percent.[59] But respondents in a recent poll seem far less sanguine. Four in 10 Americans believe marriage is becoming obsolete, proof of a growing perception that "marriage's best days are behind it."[60] Forty-six percent of unmarried adults say that they want to get married, 29 percent are not sure, and 25 percent do not want to marry. At the same time, married people report greater satisfaction in their lives than do members of all other family types.

As we discussed in chapter 2, there is no one reason for marriage's loss of preeminence in American life. Certainly, beginning in the late 1960s, the use of safe, reliable contraception dissolved the linkages between love, sex, and matrimony. Young adults could choose to live alone, to delay marriage, to cohabit, or to bear children outside of marriage. Neighborhood and community ties have eroded even further since Ernest Burgess's day, and according to Andrew Cherlin, this increases the burden on intimate relationships. Having become "the main setting in which to develop a sense of meaning and identity,"[61] marriage is now a forum for enhancing individual satisfaction and maximizing personal growth. Companionate marriage has ruptured and grown individualistic, with the desire for self-development and self-fulfillment threatening to replace "mutual satisfaction and successful team effort as the basis for marriage."[62] A heightened expectation of intimate relationships produces greater sensitivity to their defects. The constant "self-appraisal of how your personal life is going," noted Andrew Cherlin, "is like having a continual readout of your emotional heart rate."[63]

Despite these allegedly self-seeking tendencies, Americans cling to the romantic ideal. Married people continue to place the highest value on love, lifelong commitment, and companionship, even more than they cherish having children or achieving financial stability. In acknowledgment of this, Betsey Stevenson and Justin Wolfers have proposed an alternative model, "hedonic marriage."[64] Because families are no longer self-sustaining economic units of production, they have shifted their focus to shared consumption. Partners in hedonic marriage are likely to be of similar age and educational background, drawn together by shared values and activities as well as the desire for intellectual stimulation. Couples who are less educated and affluent may be ill-served by hedonic or "soul mate" models of marriage.[65] With women outpacing men in pursuit of college degrees, careers, and financial independence, visions of shared personal growth can breed mutual disappointment and resentment. Further, the demand for companionship in pursuit of life's pleasures presupposes the leisure time and standard of living with which to support it. In this sense, marriage has come to more closely resemble an exclusive club than the homey, welcoming refuge once embraced by generations past.

The United States leads the Western world in both marriage and divorce. For most Americans, "marriage is the highest expression of commitment they can imagine," and it is "taken more seriously . . . than ever before."[66] For both men and women, however, it is losing its status as the "gateway to adulthood and respectability."[67] Less exalted but far more accessible, cohabitation is now marriage's main competitor in the relationship arena.

Marriage and Cohabitation Compared

To hear Linda Waite and Maggie Gallagher tell it, marriage is the surest route to longer, happier, healthier, wealthier lives.[68] At its best, marriage helps to stave off early death, suicide, alcoholism, and depression and can aid the functioning of the immune system. Over time, the higher earnings and accumulated assets of a wedded couple lead to higher net worth and greater financial security. In itself, marriage "seems to encourage the creation and retention of wealth."[69] No such paeans are sung to cohabitation. Regardless of the length of their relationship, unmarried couples do not accrue savings and assets at a level approaching that of married couples. Although live-in lovers may experience some of the emotional benefits usually conferred by marriage, these perks are largely transitory. In the United States, "long-term cohabiting relationships are far rarer than successful marriages."[70] If marriage is the good son, cohabitation is its wayward younger brother.

Cohabitants, in turn, may be more likely to agree with Ambrose Bierce's definition of matrimony: "The state or condition of a community consisting of a master, a mistress and two slaves, making in all, two."[71] But, as James Q. Wilson noted, it is precisely the relinquishment of freedom that makes sense of the emotional and financial investment that marriage entails.[72] Couples who consent to permanent, exclusive relationships know that dissolution of their union and division of their assets will likely be costly, painful, and protracted. Issues of child custody will also be difficult, but at least the parties can expect their interests to be given legal weight and recognition. In cohabitation, "no specific procedures exist for getting into it, and none for getting out."[73] If the couple separates and has a child in common, one parent claims it, gathers its things, and walks away with it. Not only are cohabiting unions "unacknowledged by law," but they also lack the "positive vocabulary and public image that set a high standard for the couple's behavior and for the respect that outsiders ought to give to their relationship."[74]

In 2010, the number of male-female cohabiting couples increased to 7.5 million, nearly a million more than in 2009. Unlike same-sex couples, these men and women face no social or legal barriers to marrying. Yet they persist in choosing what, by all accounts, appears to be the lesser option. Many of today's cohabitants are the children of divorce, and this colors their perceptions of marital fealty and permanence. Waite and Gallagher depict a generation in which "young men and women long for stable marriage but increasingly are worried and anxious about their ability to achieve it."[75] In addition, some individuals refrain from marrying by a process of self-selection. Because of their temperaments or personality traits, they find themselves unsuited to close, lasting attachments.

The poor economic outlook, especially for men with less education, also impedes the hope and desire for long-term relationships. Modern automation and communications technologies, as well as outsourcing, have eroded the base of semiskilled blue-collar jobs. The college-educated population can generally find well-paying work, "but what's left for everyone else is a dwindling demand for routine work and a steady demand for low-paying manual work."[76] Individuals affected by chronic economic instability fear that they have too little personal and financial capital to invest in marriage. Newly formed couples in 2010 contained an even higher share of nonworking men than in the previous year. Persistent unemployment may be responsible for the increase in cohabiting couples during that same period.

Unlike their male counterparts, women with less education have better access to job opportunities. With less need of husbands to financially sustain them, they have lower incentive to marry. Among poorer women, men with weak economic prospects can be more of a burden than a benefit. As one woman explained, "I don't need a husband to help me scrape by. I can scrape by on my own."[77] Despite a growing acceptance of changing gender roles, however, we are not quite ready to let go of the archetype of the male breadwinner. Nearly 70 percent of Americans believe that a man is not ready for marriage unless he can financially support his family.

Marriage and cohabitation are alike in that the parties share lodgings, food, sex, and, hopefully, a modicum of affection. Marriage differs in its vow of mutual obligation. Spouses pledge to forever take care of each other, through illness, disability, financial hardship, and whatever other adversities they may encounter. "The promise is the heart of the matter," said James Q. Wilson. Cohabitation offers short-term gains but lacks this mechanism for "social insurance."[78] Couples at the altar also exchange promises of fidelity, a charge considerably more ambiguous for live-in lovers. One male cohabitant with no immediate plans to have sex outside of the relationship told his companion nevertheless, "I'm not going to tell you that I'm not going to be sexually involved with anyone [else] because of our relationship . . . I want to make that decision because of how I feel—not because of how you feel."[79] Such sentiments run counter to the "enforceable trust"[80] imposed by matrimony, to the assurances undertaken by wedded couples, both publicly and privately. Within a marriage, "there is no such thing as a victimless crime."[81]

A comparison of marital and nonmarital unions reveals the "mine and yours" mentality of cohabitants versus the "ours" orientation of spouses. Cohabitants tend to maintain separate bank accounts, while spouses pool their resources. Robin Fretwell-Wilson recounted an anecdote highlighting the contrast between marital and nonmarital decision making about money:[82] A married and cohabiting couple were each given $600 to spend as they chose. The married couple settled on airline tickets to Hawaii. The husband had expressed a desire to visit Maui, and the wife agreed that a vacation "would be nice for us." The cohabiting couple, without hesitation, opted for a 50-50 split, dividing up the sum in order to make individual purchases. The pooling of income underscores the trust in the relationship and "may also enhance union stability by reducing conflict about how money is spent."[83]

Marriage and cohabitation also differ in the way in which couples view social obligations external to the relationship. Wedded couples, for example, "might be expected to lead a more collectivistic lifestyle by having more mutual friends, spending more time together, and developing more common traits and interests."[84] Cohabiting couples, by contrast, "may experience more freedom to pursue an individualistic lifestyle."[85] Men, in particular, are more individualistic in their social outlook and may regard marriage as hazardous to their independence. For this reason, they may be attracted to cohabitation as the better, less confining alternative to marriage. Women, in turn, may reject the marriage option in order to avoid the risk of being trapped in traditional gender roles.[86]

As discussed in the previous chapter, the pursuit of equality can work to the detriment of long-term relationships. Cohabitants, for example, divide household tasks more equally, while married couples continually struggle to find a "comfort zone"[87] between life and work. The balance "remains elusive"[88] in dual-earner marriages where husbands' domestic contributions fail to offset wives' longer work hours. Research by Paul Amato and his colleagues indicated that spouses were happier when housework was shared equally.[89] But a strict division of labor is more characteristic of cohabiting unions than of marriage. Cohabitants strive for equality, but their inclination is toward apportioning chores quantitatively. The forward-looking, communal nature of marriage requires a more flexible, adaptive mode of egalitarianism. Waite and Gallagher have proposed a scheme of specialization whereby spouses perform chores most suited to their particular skills and talents.[90] Rather than equality achieved by 50-50 split, spouses seek a more creative allocation of tasks while minimizing stress and increasing productivity. As noted earlier, monitoring expenditures in households with separate bank accounts can produce conflict. Similarly, policing equality in marital relationships can be draining, as "the accumulated weight of decision after decision can wear on people."[91] Even those couples that claim to be egalitarian risk the perpetuation of gender inequality "by subtle, often latent processes."[92] Significant, lasting social change, the kind that truly improves marriage, is gradual rather than dramatic, "evolutionary rather than revolutionary."[93]

Decades ago, a couple's choice to live together without marrying seemed revolutionary. Today, cohabitation has increased throughout the Western world. Once it has taken root in a culture, averred David Popenoe, "cohabitation seems gradually to be corroding the desire of couples to move to marriage."[94] To a certain extent, the strength of this perception depends on the culture and the couple in question. Among Americans who have ever lived in a cohabiting union, 64 percent say they considered it as a step toward marriage. Adults with higher incomes and more education are significantly more likely to cohabit with a view toward matrimony. Among those currently residing with a nonmarital partner, 69 percent say they expect they will someday wed their live-in companion. In the United States, the desire to marry is alive and well. But it is sometimes unmoored from the personal will and financial capacity to make it a reality. Cohabitation is "still a pathway to marriage for many college graduates, while it may be an end in itself for many less educated women."[95]

The "meaning of marriage has changed"[96] from a haven for childbearing and child rearing to one of self-fulfillment. For poor women raising families alone or with a live-in partner, dreaming about marriage is "a guilty pleasure."[97] Without money and a strong, committed relationship, marriage is "impractical."[98] Wealthier, more educated couples are well acquainted with notions of self-fulfillment. For them, marriage is not just practical; they have the personal and economic capital to make it hugely profitable.

In the middle are the many who would marry if they had more education and better career prospects and could afford a lavish wedding and a nicely furnished house. For these couples, to marry is to display "the ultimate merit badge,"[99] proof that one is capable of gleaning the necessities for married life—material resources and a willing partner. Andrew Cherlin has suggested that these couples are enamored of the trappings of matrimony but not necessarily of its substance. Because they are more concerned with "*getting* married" than "*being* married,"[100] the mood of these cohabitants seems covetous rather than aspirational, as if marriage were a prize to be won rather than a bond to be developed and perfected over time.

Within three years, cohabiting unions generally break up or transition to marriage. Couples who live together prior to marrying "are less likely to stay married"[101] than those who do not. More and more, however, couples find it unthinkable to head straight for the altar without cohabiting first. If, for them, living together is a platform for marriage and a testing ground for compatibility, it seems counterintuitive that they would risk wedded unions that are less stable. David Popenoe has posited that "attitudes and behaviors developed through cohabitation may be inimical to long-term marriage."[102] Cohabitants' habits of problem solving, division of labor, and sharing of resources may be fitted to short-term relationships but not to those that are highly codependent and open-ended. Further, couples who are drawn to nonmarital living arrangements may be less comfortable with traditional family values and close, committed attachments. To view cohabiting relationships as vehicles for testing compatibility is "an attitude poisonous to long-term marriage."[103] It leads to expectations and assumptions that may be valid in the short-term but not for a long, eventful wedded life. Compared to couples who are dating, live-in lovers may find it harder to separate due to household, economic, and emotional issues, and "[t]hey therefore may drift through inertia into inappropriate marriages, only to break up further down the line."[104]

To a generation of adults who came of age in a divorce culture, trusting in cohabitation as a grounding for marriage manifests "the mistaken belief that it will provide divorce insurance."[105] Notably, couples who are already engaged when they begin living together improve their chances of marital stability.[106] Perhaps they have moved beyond tentative, trial-basis notions of sharing a living space toward carrying out an actual promise to build a life together. Psychologist Meg Jay has observed a "gender asymmetry" in the ways in which men and women approach cohabitation.[107] Women are more prone to view it as a prologue to marriage, while men tend to consider it a means for testing the waters or postponing commitment. These divergent outlooks can render the relationship unsatisfying for both parties. When seen as a "multiyear, never-ending audition"[108] for marriage, the act of cohabiting casts doubt on whether the partners were ever personally invested in each other in the first place.

Children and Family Diversity

Humans are genetically predisposed to form close attachments, but "it is a predisposition that can be facilitated or impeded by the environment."[109] In terms of child well-being, the relevant environment is the family, and it currently assumes various forms, including a single parent, two married or cohabiting biological parents, or a stepfamily created either by cohabitation or marriage and in which only one parent is biologically related to the child. Because of cohabitation's rapid breakup rate, children rarely live continuously with two unmarried biological parents. Single motherhood is sometimes hard to classify, because nearly 30 percent of single mothers in 2010, for example, were found to be residing with an unmarried partner of the opposite or same sex.[110] Currently, about 40 percent of cohabiting unions contain children, half of whom are not biologically related to both live-in partners.[111] Since cohabitation is becoming the first union of choice for young adults, the prevalence of nonmarital childbearing is increasing.

The question arises as to whether these developing trends are beneficial for children. The short answer is no. In nearly every study done to date, children who live with two married biological parents "fare better on average than other children, along almost every index."[112] Compared to those born and reared in nuclear families,

> children born outside of marriage reach adulthood with less education, earn less income, have lower occupational status, are more likely to be idle (that is, not employed and not in school), are more likely to have a nonmarital birth (among daughters), have more troubled marriages, experience higher rates of divorce, and report more symptoms of depression.[113]

Not every social science or legal scholar seeks to blame family diversity for deterioration in child well-being. One expert states that, in and of itself, "the increasing diversity of family structure does not lead to family decline."[114] Others suggest that "family processes and the qualities of relationships are more important than family structures."[115] Still others may concede the role of family forms in child outcomes but also look to "other factors that distinguish one type of family form from another."[116] Even those who clearly implicate family structure in lower child functioning can name "[n]o single factor that explains its effects."[117] But whether by cause or association, family diversity is linked to declining child well-being. One need not draw a straight line between them to see that they are connected.

Children crave stability and function best when their lives are predictable. Cohabiting family structures appear to be inherently unstable. As a result, children in these households risk exposure to multiple transitions. Children may be required to "adjust repeatedly to the loss of coresident parents and parent-figures or the introduction of cohabiting partners and stepparents."[118] Stable, single-parent families may actually promote less stress than does movement in and out of cohabiting partnerships and stepfamilies.[119] For children, the effects of negative change are cumulative and may resound throughout adulthood. In the long run, "changes in household composition" matter less to children than "the stress associated with moving from one form to another."[120] Of course, these lessons are nothing new. We began to learn them decades ago by studying the effects of divorce.

The current proliferation of newer family forms was preceded by an era of seemingly rampant divorce. Parental breakup became so common that even children affected by it no longer found it stigmatizing. Yet a whole generation could not help but be imprinted by it. Judith Wallerstein observed that divorce "changes the entire trajectory of childhood."[121] Divorce is "not a single event" but begins with domestic discord, proceeds through an often chaotic marital dissolution, and "extends even further, often over many years of disequilibrium."[122] Compared to children from intact families, children of divorce experience greater levels of aggression and antisocial behavior, more difficulties with peer relationships, more depression, more learning problems, and higher educational dropout rates.[123] Loss of contact with the noncustodial parent, usually the father, is particularly painful. Many men are apt to "disengage from their children when they disengage from their former wives,"[124] causing them to abandon their children both emotionally and economically. Boys, who tend to be less communicative about their grief, are more vulnerable than girls to the stresses of parental breakup. Men whose parents divorced before they reached age 18 "are two to three times more likely to seriously consider taking their own lives as men whose parents were not divorced by that age."[125]

Children who reside in high-conflict households are generally worse off than those whose parents are divorced. Curiously, children of low-conflict marriages are especially at risk of upheaval.[126] Characterized by emotional estrangement rather than overt hostility and aggression, low-conflict marriages comprise a majority of divorces.[127] Parents who leave their families in search of greater happiness elsewhere often view the transition as positive. Their children, however, are more likely to regard the change as "unexpected, inexplicable, and unwelcome."[128] Children and their parents have markedly "different interpretations of family transitions."[129] In situations like these, children might be better off if their vaguely unhappy and dissatisfied parents remained together.[130]

Although most children do recover from the effects of divorce, their own rates of marital dissolution exceed those of adults who grew up in intact families.[131] When children live in stable, two-parent homes, they benefit from the consistency of what Paul Amato calls a "cooperative co-parental relationship."[132] Children absorb successful communications and interpersonal strategies as modeled by their parents, as well as the ability to resolve disagreements through compromise and negotiation.[133] Children then employ these skills to cultivate their own peer interactions and, later, intimate relationships. Parents who reside in separate households often lose the ability to communicate effectively with each other. As a result, "children living with single adults experience 'parallel' parenting rather than cooperative co-parenting."[134]

Relying exclusively on statistics for the divorce rate "seriously underestimates the amount of family breakup that prevails."[135] Children born in cohabiting unions face twice the risk of parental breakup than those born to married couples.[136] When intact families dissolve, most children reside, at least for a period of time, with a single parent, generally a single mother. Due to this transition, many of these families encounter loss of income as well as the necessity to move from place to place in search of affordable housing. Children suffer the disintegration of important ties—to home, school, neighborhood, and friendships.[137] Single parents of either gender "commonly experience strain in fulfilling tasks traditionally assumed by the opposite-gender parent."[138] They may have problems communicating with their children, show less affection, and be inconsistent in imposing discipline. Children in single-parent families may find themselves burdened by tasks and roles inappropriate to their age and status as children. Teenagers, in particular, "may worry about and feel a need to take care of their parents."[139] In turn, the normal "hierarchical relationship between mother and child" risks disruption when mothers "rely on their children for friendship and emotional support."[140]

Single-parent households undergo still more change when parents enter into subsequent marital or cohabiting relationships. While this may help to ease economic worries, it "is not a simple reconstitution of the two-parent family but is instead yet another difficult transition for biological parents, stepparents and children."[141] The fragility of second marriages[142] as well as of cohabitation in general exposes children to repeated cycles of uncertainty and readjustment.

Nearly half of all children who ever live in a cohabiting household "transition to a single-mother family without their mother every marrying."[143] Many are born to single mothers who later cohabit but never marry.[144] Children raised in cohabiting families are more likely to form their own cohabiting unions than those reared in other family types.[145] Although cohabiting families may be better off financially than single-parent households, they compare unfavorably with married families in income, education, satisfaction, and quality of relationships.[146] Children born in cohabiting unions are more likely to be unplanned than those born to married couples.[147] There is also some evidence that cohabiting biological fathers devote less time to activities with their children than married biological fathers.[148] More research is needed to determine the extent to which cohabiting biological fathers support and maintain contact with their children after dissolution of the live-in relationship.

Cohabitation's "unique stresses"[149] may also stem from its failure to achieve broad societal and governmental sanction. Within cohabiting unions, family roles and "even language to refer to family members"[150] remain ambiguous. Rights and obligations owed by cohabiting couples to each other as well as to their children have yet to be clearly defined.[151] Cohabitation's "walk-away prerogative"[152] is perhaps its most attractive feature for adults. But it leaves children at the mercy of their parents' inclination to invest in often tenuous attachments. Cohabiting biological parents who later marry decrease their odds of breakup by 35 percent.[153] This extra margin of commitment can be vital to children in need of a "buffer against instability."[154]

If cohabitation is an "unstable family form,"[155] cohabiting stepfamilies are "arguably the most unstable family form"[156] of all. Two-thirds of children entering stepfamilies do so in the context of cohabitation rather than marriage, although some of these couples will later wed.[157] Half of currently married stepfamilies began as cohabiting unions.[158] Second marriages containing children from a prior relationship are particularly unstable and subject to high rates of divorce. Children living with a remarried parent have a 40 percent probability of witnessing another parental breakup.[159] This represents "yet another disruptive marital transition for children, most of whom have undergone at least one divorce."[160] Higher-order marriages may be more fragile than first marriages, because they tend to attract people who have already experienced marital failure. Thus, the "pool of single people on the marriage market" carries an "elevated risk of subsequent marital dissolution. In this sense, marital instability breeds more marital instability."[161]

Children in stepfamilies may have outcomes no better than those in single-parent families. Compared to children from intact two-parent households, stepchildren experience more problematic behavior, higher dropout rates, more delinquency, and lower emotional well-being.[162] Children entering stepfamilies encounter changes in household composition, perhaps the "addition or subtraction of grandparents or siblings."[163] They undergo alterations in family routine as well as reorganization of family roles. Stepchildren may resent a stepparent's effort to impose authority or may fear that developing a relationship with the stepparent represents a betrayal of the noncustodial biological parent.[164] Some stepchildren "become jealous because they must share parental time and attention with the stepparent."[165] For some, remarriage "ends any lingering hopes that the two biological parents will one day reconcile."[166] Stepdaughters pose particular challenges to these parenting relationships, presenting greater conflict and more negative interactions than stepsons.[167]

A person who enters a cohabiting union as stepparent may be all too cognizant of the relationship's potentially short-lived nature. He or she may be reluctant to invest emotionally in another person's children, especially if he or she risks losing contact with them later on.[168] Adding a cohabiting parent to a single-family household appears to provide little or no benefit to children.[169] In fact, cohabiting stepfamilies "may compromise adolescent well-being, regardless of whether they are stable or even formalized through marriage."[170] Additional findings suggest that cohabitation following divorce is no more unstable than remarriage without cohabitation, as "[b]oth trajectories are associated with high levels of instability."[171] There is contrasting research, however, indicating that married versus cohabiting stepparents may have "a more clearly defined obligation to their stepchildren" and a "more pronounced expectation" that they will spend time with their stepchildren and contribute financially to their support.[172]

The distinction between the legal status of stepparents and the rights and obligations of natural parents is "remarkable."[173] The biological tie alone, regardless of the actual quality of the bond, imposes support obligations and confers custody and inheritance rights. In most states, stepparents "have no obligation to support their stepchildren, nor do they enjoy any right of custody or control."[174] The stepparent's relationship to the child terminates upon divorce or the death of the custodial parent. In general, a residential stepparent has "fewer rights than a legal guardian or foster parent."[175]

Stepfamilies may be America's fastest growing family form,[176] but they have yet to achieve statutory or judicial legitimacy. Only a few jurisdictions expressly grant stepparents standing to seek visitation or custody upon the dissolution of the adult relationship.[177] In other states, stepparent visitation is subsumed within broader grants of standing to third parties.[178] A married stepparent is more likely to receive visitation than a second parent in a cohabiting union,[179] and visitation is awarded far more commonly than custody.[180] State laws on the rights and obligations of stepparents are disparate and inconsistent. In the absence of statutory authority, courts are generally reticent about granting equitable relief, even where the child and stepparent have clearly formed a long-term loving relationship.[181] As third parties with no parental status, stepparents pose a particular challenge to the norm of the two-parent family.[182]

No one knows what the next social revolution will bring, but it does seem as though nontraditional families have dug into the culture for the foreseeable future. The legal system will eventually grow to accommodate them, if only to clarify and protect the parent-child relationships conceived in family diversity. But it does seem faintly ironic that couples who deliberately aim to avoid legal entanglements when building their families should seek shelter in that very system to resolve their disputes.

Terms denoting instability appear with dismaying regularity throughout the literature on family diversity. It may well be that families are in a state of transition and, in time, will settle more comfortably into their various functional forms. Cohabitant parenting is "a relatively recent phenomenon"[183] and has yet to evolve norms to "guide the couples in the relationship."[184] Marriage is still, without doubt, the most hospitable environment for child rearing and intimate relationships. But while the "absence of a stable marriage is a risk factor in a child's life," it is "not a prophecy of certain doom."[185] Most children are adaptable, although "resilience is not the same as invulnerability."[186] In a more secure, rational, and family-centered world, we would not repeatedly test the resilience of children by making them vulnerable.

Steven Mintz has suggested that panics about child well-being "are nothing new."[187] Twentieth-century parents obsessed over latchkey children, juvenile delinquency, youth gangs, and even "the supposedly deleterious effects of comic books."[188] Young people are better educated and better off today "than in any previous generation."[189] Mintz concluded that any current increase in public anxiety about the well-being of children "simply represents the latest example of American nostalgia for a mythical golden age."[190]

Remnants of that "mythical golden age" live on in our fondest conceptions of matrimony. Depending on the era in which it finds itself, marriage transforms and evolves but never quite sheds its allure. To arrive at its current incarnation, marriage has traversed the realms of the institutional, the companionate, the individualistic, and even the hedonistic. Couples approaching the altar today seem to expect a ready-made paradise waiting there to greet them. With the requisite wealth and educational credentials, they just might find it. Economic stability has become "the precondition rather than the consequence of marriage."[191] But marriage confers far too much good to confine its benefits to an elite or to have grown so inaccessible as to lose its universal, more democratic appeal. Indeed, "the growing marriage gap in this country is aligned with a growing socioeconomic gap."[192] The less privileged and less educated, those with a lower sense of self-entitlement, get cohabitation, the "poor man's marriage." The rich get richer.

CHAPTER 4

The Children of *Baby M*

Alternative Reproductive Technologies and the Remaking of Contemporary Families

Nontraditional families, those that are formed apart from and outside of marriage, have their limitations and fallibilities. As we saw in the previous chapter, cohabitation has made family bonds more tenuous and has not produced the best argument for recognizing and supporting nontraditional relationships. Family diversity often begins with unconventional adult romantic liaisons. It also occurs when children are created by unconventional means. Thanks to reproductive technology, children have sprouted in soils once thought inhospitable to family building—among same sex couples, single men and women, the infertile, and those too advanced in age to conceive or bear offspring on their own. In the context of childbearing, technology's challenge to tradition has spurred a family-centered, life-affirming revolution. Assisted reproduction has yet to obtain the full blessing of the legal community. But, even though erratically policed and largely unregulated, it has become an unstoppable global phenomenon.

In this chapter, we discuss the rise of childbearing markets and the network of would-be parents, surrogates, and donors that makes the industry hum. Although, for the most part, it is a highly successful operation, assisted reproduction remains an imperfect solution to childlessness. Egg donors may be subject to medical risks, and most clinics lack adequate tracking and monitoring systems of donor and offspring health. Further, there is no clear policy in place concerning disclosure of donor identity. As a result, children are often left with no clue as to their genetic origins and predispositions. Many are curious about their parentage and wonder about the possible existence of half siblings. Still, most of these children are loved, happy, and well-adjusted. With the help of donor registries, some have managed to connect with their genetic parents and, depending on the popularity of the donor, a sometimes vast array of half brothers and sisters. Science has not altered the essential building materials of family, but it has radically redistributed them.

We begin with a famous New Jersey case, one that, despite its bitter and unqualified opposition to it, will forever be linked with the age of assisted childbearing.

Baby M Then and Now

In the late 1980s, the world witnessed an "emotional legal battle between a housewife who had dropped out of high school and a couple with graduate degrees and professional careers who sought to have a child with her assistance."[1] At times, the drama swelled to soap-operatic proportions. In the *Baby M* case, William Stern contracted with a surrogate, Mary Beth Whitehead, to be artificially inseminated with his sperm and to bear a child for him and his wife, Elizabeth.[2] Whitehead further agreed to surrender the child to the Sterns for adoption. Suffering an emotional crisis that made it impossible for her to comply with the contract, Whitehead absconded with the baby, Melissa, returning her to the Sterns only in response to court order and after Whitehead's own arrest. The New Jersey Supreme Court reversed the trial court's validation of the contract and its authorization of Melissa's adoption by the Sterns.[3] In doing so, the supreme court not only declared the contract invalid but also pronounced it evil.

> It guarantees the separation of a child from its mother; it looks to adoption, regardless of suitability; it totally ignores the child; it takes the child from the mother regardless of her wishes and her maternal fitness; and it does all of this, it accomplishes all of its goals, through the use of money.[4]

Numerous amici curiae joined in support of Whitehead, several prominent feminists among them.[5] Confronting a divisive issue and a relatively uncommon reproductive practice, *Baby M* was very much a creature of its time. The decision deplored the commodification of children, the treatment of women's bodies as "childbearing factories,"[6] and the way in which surrogacy "degraded the mother-child relationship by paying women not to bond with their children."[7]

We have come to expect that technology will outpace the law's ability to comprehend it and regulate it. This lag time is not necessarily harmful: it allows new trends to take root in the culture, to reveal how they operate, and to expose their benefits and limitations, as well as areas needing further study. As Elizabeth Scott noted, the making of law and policy in a climate of controversy and intense political pressure will seldom promote society's long-term interests.[8] At the same time, an awareness of innovation and its influence on cultural norms is what keeps the judicial and legislative processes relevant and vital. We do not ask courts to sanction every new idea that comes along; we ask only that when novel issues arise, courts do not take refuge in unproven assumptions and outdated precedent.

Twenty-one years after the *Baby M* decision—nearly the span of a generation—a New Jersey trial court revisited the surrogacy issue. As in *Baby M*, the court roundly repudiated surrogacy contracts as void and unenforceable. The later case, *A.G.R. v. D.R.H. and S.H.*, concerned a gay male couple, Donald and Sean Hollingsworth, who legally married in California and registered their domestic partnership in New Jersey.[9] The surrogate, Angelia Robinson (Donald's sister), agreed to carry eggs from an anonymous donor that had been fertilized by Sean's sperm. After giving birth to twins, Robinson claimed entitlement to the status of parent. In voiding the surrogacy contract and granting parental status to Robinson, the court relied almost exclusively on *Baby M*.[10] For the court, the fact that Robinson, unlike Whitehead, was genetically unrelated to the twins was "a distinction without a difference significant enough to take the instant matter out of Baby M."[11]

The court that heard *A.G.R.* appeared oblivious to the revolution in reproductive demographics that had occurred since *Baby M*. Many of these changes were tied to the rise of a thriving industry in assisted reproductive technology (ART).[12] During the last decade of the 20th century, the number of gay and lesbian families more than tripled.[13] The birth rate increased for women aged 35 and over, doubled for women aged 40 to 44, and tripled for women aged 44 to 49.[14] The number of children born to women aged 50 to 54 rose from 117 in 1997 to 417 in 2005.[15]

Collaborative reproduction, with its constellation of sperm, egg, and embryo donors and gestational carriers, had transformed the concept of legal parentage.[16] No longer could the term *parent* be determined solely by biology or genetics.[17] The use of ART, especially in nontraditional families, was leading courts away from biological and gestational models and toward "a more functional view of parenthood."[18] As early as 1992, a Pennsylvania appellate tribunal admonished courts for failing to validate "unusual or complex" family arrangements and for perpetuating "the fiction of family homogeneity at the expense of children whose reality does not fit this form."[19] The court was addressing a mother's right to visit her son in the company of her lesbian partner, but the call for tolerance could easily apply to any nontraditional family, including those formed by surrogacy and ART.

Particularly in states where surrogacy contracts are invalid, courts continue to fall back on genetic or biological connections when parentage and custody disputes arise.[20] In Michigan, where surrogacy contracts are illegal, a gestational mother unilaterally declared herself the better parent for twins she had borne for an infertile couple.[21] Without the couple's financial provision for eggs, sperm, and gestational services, the twins would not have existed. Yet, based on tenuous allegations of the intended mother's mental unfitness, the court awarded custody to the surrogate—the only one of the parties who could claim a biological connection to the twins.[22] "Shotgun marriage may be dead," noted June Carbone and Naomi Cahn, but when the functional clashes with the biological, "shotgun parenthood is not."[23] The "widely disparate" nature of state laws on surrogacy and ART obstructs uniformity and makes consistency unlikely in determining matters of parentage.[24]

The shrinking supply of adoptable babies, rising infertility, and the growing number of same-sex couples drive the demand for assisted procreation. Though not without problems for the families they create, these reproductive practices are here to stay, and law and culture must make room for them. Despite earlier fears, empirical evidence disputes the notion that surrogacy and ART make childbearing slaves of women and commodities of children. Surrogates, in general, are the victims of neither coercion nor exploitation. The children of ART, however, require greater attention and sensitivity to their need to know more about their origins. Many of them are now of an age to teach us how to most humanely and intelligently direct the future of ART.

Shopping for Parenthood

In *Baby M,* amid a meditation on the irrelevance of voluntariness in paid surrogacy arrangements and the price of "labor, love, or life," Justice Wilentz opined for the court, "There are, in a civilized society, some things that money cannot buy."²⁵ Wilentz was misinformed. Even before the advent of the ART boom, it was apparent that "the wall between commerce and adoption is not completely impenetrable," that adoption fees "vary dramatically," and that some adults are willing to expend "huge sums" on adopting a child.²⁶ The cost of domestic private adoption ranges from $4,000 to $30,000, compared to $7,000 to $30,000 for international adoptions.²⁷ Children who are racial minorities are sometimes less expensive to adopt than white children, indicating that, "like price in other markets," adoption cost is one factor influencing people to adopt one baby rather than another."²⁸ On display with reproductive technologies is not the children but, instead, the means to produce them. In ART, "egg and sperm are sold, and the rights to their contents and reproductive energy legally transferred."²⁹ Whether it is through adoption, surrogacy, egg donor, artificial insemination, or in vitro fertilization (IVF), the exchange of money for parental status has become routine. There is, in short, a "functioning market" in parenthood.³⁰

In the United States, this seemingly unquenchable thirst for offspring began in the mid-20th century, with the rise of the nuclear family as the ideal of "domestic perfection."³¹ Infertile couples in the post–World War II years turned to adoption to erase "the stigma of childlessness in an era of 'compulsory parenthood.'"³² The use of artificial insemination began to take hold in the 1930s, becoming more prevalent after World War II.³³ The first successful IVF took place in 1978, followed by the emergence of surrogate motherhood practices in the 1980s.³⁴

The treatment of infertility accelerated as the supply of adoptable children, especially healthy white infants, diminished. By 1988, only 3 percent of babies born to single white women were relinquished for adoption, compared to 19 percent before 1973.³⁵ Many people have been barred from adopting because of their sexual orientation, age, or marital status, and in the United States, mothers who give up their children "often hand-pick the adoptive parents."³⁶ For infertile couples, ART became an alluring alternative to adoption.³⁷ Aside from the shortage of available white babies, the adoption process could be costly, risky, and subject to disruption by the birth parents. By the end of the 20th century, the combined annual birth rate from donor insemination, IVF, and surrogacy arrangements was 76,000, while only 30,000 healthy children were available for adoption.³⁸

In the 20th century, child rearing began to change from "a community endeavor ... designed to produce good citizens for the future" to a "route to personal satisfaction and private happiness for adults."[39] As infertility became increasingly "medicalized," ART marketers instilled in the infertile a sense that they were personally responsible for their undesired childlessness, fueling "the drive to pursue treatment after treatment."[40] Today, the patient base for ART is comprised, first and foremost, "of men with fertility problems followed by women who suffer from conditions like endometriosis, fibroids, missing uteruses, ovulation difficulties, or advanced maternal age.[41] Doctors at fertility clinics treat "plumbers, schoolteachers and lawyers," as well as patients whose desire for children has been hampered by psychological problems, life-threatening diseases, or crippling accidents.[42] Among the fastest-growing clientele are single mothers, lesbians, and gays—driven less by infertility than by the absence of a willing or viable reproductive partner.[43] When a lesbian couple's relationship dissolves, the nonchildbearing partner often risks losing access to a child she planned for, cared for, and supported.[44] A technique known as ROPA (Reception of Oocytes from PArtner) allows both women in a lesbian couple to share in the pregnancy.[45] Eggs retrieved from one partner can be fertilized and implanted for gestation in the other.[46] Or if both women are fertile, they can exchange embryos, with each woman gestating her partner's fertilized eggs.[47] The new reproductive technologies are part of "modernity's impulse to control the body and extend choice,"[48] and they are spurring the proliferation of nontraditional families.[49] ART has reconfigured parenthood by compartmentalizing it. At the same time, for countless couples and individuals, it has made parenthood "deliciously possible."[50]

In 2007, the rate of births to unmarried women reached a record 39.7 percent of all U.S. births.[51] A good many of these women, perhaps "tens of thousands," are single mothers by choice.[52] Some of them have grown impatient in their search for reproductively willing partners, having endured "too many years of uncertainty from too many noncommittal males."[53] Liza Mundy half-jokingly mused, "Reluctant single men. Where are the cover stories agonizing about the threat they pose to the traditional American family?"[54]

But, as single-mother-by-choice Lori Gottlieb noted, ambivalence lies on both sides of the gender equation.[55] A lot of Generation X women "took it for granted that we could do anything we wanted" and ended up paralyzed by indecision.[56] Unwilling to compromise on their choice of mate, they forgot "that if you don't choose anything, eventually you're left with nothing."[57] In the new millennium, women in their 30s see themselves confronting a choice "between love and offspring."[58] As Gottlieb perused the profiles of sperm donors, she found it "liberating to have the pick of the genetic crop."[59] Instead of "marrying a schlubby but lovable man" with less than stellar physical attributes, she could "indulge hubristic fantasies of genetic engineering."[60] Ironically, after becoming pregnant, Gottlieb attracted the attention of a surprising number of men in their 30s. She believed they were charmed by her lack of ulterior motive and by the chance to be liked for their innate qualities rather than their procreative potential. "The men I'm dating realize that I already have everything else I want," explained Gottlieb, "so now I'm in this purely for a chance at love."[61]

Sex has become increasingly divorced from marriage and reproduction, to the extent that the labels *marriage* and *family* no longer predictably reveal the inner workings of the relationships they are used to describe. ART has burrowed deep into our social institutions and extended its reach around the globe. At an estimated rate of 250,000 per year,[62] more than 3 million ART babies have been born worldwide, making up 4 percent of all live births.[63] Israel is the IVF capital of the world, followed, somewhat distantly, by Iceland.[64] In Israel, all citizens, including Arabs, are entitled to "free, unlimited IVF procedures for up to two 'take-home' babies until a woman is 45."[65] The largest sperm bank in the world is in Denmark, and it exports three-quarters of its product overseas.[66] Patients from Spain, France, Australia, and elsewhere travel to California clinics, eager to take advantage of ART regulations more liberal than in their own countries. Couples—straight and gay—from Canada, the United States, Israel, Europe, and other countries "can combine eggs and sperm (their own or someone else's) and have the resulting embryo carried by a village woman in India for a fraction of the cost" in America.[67] Fertility tourism has produced a "pulsing commerce, with dollars and Euros flying around the world."[68] A growing number of 21st-century babies are "global citizens"[69] in ways that our ancestors could never have envisioned or comprehended.

ART has come a long way since *Baby M*'s excoriation of the childbearing marketplace. Surrogacy has slipped most of its moral constraints,[70] and many of ART's children are now old enough to speak for themselves.[71] Along with aspiring parents and the clinics that serve them, the donors, surrogates, and children are the major players in ART's unfolding history. Their insight and experience are crucial to an understanding of the ways in which these new technologies have infiltrated our culture and molded our reproductive future.

Participants and Products in the Reproductive Marketplace
The Surrogates

Reproductive technologies do not alter the desire for parenthood, but they do create a gulf between marriage, on the one hand, and motherhood and the "drives, emotions, and desires of pregnancy," on the other.[72] In our contemporary culture, the yearning to become a parent is sufficient pretext for setting in motion the mechanisms for achieving pregnancy and parenthood. At times, this can only be accomplished through collaborative reproduction and by "borrowing the reproductive capacity of another woman."[73] Ties of kinship are forged no longer by nature and instinct alone but also by "choice, love and intention."[74] Surrogate motherhood helps to form families when desire and intent are impeded by nature.

The "moral panic"[75] that ensued in the aftermath of *Baby M* produced laws designed either to prohibit surrogacy or to discourage it by forbidding payment to the gestational mother.[76] In deciding *Baby M,* Justice Wilentz had no problem with the practice of surrogacy as long as the surrogate mother acted voluntarily, received no remuneration, and obtained the right to change her mind and to assert her parental rights.[77] The trial court in *A.G.R.* engaged in identical reasoning when it voided a surrogacy contract, even though the gestational mother had carried the eggs of an anonymous donor.[78] In its haste to condemn the practice of surrogacy, the *A.G.R.* court seemed more concerned with the emotional harm to the surrogate mother than with the long-term needs of the children. Noting that the legislature in *Baby M*'s time was silent on the legality of surrogacy contracts, the *A.G.R.* court concluded that "the additional twenty one years of silence as to surrogacy agreements speaks even louder."[79] In those intervening years, however, surrogacy changed dramatically. Today, 95 percent of surrogates carry embryos created by genetic materials other than their own.[80] In fact, most surrogacy agreements "stipulate that the woman who carries the baby cannot also donate the egg."[81]

Cases like *Baby M* are rarities today. *A.G.R.*'s facts are more problematic, though its principal defect is its rote adherence to *Baby M* and its failure to distinguish between the fact that Whitehead was genetically related to the subject child whereas Robinson was not.[82] The court was well aware of the obligations that parental status imposes.[83] Awarding parental rights to a person with no genetic bond and no clearly stated intention of becoming a parent serves neither personal nor policy interests. The parties in *A.G.R.*

also suffered because of their unfortunate choice of a gestational mother. Robinson, the surrogate, appears to have been psychologically unprepared to give up the twins, or perhaps the intended parents never plainly specified her role in regard to the children.[84] Additionally, her familial relationship to the children—she is their paternal aunt—created a continuing obstacle to the Hollingsworths' unfettered assertion of their intended parental rights.[85] As it is practiced today, surrogacy strives to avoid the perils of both *Baby M* and *A.G.R.*[86] When it works—and it most often does—surrogacy strengthens the concept of family as surely as it transforms it.

Although today's surrogates admit that separating from the baby "is still the hardest part of the job,"[87] they rarely refuse to relinquish a child after giving birth.[88] Given the estimated 1,000 surrogacy agreements entered into each year in the United States, "the lack of litigation is remarkable."[89] In many states, lawmakers are now less concerned with discouraging and "punishing a pernicious practice"[90] than with issues that are more pragmatic, such as clarifying parental status and "protecting all participants, especially children."[91] The evolution of surrogacy's image from a coercive, commodifying moral threat to a socially accepted practice illustrates the triumph of the empirical over the theoretical.

This is not to suggest that the commodification question has been definitively resolved, even in the minds of the surrogates themselves. Katherine Drabiak and her colleagues defined commercial surrogacy as "a contractual relationship where compensation is paid to a surrogate and agency, excluding any reasonable medical, legal, or psychological expenses, in exchange for the surrogate's gestational services."[92] When a practice like surrogacy has yet to attain full cultural consensus, contractualization "insulates socially marginal transactions from the bias in majoritarian morality."[93] For nontraditional seekers of parenthood—single people, lesbians, and gays—contractualization offers privacy and a "safe haven" in which to pursue one's dreams "relatively free from the constraints imposed by the lowest common denominator of public opinion."[94] In view of the public's distaste for baby selling, contractualization avoids commodification claims by defining the gestational services, not the baby, as the "item for sale."[95] One surrogate mother explained, "If you're being paid for your time, it's like a contract and it severs it completely at the end because it is a job done and you're paid for it and that's the end of it."[96]

The preceding statement highlights two of the main perplexities facing surrogates: the acceptance of money for bearing a child and the act of relinquishing that child as part of the contractual obligation. To do her job, a surrogate has to make peace with her conscience on both of these issues. On the matter of fetal attachment, discussed more fully shortly, she succeeds by firmly believing the baby is not hers to keep.[97] On the issue of compensation, she frames her motive as altruistic rather than financial, the "desire to help a childless couple" or to "create a family for a person who otherwise would have no way" of doing so.[98] The payment, generally a modest sum of $20,000 to $25,000,[99] only serves to facilitate the preexisting altruistic plan.[100]

Research shows that although surrogates are not poor, they are usually of lower income and are less educated than the intended parents that employ them.[101] Most agencies decline to accept women on public assistance, and there is no empirical evidence that women are driven to surrogacy by financial crisis.[102] The vast majority of surrogates have already had two or three children and completed their families.[103] Payment for gestational services allows these women to work part-time or to remain at home to raise young children.[104] With the money earned, surrogates can supplement their family's income. They can also afford to indulge in such things as a family trip to Disney World or to meet special personal expenses, as in the case of one gestational mother who used the funds to build an occupational therapy gym for her autistic son.[105] In states like Texas and California, surrogacy agencies actively recruit military wives by distributing leaflets at military housing complexes and advertising in military publications. With a single pregnancy, a military spouse can earn more than her husband's annual base pay, which ranges from $16,080 to $28,900 for new enlistees.[106] The fact that the gestational process takes less than a year "gives them enough time between postings" to work as surrogates.[107]

In terms of their personality profiles, surrogates tend to be "sociable, assertive, active, energetic and optimistic."[108] They are also likely to be "self-sufficient, independent thinkers and nonconformists" who are less troubled by social taboos than are other women.[109] Rather than feeling demeaned or exploited, surrogates find the experience empowering—one that enhances self-esteem and instills "a sense of uniqueness and accomplishment."[110] They take pleasure in being pregnant, are skilled and knowledgeable about it, and often regard surrogacy as a "vocation or calling."[111]

Altruism is self-gratifying, but surrogates also want to be thanked and appreciated and to have their altruism "celebrated and acknowledged."[112] A personal relationship with the intended parents, "even though limited to a few visits or some telephone contact," brings greater satisfaction to the surrogacy experience.[113] "I really wanted to feel as though the people I was doing this with were my friends," said one gestational mother, who added, "That's how I wouldn't feel used."[114] When treated with "respect, honor and care,"[115] surrogates find that their bond with the intended parents, not a bond with the baby, is of the utmost value.[116]

One of *Baby M*'s prime objections to contractual surrogacy was that "the natural mother is irrevocably committed before she knows the strength of her bond with her child."[117] Here, the operative term is *natural mother*, meaning a woman who carries her own egg. In a natural pregnancy, in utero bonding maximizes survival because "the fetus carries the genes of the woman who gestates it."[118] In the age of reproductive technology, the dictates of evolution are yielding to functionalism.[119] Today's surrogates, who rarely carry their own egg, do not regard the fetus as their own, and it is clear that "bonding does not constitute an impediment to surrogate motherhood."[120] If fetal attachment were such a "fundamental biological reality," the practice of surrogacy would be "unsustainable."[121] If bonding is not consequential in surrogate pregnancies, other mechanisms must be at work to "counteract the surrogate's impulse to identify the child as her own."[122] In her research, Heléna Ragoné discovered these mechanisms in the surrogates' main motivations: "They wanted to help infertile couples, they wanted to earn money at home, and they loved being pregnant."[123] Because the circumstances preceding, rather than following, impregnation provide the inducement, bonding is not obstructive to surrogate motherhood.[124] The "opportunity to have a pregnancy and birth without the responsibility of having a child to bring up after it" attracted one gestational mother.[125] Another felt more "like a caring babysitter" than a mother, while still another "almost felt guilty for not feeling bad about giving up the baby."[126]

In the course of his research, Hal Levine monitored an electronic mailing list for surrogate mothers.[127] This network of support, encouragement, and shared experience helped surrogates overcome in utero bonding.[128] One surrogate asked, "Do you think it will sound crazy if I say I want to be able to keep the baby in my room for a little while after the parents have decided to leave the hospital and go home for the night?"[129] A member of the list responded, "They are the parents. I hate to sound like I'm minimizing our job, but we are just there to carry babies. When the baby has its first cry our job is over."[130] In addition to supplying a ready conduit for advice and empathy, this organization of surrogate mothers helps surrogates, their families, and the intended parents accomplish a sense of closure at the end of the process.[131]

A drive for legitimacy and professionalism motivates all of surrogacy's participants, including the surrogates' husbands, the staff of surrogacy agencies, and intended parents, as well as the surrogates themselves.[132] Psychological screening of potential surrogates is imperative, described by one applicant as one of the most "grueling" and "invasive" aspects of the process.[133] One president of a surrogacy agency asserted that parents who seek out reputable agencies that carefully select their surrogates have a "99 percent chance of getting a baby and a 100 percent chance of keeping it."[134]

Baby M discerned no legal prohibition against unpaid surrogacy.[135] But while the absence of payment might have soothed the moral qualms of Justice Wilentz, it does little for a gestational mother who spends a minimum of nine months on the job and is "on task twenty-four hours a day altering her nutrition and other behaviors, risking physical injury, undergoing profound emotional and hormonal changes, and also enduring extraordinary physical pain and hardship while giving birth."[136] It is not unusual for surrogates to construe their services as "a type of gift-giving"[137] (albeit with modest compensation), and some have likened it to organ donation.[138] Janet Dolgin observed that "gifts bind," while "contracts separate."[139] Gifts "transform relationships," while "contracts leave them untouched," and "while gifts bespeak attachment, contracts bespeak freedom."[140] Dolgin further suggested that because surrogacy agreements are a hybrid of gift and contract, legal approaches must address each of these elements.[141] Katherine Drabiak and her colleagues suspected that surrogates "feel socially pressured to provide a socially acceptable justification for their activity."[142] Thus, notions of altruism and gift giving serve to obscure "economic self-interest."[143] If children are "priceless gifts"[144] and if putting a price on them is distasteful, surrogates may tend to subordinate their own financial interests. This places them at a disadvantage when negotiating contract terms.

Katherine Drabiak and her colleagues proposed a regulatory scheme determining reasonable compensation to surrogates.[145] Along with disparity in state surrogacy laws, there is also no uniform regulation of the practice.[146] The use of the Internet has made surrogacy "a distinct interstate business,"[147] and the absence of uniform industry standards exposes both surrogates and parents to exploitation by surrogacy agencies.[148] Further, surrogates lack standing to bring contract claims in states that penalize, prohibit, or simply ignore the practice.[149]

Surrogacy succeeds when the parties clearly understand what is expected of them. The Canadian Bar Association recommended that all surrogates obtain legal advice before entering into contracts and that fees for such legal advice be considered a compensable expense.[150] Legal advice is not, however, "a substitute for screening or separate and joint counseling" of surrogate applicants and parents.[151]

Surrogacy has achieved legitimacy unanticipated in *Baby M*'s time. The practice continues to be vulnerable to charges of commodification and baby selling, and there is lingering aversion to commerce in women's bodies as childbearing vessels.[152] But the surrogates' deeply felt motives and convictions seem to make these accusations sound, at the very least, ill informed. As to whether contractualization demeans parenthood, one might answer, "It is hard to follow the argument that pre-conception agreements reduce parenthood to a transaction. That 'transaction' is but the first step to becoming a parent, with most of the work of 'family and parental responsibilities' yet to come."[153]

The Donors

From 1998 to 2007, the number of ART cycles performed in the United States nearly doubled, producing 57,569 infants in 2007.[154] The "exploding market"[155] in human eggs is fueled by demands for stem cell research[156] as well as by infertility in women who wait until advanced age to begin bearing children.[157] It is estimated that 100,000 young women have been recruited to sell their eggs to the nearly 500 IVF clinics in the United States.[158] Fees typically range from $8,000 to $15,000 but can run as high as $100,000.[159] The egg donor industry, largely unregulated, is a lucrative business for physicians, fertility clinics, and the university obstetrics and gynecology departments connected with them.[160]

Unlike surrogates, who are esteemed for their gestational abilities as well as for their social and communications skills, egg donors market their brains, physical assets, ethnic backgrounds, educational levels, psychological stability, and health histories.[161] Although egg donation sports a veneer of altruism, most young women involved in it are "savvy"[162] and financially motivated. Like sperm donors, they want to help people, but they also share a desire to play a role in the gene pool.[163] In the words of one egg donor, "Men have always been able to spread their genes. Now I can spread my genes."[164] But unlike sperm donation, which carries little or no physical risk,[165] the effects of hormonally stimulated egg production, especially in the long term, are mostly unknown. An egg donor survey conducted by Wendy Kramer and her colleagues found that more than 30 percent of respondents experienced ovarian hyperstimulation syndrome (OHSS), with 11.6 percent of them requiring medical treatment, hospitalization, or both.[166] More than a quarter (26.4 percent) reported new infertility problems, changes in their menstrual cycle, or both.[167] The risks associated with hormonal ovarian stimulation appear to increase "with the number of cycles undergone."[168] The study's authors concluded that there is "clearly a need for an oocyte donor registry" to track the effects of egg retrieval on donors and to monitor the continuing state of their health.[169]

For the most part, egg and sperm donors are anonymous.[170] While the Centers for Disease Control and Prevention collects data on pregnancy outcomes, multiple births, and technologies used, it does not require fertility agencies to track the health of individual donors.[171] Wendy Kramer and her colleagues found that only 2.6 percent of egg donors responding to their survey reported being contacted by their IVF clinics for medical updates. More than a third of the respondents experienced medical changes of potential concern to donor children.[172] Roughly half of these women did not attempt to contact their fertility clinic to update them, due to "lack of education about the value of providing such information, along with the lack of encouragement by the fertility clinic to do so."[173] Of those who attempted to contact their clinics with medical updates, several encountered "a missing or destroyed chart; a clinic that had closed or relocated and could not be found; and a clinic that declined to notify oocyte recipients on the basis of anonymity."[174] The fertility industry's lack of diligence in tracking donor health starts at the beginning of the process, with a tendency to understate the risks of oocyte donation. Because of the IVF clinics' close financial bond with ooctye recipients, a potential conflict of interest prevents them from fully disclosing to donors the medical risks of the procedures used for egg retrieval.[175] Even when clinics fully discuss known risks and inform donors that long-term risks are unknown, donors "may not clearly understand the difference between 'there are no known risks' and 'there are no risks.'"[176]

The long-term health of sperm and egg donors is of profound interest to their donor offspring, particularly in regard to genetically related medical conditions.[177] While Great Britain, Sweden, Austria, Switzerland, the Netherlands, and parts of Australia maintain centralized donor registries,[178] the United States does not.[179] In the American fertility industry, which seems to prize donor anonymity above all else, experts fear that a mandatory registry would "scare away" potential donors.[180] It would undoubtedly scare away some, perhaps even half,[181] but the United States is slowly beginning to embrace disclosure of some aspects of donor identity. In 2009, the Ethics Committee of the American Society for Reproductive Medicine (ASRM) strongly encouraged fertility programs to maintain accurate records of donor health, to enable information to be shared with donor offspring.[182] In addition to promoting the informed consent of donors, the committee advised programs to gather from donors medical updates that are pertinent to the health of their offspring.[183] It also counseled programs to "give consideration to the fact that donors may have interests in learning the outcome of their donation, especially when information sharing or contact between donor and offspring are possible in the future."[184]

The question of whether donors and their offspring should share information and possibly establish contact is frequently debated in the literature on ART. Jennifer Schneider and Wendy Kramer noted that as donors age, they begin to wonder about the outcome of the pregnancies to which they contributed.[185] Donors initially place great value on their anonymity, but they often later wish to know more about their genetic offspring.[186] Informing donors at the outset that this opportunity might be available to them underscores the long-term impact of their decision to donate.[187] It gives them a glimpse into the future and transforms an altruistic or economic abstraction into a living, breathing being.

For the first generation of ART's children since *Baby M*, the veil of donor anonymity seems to be lifting, illuminating linkages to their genetic parents, the parents who raised them, and the half siblings they might one day meet—the strange new conglomeration we are coming to know as "family."

The Children

Although the court in *Baby M* ultimately awarded custody to the Sterns, it clearly recognized the magnitude of what Whitehead was expected to relinquish under the surrogacy agreement. Justice Wilentz termed it "beyond normal human capabilities" to suppose that Whitehead would give up her newborn child "without a struggle."[188] The justice asked, "Other than survival, what stronger force is there?"[189]

The human gift for adaptation keeps us, for the moment at least, one step ahead of extinction. Neither survival nor mother-child bonding is rule bound, and creatures of all species, including our own, will look for nurturing in any parent figure that seems willing and able to provide it.[190] The acts of "recognizing and bonding with a parent are more dependent on exposure and learning than on a genetically programmed response."[191] Absent "such a promiscuous capacity for trust," an infant who is abandoned or orphaned shortly after birth "would face certain doom if it were unable to swap preferences for an adoptive parent."[192] Experience with surrogacy, adoption, and ART reminds us that what is most "natural" about parent-child bonding is its capacity to flourish in "unnatural" situations.

Research by Susan Golombok and her colleagues revealed that solid maternal bonding is less dependent on genetic or gestational relationships than on "a strong desire for parenthood."[193] When compared to parents of naturally conceived children, surrogacy parents exhibit greater warmth and emotional involvement with their children, as well as lower stress levels.[194] The presence or absence of prenatal bonding is not determinative, and pregnancy "is not a prerequisite" for "positive maternal representations of the mother-child relationship."[195] Surrogacy parents have "gone to great lengths to have a child," which results in higher motivation and commitment to parenthood.[196] Greater levels of warmth and emotional involvement were also seen in parents of children conceived by IVF and donor insemination (DI).[197] As is true in families that exist because of surrogacy or egg donation,[198] IVF and DI parents are "generally older than first-time parents of a naturally conceived child."[199] Possibly due to an absence of siblings, IVF, surrogacy, and DI children experience greater commitment and emotional involvement from their parents.[200]

Despite these enhanced levels of warmth, emotional involvement, and parental interaction, Susan Golombok and her colleagues concluded that ART children "did not differ from the naturally conceived children with respect to socio-emotional or cognitive development."[201] Further, these positive parental factors do not necessarily "result in even greater well-being for the child."[202] Lutz Goldbeck and his colleagues, however, suggested that the higher socioeconomic status and educational levels of many ART parents contribute to a more stimulating developmental environment in which to raise children.[203]

Children conceived by intracytoplasmic sperm injection (ICSI) appear to have "an elevated risk of borderline delayed cognitive development compared with singletons conceived by IVF."[204] In ICSI, a single sperm is injected directly into an unfertilized egg and, unlike in IVF, bypasses the natural selection process that occurs during conception.[205] Perhaps the ICSI process results in genetically based cognitive problems.[206] After adjusting for the educational and socioeconomic advantages of ART parents, researchers found no significant statistical differences in cognitive development between naturally conceived and ART children.[207] A comparison study of IVF and naturally conceived children at ages 9 to 10 showed no significant difference in IQ or cognitive performance but did show somewhat higher levels of depression, anxiety, and aggression in IVF children.[208] Except for recent research discussed shortly, no other studies have reported poorer socioemotional adjustment in children conceived by IVF.[209]

Children conceived by ART are at higher risk for preterm birth and low birth weight.[210] Because earlier ART procedures often resulted in multiple births, it was thought that limiting the number of embryos implanted after fertilization would reduce the risk to the fetus.[211] Surprisingly, however, even singleton ART infants are disproportionately born preterm and at low birth weights.[212] Adverse neurological outcomes such as epilepsy and cerebral palsy may be associated with preterm birth and low birth weight,[213] but no strong association exists between cerebral palsy and ART.[214] Data collected from five European countries showed more childhood illness up to age five in ART-conceived children than in those naturally conceived.[215] Because these findings have not been sufficiently replicated, they are not definitive.[216] There is some evidence of increased risk of birth defects in ART children,[217] as well as epigenetic disorders such as Angelman and Beckwith-Wiedemann syndromes.[218] Further study is needed to determine whether health risks to ART-conceived children are caused by parental infertility, the IVF procedures themselves, or a combination of the two.[219] In addition, because adult-onset diseases such as cardiovascular disease and type 2 diabetes may be linked to babies that are small for their gestational age, long-term tracking of children conceived by ART is essential.[220]

Despite medical concerns requiring further research, reports about the health of ART-conceived children are, overall, "reassuring."[221] As for emotional adjustment, children conceived by donor insemination within lesbian relationships are doing quite well. A longitudinal study of adolescents in planned lesbian families revealed significantly high levels of social and academic functioning and significantly low incidences of aggressive and rule-breaking behavior.[222] The study's authors credit parental engagement, educational involvement, and effective disciplinary styles for the successful adjustment of these children.[223] Data on gay fatherhood is much scarcer, because the high costs of adoption and surrogacy make these households less common than those headed by lesbians.[224]

In their survey of adults aged 18 to 45 who were conceived by donor insemination, Elizabeth Marquardt and her colleagues reported decidedly mixed and complex results.[225] A majority of donor-conceived adults described a sense of incompleteness, the feeling of having a "piece missing."[226] One respondent explained that rather than looking for a dad, she had questions about "who I am and why I do what I do."[227] Understandably, many of these donor offspring wanted to learn about their genetic origins but feared hurting or angering the parents who raised them.[228] Some worried about unknowingly becoming romantically involved with someone related to them, while others felt confused about who their real families were.[229] Fifty-nine percent of respondents said their parents were always open with them about their means of conception, while 16 percent said their parents told them either before or after age 12.[230] Twenty percent of respondents learned about their conception in an unplanned or accidental manner.[231] Of this latter group, a sizable portion reported problems with the law as well as substance abuse and mental health issues.[232] Among those who had always known about their origins, about one in five reported substance abuse issues and problems with the law.[233]

Despite these adjustment difficulties, Elizabeth Marquardt and her colleagues discerned a "strikingly libertarian"[234] attitude in their study subjects toward reproductive technologies in general: 61 percent said they favored the practice of donor conception, while 75 percent agreed that "every person has a right to a child" and that ART is "good for children because the children are wanted."[235] Equally "startling" was the finding that 20 percent of these adult DI offspring had already donated their own eggs or sperm or become surrogate mothers.[236] The study's authors appear unable to convincingly reconcile these contradictory findings in which donor offspring feel troubled about their origins but embrace the technology.[237] Clearly, however, the majority of donor offspring support the right of DI children to know the truth about their origins.

[A]pproximately two-thirds of grown donor offspring support the right of offspring to have non-identifying information about the sperm donor biological father, to know his identity, to have the opportunity to form some kind of relationship with him, to know about the existence and number of half-siblings conceived with the same donor, to know the identity of half-siblings conceived with the same donor, and to have the opportunity as children to form some kind of relationship with half-siblings conceived with the same donor.[238]

Research in 1996 on IVF and DI children and their family functioning showed that none of the parents had told their children about how they were conceived.[239] Seventy-five percent of the parents decided not to tell their children, 13 percent were undecided, and 12 percent planned to tell them.[240] Although the majority of these parents elected not to inform their children of their origins, more than half of them told a friend or family member.[241] It is now well recognized that secrecy and accidental discovery produce stress, bewilderment, and feelings of betrayal in children of ART.[242] Arguing in favor of disclosure, one donor-conceived child eloquently stated, "We didn't ask to be born into this situation, with its limitations and confusion. It's hypocritical . . . to assume that biological roots won't matter to the 'products' of the cryobanks' service when the longing for a biological connection is what brings customers to the banks in the first place."[243] In 2004, ASRM's Ethics Committee announced its support of disclosing to children the facts of their donor conception, the available characteristics of the donor, and, when all parties agree, the donor's identity.[244] Secrecy and anonymity are slowly giving way to more open, expansive concepts of family connection.

Parents who disclose the facts of donor conception to their children have to overcome a number of concerns. They worry that they will damage their child's trust or emotional development or that their child will reject them.[245] They fear their child will be stigmatized or will compare himself or herself unfavorably to other children and families.[246] Parents often struggle to find comfortable, expressive language with which to explain the use of a donor. Two basic strategies appear to predominate: the "seed-planting" strategy and the "right time" strategy.[247] Parents who choose the "seed-planting" strategy—begun at age three or four—believe that its result will be children who feel as if they have always known about their origins. Disclosing early avoids the danger of waiting too long and giving the appearance of shame or concealment. Parents who prefer the "right time" strategy—

usually initiated at age six or seven—want to ensure that the child is emotionally able to process the information and formulate appropriate questions. When disclosure fails to occur by age eight, the chances of it occurring at all diminish as the child gets older. Regardless of the chosen method, none of the parents who were candid with their children and studied by Kirstin Mac Dougall and her colleagues reported a negative outcome, and none regretted the decision to disclose.[248]

In the United States, traditional gamete donation programs provide only nonidentifying donor information—the type of data, such as physical and personality traits, generally used to match donors and recipients.[249] An increasing number of programs allow recipients to opt for open-identity donors who agree to permit disclosure of their identities to offspring who request it. The Identity-Release Program, offered by the Sperm Bank of California, authorizes donors to release their identities to offspring at least 18 years of age but imposes no obligation to meet them. Research on DI offspring aged 12 to 17 with open-identity sperm donors found that most described themselves as having always known about their origins, with the average age of disclosure at less than seven years. Most felt comfortable with their origins and overwhelmingly curious about their donor. They wanted to know what he was like as a person, what he looked like, whether he had a family and what they were like, and whether the donor resembled them in any way. The primary thing they wanted was a photograph, and on average, they reported being moderately to very likely to request their donor's identity. About two-thirds envisioned forming a relationship with their donor, most often a friendship, rather than a parent-child relationship. The study's findings "provide little support for the stereotype that offspring are looking for a father in their donor."[250]

In 2000, Wendy Kramer and her donor-conceived son, Ryan, created the Donor Sibling Registry (DSR), a website aimed at bringing donor children together.[251] By posting the name of the sperm bank or egg donor program and the number assigned to the donor, DSR registrants can look for matches between half siblings and possibly donor parents. As of 2013, DSR's registrants numbered nearly 39,000, with more than 9,800 matches among registrants, half-siblings, and donors.[252]

Less is known about donor interest in establishing relationships with offspring, although most are curious to know what their offspring are like.[253] Mike Rubino is a donor father who agreed to meet his offspring Aaron, age seven, and Leah, age three.[254] Accompanied to the visit by their single mother, the children, especially Aaron, seemed primed to accept this new acquaintance into their lives.[255] The feelings about donors among children of single-parent households, compared with other types of households, are significantly more positive.[256] Aaron, whose wish for a dad was for someone "to play with me," bonded with Mike almost immediately.[257] The two discovered much in common and, despite a promise to keep in touch, found it painful to separate at the visit's end. Mike, an artist who treasures his solitude, later established contact with several more offspring.[258] But his fatherly welcome has its limits. "I'm a little concerned if any others come forward," he said, "only because I don't know how much time I could spend with everyone."[259] Although there are no legal limits, ASRM guidelines recommend restricting conceptions by individual donors to 25 births per population of 800,000.[260] But these guidelines are not always observed. The children sired by Fairfax Donor 1476 number at least forty-five, and the mothers of those children have their own website.[261] Another donor is reported to have 150 offspring.[262] Several donors, overwhelmed by contact requests from donor offspring, have withdrawn their identifying information from the DSR. "Not everyone," observed Liza Mundy, "wants to be part of an unprecedented extended family."[263]

Whatever our assumptions about surrogates, donors, and the children of ART, the empirical realities are sometimes surprising or even counterintuitive. Questions of familial ties, rights, and responsibilities have never been simple, and these new reproductive technologies roil the waters even more. As the culture more fully absorbs family-fashioning innovations, law and policy will, eventually, catch up with them. In the interim, our notions of what is ideal and what is functional drift further apart, exposing discomfiture and ambivalence in legal and legislative thinking. Clarity and certainty are still a long way off. But in the years since *Baby M*, practical experience and research have aimed to unseat moral rhetoric and blind theorizing, lighting a path toward fashioning law and policy for the known world of living families.

CHAPTER 5

Parenthood in the 21st Century

The Evolving Functional Norms

The use of reproductive technology gives rise to legal complexity, but not because the science of it is so frightening or difficult to grasp. Altering the biological connections between parent and child disrupts our understanding of family relationships. Is a woman who bears a child containing none of her genetic material still the biological mother? What, if any, are her legal rights to the child? What, if any, are the rights of individuals who purchase the materials, resources, and services to create a child but who are biologically unrelated to the child? Childbearing within same-sex unions also jars accepted notions of the parent-child bond. Is parenthood genetically determined, or may it also be defined by consistent and purposeful nurturing behavior? Biology alone is no longer a valid or reliable standard for assessing and legitimating today's parental relationships.

In this chapter, we discuss what courts should do when legislatures fail to act in accommodating novel family structures. We apply a brace of norms, *intention plus behavior,* to cases where genetic ties are lacking but where acts in furtherance of parenting are undeniably present. We conclude the chapter with two emblematic stories from the parenthood wars. One features lesbian coparents and an all-too-common "chutzpah argument," and the other features an unmarried heterosexual couple struggling to assert the proper scope of parentage in this century.

The central difficulty with contemporary family law is that the subject matter has changed faster and more thoroughly than the formal legal principles. The central aims of family law "cannot be fully accomplished when 'family' is defined in law to exclude a significant part of the population of actual families."[1] Even though married couples and their children now form a minority of households, most state statutes still envision a 1950s sitcom world in which families consist of two heterosexual spouses and their biological children.[2] As the Colorado Supreme Court noted, however, "Parenthood in our complex society comprises much more than biological ties, and litigants increasingly are asking courts to address issues that involve delicate balances between traditional expectations and current realities."[3]

Major changes are stirring as the legal system shifts from biological to functional norms. Nurture is dislodging nature as the primary determinant in the resolution of legal disputes within these new family forms. Although their legal status is often contested, families are increasingly characterized as "two or more persons related by birth, adoption, marriage, or choice."[4] The core concept involves "the creation of 'an intimate familial relationship that is stable, enduring, substantial and mutually supportive, . . . one that is cemented by strong emotional bonds and provides deep and pervasive emotional security.'"[5] New Jersey Supreme Court justice Virginia A. Long has sensitively described these emerging family norms.

> Those qualities of family life on which society places a premium—its stability, the love and affection shared by its members, their focus on each other, the emotional and physical care and nurturance that parents provide their offspring, the creation of a safe harbor for all involved, the wellspring of support family life provides its members, the ideal of absolute fealty in good and bad times that infuses the familial relationship (all of which justify isolation from outside intrusion)—are merely characteristics of family life that, except for its communal aspect, are unrelated to the particular form a family takes.[6]

When these modern families experience legal turmoil, they must turn to judges who have little or no statutory guidance in dealing with these new domestic configurations. Courts are the beachhead for this revolution, because society is evolving faster than legislatures can—or choose to—keep up.[7] The rapid pace of change in reproductive technologies has created a yawning gulf between the realities of family life and most statutorily prescribed norms.[8] The dilemmas of assisted conception cut to the heart of our legal identity, as the Connecticut Supreme Court pointed out in expressing a measure of frustration with legislative quiescence.

> [N]o one can deny that assisted reproductive technology implicates an essential matter of public policy—it is a basic expectation that our legal system should

enable each of us to identify our legal parents with reasonable promptness and certainty. Despite the fact that assisted reproductive technology has been available for some time, and that the technology implicates the important issue of the determination of legal parentage, our laws, and the laws of most other states, have struggled unsuccessfully to keep pace with the complex legal issues that continue to arise as a result of the technology.[9]

Perhaps our family relations are developing too quickly to be properly codified in statutory form. Although gestational surrogacy contracts are increasingly common, these agreements "seem beyond the boundaries of settled law, reaching into a morass of issues and rights involving morality, ethics, and responsibility."[10] In declaring a common-law status of de facto parentage in the face of a legislative gap, the Washington Supreme Court remarked that the state's "current statutory scheme reflects the unsurprising fact that statutes often fail to contemplate all potential scenarios which may arise in the ever changing and evolving notion of familial relations."[11] Given the rising tide of nontraditional family cases, the legislative hiatus is necessarily resulting in a transformation in the judicial allocation of parenting rights and obligations.

Many courts have recognized that "[t]he changing realities of modern family life, and the increasing use of collaborative reproductive technology to procreate children by asexual means, has forced a reconsideration of the meaning of parenthood."[12] When statutory means are ill fitting or entirely absent, courts may not—as legislatures often do—simply postpone dealing with the difficult issues presented to them. Instead, judges must often craft equitable remedies in an effort to achieve substantial justice between the parties and for their children and society at large. In these broad policy areas, courts often employ case-by-case adjudication when they find "statutory silence regarding the interests of children begotten by artificial insemination, and the rights and responsibilities of adults in such parenting arrangements."[13]

Silence is a two-edged statutory sword, however. Some judges see legislative silence as a golden opportunity to behave like traditional common-law judges, filling in the interstices with the accumulated wisdom of similar cases in light of evolving norms.[14] Other judges find a different solace in silence. They limit their job to applying the statutes as written, and they toss the policy dilemmas back to the legislature.[15] In doing so, however, these dodging jurists reject the family structure that the parties created, in favor of the idealized and drastically out-of-date family model the legislatures had in mind a generation or even a century ago.

Equitable Relief: How Judges Deal with Missing or Ill-Fitting Statutes

Reproductive technology cases are not unique in forcing a reexamination of what constitutes a family.[16] Nor are they the first domestic phenomena to pit judicial reticence against legislative inertia, prodding one or the other into finally taking up the reins of decision making.[17] Given the flood of nontraditional family cases, the legislative vacuum is leading to a transformation in the judicial allocation of parenting rights and obligations. A selection of recent cases—many of them controversial—illustrates the broad dimensions of the rift between formal law and contemporary culture in the construction of the modern family and suggests an eventual resolution premised on functional norms. The variety of these parentage cases bespeaks the wide range of family forms in the 21st century. Here is a sampling of the cases involved:

- A stepparent assumed the role of a coequal parent with the consent of the natural parent.[18]
- A married heterosexual couple arranged to implant an embryo created with their genetic material into the wife's sister, who bore the child as a gestational surrogate.[19]
- A gay male couple contracted with a gestational surrogate to bear them a child, using a donor egg and the sperm of one of the partners.[20]
- One partner in a lesbian couple gave birth via artificial insemination, while the other partner coparented the child with the consent of the natural parent.[21]

If the couples in the preceding examples come to a parting of the ways and dispute child custody or visitation, should the courts provide legal recognition to the family that the parties and children have constructed? When the questions is phrased in that way, an affirmative answer appears obvious.[22] It bears emphasizing at the outset that allowing the family members to construct and maintain their own family on their own terms is an essentially *conservative* notion, one that preserves the structure in place and counsels against state power interfering with family organization. Courts are tending to agree and increasingly aim at preserving the parental status quo in these cases.

Terms such as *de facto parent, equitable parent,* and *psychological parent* were initially unknown to the common-law world, rooted as it was on biology, with the later addition of adoption. But the courts (and a handful of legislatures) that designed and now employ these terms are not seeking to inject a stranger into the natural family. To the contrary, every case in this area seeks to answer three questions at the heart of family reconstruction: (1) whether the petitioning party claiming legal parenthood status was accorded that status by the other legal parent during the time they lived together as a family with the child; (2) whether that adult has been performing as a parent for a sufficiently long period of time; and, critically, (3) whether that adult and the child have established a parent-child relationship. What is new and strange in these cases is the nonbiological or adoptive origin of the parent-child bond, not the essential nature of that bond or the lived experience of family life.

The Supreme Judicial Court of Massachusetts has provided a practical definition of a de facto parent, "one who has no biological relation to the child, but has participated in the child's life as a member of the child's family."[23] The de facto parent "resides with the child and, with the consent and encouragement of the legal parent, performs a share of caretaking functions at least as great as the legal parent."[24] The de facto parent "shapes the child's daily routine, addresses his developmental needs, disciplines the child, provides for his education and medical care, and serves as a moral guide."[25]

Maintaining the parent-child bond in cases where families break up is a charge that family courts have undertaken for generations. Where the children's welfare is in jeopardy, the premise for court intervention is found in most states' general equity powers. Equitable recognition of de facto parenting is grounded in the principle "that disruption of a child's preexisting relationship with a nonbiological parent can be potentially harmful to the child" and, thus, that state intervention is warranted to safeguard that parent-child bond.[26]

Courts crafting equitable resolutions in these cases are sometimes charged with engaging in "judicial lawmaking."[27] But that accusation is an oddly inapt way to describe the process of enforcing the rules the family created for itself and lived by long enough to establish a cognizable family structure.[28] It is difficult, for example, to make sense of a dissenting justice's use of the label "antifamily" to describe a court decision awarding parenting rights to a women who lived in an intimate relationship with the child's biological mother, shared in the decision to bring the child into the world, helped plan the birthing, helped create a nursery in which to care for the child upon his arrival, and "mothered" the child from birth until the death of his biological mother.[29] Such a court ruling may contradict a homophobic view of what constitutes an appropriate family life, but it clearly affirms the family in which this child was raised and allocates parenting rights to the only living parent the child has ever known.

A recent example of this type of equitable relief may be found in a 2009 Montana Supreme Court decision on whether to award parenting rights to a lesbian coparent.[30] In *Kulstad v. Maniaci*, the majority considered a state statute that allowed a third party to acquire parental interests under the following conditions: the "natural parent has engaged in conduct that is contrary to the child-parent relationship"; the third party "has established with the child a child-parent relationship;;" and "it is in the best interests of the child to continue that relationship."[31] The majority found that the natural parent had fostered the parent-child relationship between her lesbian partner and her child, that the partner and the child had developed a parent-child relationship, and that continuing that relationship was in the best interests of the child.[32]

Another argument against the expansion of equity jurisprudence targets the judiciary's supposed lack of expertise in family policy. The argument insists that judges are ill equipped to draft the substantive and procedural rules governing when child welfare provisions should apply and when and how they may be modified. Under this view, fashioning an equitable parent doctrine forces a court "to improvise, as it goes along, substantive standards and procedural rules about when legal custody may be modified, what terms and conditions may be set, and other matters that already have well-charted passageways under state statutes and related court decisions."[33]

The problem with this view is that the "well-charted passageways" are chock-full of nontraditional families whose very composition challenges established notions of family law. Our "dominant legal norm" posits that "family is a heterosexual, marital, biological unit, [but] our social and cultural patterns expose a culture that is largely at odds with that nuclear, marital family norm."[34] Three and a half centuries of domestic life in America have yielded a cornucopia of family arrangements, and the bounty is not likely to diminish. As legal historian Michael Grossberg has observed, our history reveals "the constant reality of American family diversity."[35]

When the patterns in our lives diverge from the pathways in our laws, what are courts to do? Parents receive the law's imprimatur because society considers them central to family life.³⁶ That parenthood was once framed in biological terms was a historical inevitability—practically a tautological position. But the argument that parenthood has now been uprooted from its biological grounding and transplanted into functional soil does not stem from a new conception of families. Rather, it grows out of the same core family tradition of parents nurturing children into adulthood, and that difficult task remains a central socializing fact of our culture.³⁷ The "equitable parent" cases all attempt to answer the same question that biological parenthood presupposed: who is actually raising the child?

Consider the "psychological parenthood" test adopted by the New Jersey Supreme Court. For a "third party" to become legally recognized as a coparent, four steps are required. The legal parent "must consent to and foster the relationship between the third party and the child; the third party must have lived with the child; the third party must perform parental functions for the child to a significant degree; and most important, a parent-child bond must be forged."³⁸ The Maine Supreme Court has adopted a similarly high standard: a de facto parent must have "undertaken a permanent, unequivocal, committed, and responsible parental role in the child's life," and the individual must be "understood and acknowledged to be the child's parent both by the child and by the child's other parent."³⁹

Some judges justify a key role for equity jurisprudence on the ground that the primary institutional expertise in family law resides in the courts, not in the legislatures, which are "ill-equipped to deal with the myriad situations in which children find themselves."⁴⁰ The psychological or de facto parent analysis exemplifies how courts act to protect children who may be harmed unless creative judicial solutions are developed to fill the gaps in statutory enactments.⁴¹ The accusations of "judicial lawmaking" ring particularly hollow when applied to this equitable doctrine. In application, this set of guidelines mirrors the traditional norms of family governance and child welfare. The issue of psychological or de facto parenthood is raised only if coparenting was intended and acted on by the original biological or adoptive parent. The creation of a shared parenthood status is thus entirely within the control of the original legal parent of that child.⁴²

However, the legal parent cannot have it both ways. He or she cannot "invite a third party to function as a parent" to his or her child and then later pretend, once that parent-child relationship has matured, that the family the third party helped bring into being never existed.⁴³ As the Pennsylvania Supreme Court forcefully observed, "a biological parent's rights 'do not extend to erasing a relationship between her partner and her child which she voluntarily created and actively fostered simply because after the parties' separation she regretted having done so.'"[44] Rejecting this argument is implicit in the central child welfare task of the courts: avoiding injury to children. Severing an established parent-child relationship harms a child, whether that relationship began through biological means or social ones following the invitation of and cultivation by the legal parent.

Every matrimonial lawyer and judge knows that child custody battles in divorce courts frequently involve the cruel display of one parent trying to deny the other parent contact with their child.[45] When the second parent is a psychological or de facto parent, the spectacle is no less barbaric, and the potential harm to the child is no less ruinous. As the New Jersey Supreme Court observed, the law should follow the necessities of family life: "At the heart of the psychological parent cases is a recognition that children have a strong interest in maintaining the ties that connect them to adults who love and provide for them."[46] The South Dakota Supreme Court agreed, emphasizing that "the temporal, mental and moral welfare of children are paramount" in these cases.[47]

This acceptance of the familial status quo also has constitutional moorings. The U.S. Supreme Court has acknowledged that "freedom of personal choice in matters of . . . family life is one of the liberties protected by the Due Process Clause of the Fourteenth Amendment."[48] Equity powers may be employed creatively under these circumstances, but they are designed to conserve, to the extent feasible, the family structure the parties themselves adopted when they were contemplating and carrying out a shared family life, rather than when they were later devising a tactical litigation position. The goal is always to maintain the particular family structure that the children experienced before the breakup of the adults who had parented them. This aim guides family courts in allocating parental functions (making custody and visitation orders) in cases in which the parents had married. Children of nontraditional families deserve no less. Equity in these cases begins by recognizing "the emotional bonds that develop[ed] between family members as a result of shared daily life," particularly the parent-child relationships.[49]

These nontraditional families include those formed by same-sex couples, but heterosexual couples are often locked in the same dilemmas. For example, parenting issues abound in heterosexual stepfamilies, the fastest growing family type in America, composing approximately 30 percent of all households with children under age 18.⁵⁰ Traditionally, a stepparent could only receive custody of or visitation with a stepchild if the natural parent was declared unfit as a parent.⁵¹ Indeed, the "starting premise under the traditional model of parenthood and family is that claims for legal recognition of the stepparent-child relationship will be denied."⁵² Stepparents have gradually achieved some measure of rights vis-à-vis their stepchildren, but their status remains unresolved in family law.⁵³ A number of state statutes grant stepparents standing to seek orders of visitation.⁵⁴ Some courts have developed an in loco parentis doctrine to afford some parental rights to stepparents who have demonstrated a parent-child relationship.⁵⁵ A few courts go further and contemplate awarding custody to a stepparent who has established a psychological parent relationship to a stepchild.⁵⁶

The emerging trend reflects the view that any adult who has been treated for a sufficiently long period as a coparent by the natural parent and who has established a parent-child relationship will be deemed to be the child's legal parent, whether the adult was originally a stepparent, a grandparent, or a lesbian or gay male coparent. The focus in all these instances is on the nature and quality of the parental relationship or bond between the child and the adult seeking legal recognition.⁵⁷ This analysis is necessarily a fact-laden one, and courts should look to objective indicia satisfying all the criteria for functional parenthood.⁵⁸

In terms of constitutional analysis, the determination that de facto parents may exercise full parental rights is consistent with ruling Supreme Court doctrine. That the due process clause of the 14th Amendment protects the rights of legal parents to direct and govern the care, custody, and control of their children is fundamental.⁵⁹ But the question "Who is a legal parent?" frames a quite different inquiry. In its well-publicized *Troxel v. Granville* decision, the U.S. Supreme Court held that a "nonparent" visitation statute violated a parent's due process rights as applied, because it "effectively permit[ted] any third party seeking visitation to subject any decision by a parent concerning visitation of the parent's children to state-court review."⁶⁰ But the question in the de facto parent cases does not involve nonparent rights at all. Instead, a court must decide whether the petitioner in such a case is "a legal 'parent' of [the child] who would also have parental rights to [the child]—rights that are co-equal to the [natural parent]."⁶¹

The task of apportioning parental rights and duties in a family that is breaking apart is always difficult, but it is even harder in these nontraditional cases. The painful pressure brought to bear on the family by the separation of the adult partners is often exacerbated by the argument that one of the adults who was parenting the child—and was accepted in that role by both the other partner and the child—is actually an interloper, a legal interloper in the family. Indeed, the outré legal position in these cases is not the one taken by courts deploying equity solutions to bolster the family created by the parties themselves. It is, rather, a belated legal pose adopted by some of the litigants in the lesbian coparenting cases, which we term the "chutzpah argument."[62] In essence, the biological or adoptive lesbian parent claims that the woman whom she invited to share in her life and coparent her child and who has, with the biological or adoptive parent's consent and cooperation for several years, "on a continuing, day-to-day basis, through interaction, companionship, interplay, and mutuality, fulfill[ed] the child's psychological needs for a parent, as well as the child's physical needs," should now legally be deemed a stranger to the child.[63] This argument is not creditable. Rather, equity should reject, under the rubric of "unclean hands," this position articulated by a biological or adoptive parent seeking to deny the family structure that he or she worked so hard to establish.[64]

The Challenges of Surrogacy: The Children of *Baby M* in the Courts

The legal status of surrogacy today is a muddle. Some states have outlawed surrogacy, others have regulated it, but most states have not legislated on the practice.[65] Not until recent years was there adequate common-law development to suggest a compelling rationale. This deficiency in our legal tradition should not be surprising. As one trial court aptly noted, "for millennia, giving birth was synonymous with providing the genetic makeup of the child that was born."[66] The common law was silent on alternative reproduction because "[b]irth and blood/genetics were one."[67] But for the past several decades, the assumption that giving birth aligns with a genetic match has weakened to the point that a legal overhaul is needed.[68] Collaborative reproduction is forcing a recalibration of governing norms, beginning with the fundamental question of determining parentage.[69]

Initially, courts tended to treat issues that arose in the context of assisted reproduction by ignoring the reproductive technology and its implications. For example, in a much-discussed 1991 lesbian coparenting case, the New York Court of Appeals refused to grant visitation to a woman who coparented a child for over two years with her partner who had given birth by intrauterine insemination using donor sperm.[70] The two women had agreed on a coparenting arrangement, given the child the names of both women, and fully shared in parenting the child.[71] But New York's highest court believed that only biology or adoption could establish parentage.[72] Defining one of the child's coparents as a nonparent allowed the court to reaffirm the prohibition on extending parenting rights to a nonparent, a point reinforced in a different context by the U.S. Supreme Court in *Troxel v. Granville*.[73]

Some recent cases have taken a more pragmatic view of the parentage determination. Typical is *Culliton v. Beth Israel Deaconess Medical Center*, in which the Supreme Judicial Court of Massachusetts considered how to determine legal paternity and maternity in an alternative reproduction case involving a gestational surrogacy contract.[74] The surrogate gave birth to twins who were the genetic children of a married heterosexual couple, but the state statutes did not make clear who the mother or father would be under these circumstances. This case showcased the dilemmas of technological change outstripping the pace of legislation. The Culliton twins "technically were born out of wedlock, because the gestational carrier was not married when she gave birth to them."[75] Had the surrogate been married, her husband would have been presumed to be the father of the children to whom she gave birth. Addressing the issue as a modern-day biology teacher might discuss an outdated text, the court noted that while the paternity statute presumed sexual intercourse as a predicate to parentage, "reproductive advances have eliminated the necessity of having sexual intercourse in order to procreate."[76] The court concluded that since the children were conceived by a married couple, they "should be presumed to be the children of marriage," even though another woman gave birth to them.[77]

The dispute over the Culliton twins illustrates how alternative reproduction technologies have compelled a fundamental reconsideration of parentage determinations.[78] Although a majority of states with legislation on the subject declare surrogacy agreements void, "thousands of children are born each year pursuant to gestational agreements."[79] As Joanna Grossman pointed out, the popular perception that surrogacy is problematic is mistaken, because "the vast majority of surrogacy arrangements are carried out without a hitch."[80] Some rational statutory solutions are coming to pass in response to the need to determine the status of ART children fairly. For instance, in 2004, the Illinois legislature passed the Gestational Surrogacy Act, providing for the enforcement of gestational surrogacy contracts and declaring that the intended parents automatically become the child's legal parents at birth.[81] The Illinois law contemplates a prebirth registration process, rather than a judicial proceeding, to establish the status of the intended parents.[82] It is based on the Uniform Parentage Act, which authorizes a "prospective gestational mother, her husband if she is married, a donor or the donors, and the intended parents" to enter into a gestational agreement.[83]

Statutory efforts might significantly clarify parenting rights, especially if they are modeled after the Uniform Parentage Act or the American Bar Association's Model Act Governing Assisted Reproductive Technology.[84] Even with statutory improvements, problems will remain for families who do not fit within formal legal parameters. For nontraditional families who have children through ART, a workable analogy may be drawn from the "functional" family norms articulated in the equitable parentage cases. The intended parents in a surrogacy agreement or ART procedure should be treated as the equivalent of the functional parents in a contested custody case. In many gestational surrogacy cases, the intended parents made possible the creation of the child, a child who would literally not exist were it not for the actions of those parents.

Granting parental status to intended parents in surrogacy cases is consistent with the law's movement toward valuing functional norms in all parenthood cases. In its landmark holding in *Johnson v. Calvert*,[85] the California Supreme Court characterized the actions of the parties to a contested gestational surrogacy case in clearly functional terms. Mark and Crispina wanted a child from their genetic stock but needed reproductive technology to achieve that goal. They took all the steps needed to effect in vitro fertilization. "But for their acted-on intention," the court noted, "the child would not exist."[86] Their gestational surrogate, Anna, "agreed to facilitate the procreation of Mark's and Crispina's child."[87] The zygote with the couple's genetic material was implanted in Anna. When the child was born and Anna surprisingly claimed to be the legal mother, the court rejected her claim and upheld Crispina's maternity claim. Although the legal precedents were murky, the court's analysis showed why this result is the only tenable outcome.

> Crispina from the outset intended to be the child's mother. Although the gestative function Anna performed was necessary to bring about the child's birth, it is safe to say that Anna would not have been given the opportunity to gestate or

deliver the child had she, prior to implantation of the zygote, manifested her own intent to be the child's mother. No reason appears why Anna's later change of heart should vitiate the determination that Crispina is the child's natural mother.[88]

In emphasizing the intentions and behavior of the three parties to the *Johnson v. Calvert* case, the court suggested that its role was to validate the reasonable decisions of intended parents and to preserve the resulting family.[89] This brace of norms, *intention plus behavior*, suggests a simple but perhaps workable format for approaching cases of second-parent disputes in gestational surrogacy and ART cases in general. *Intention plus behavior* means that nonparents achieve parenthood status only when both adult partners have demonstrated appropriate intent to become a parent plus sufficient behavior establishing a parent-child relationship.

In contested gestational surrogacy cases, the intended parents have typically not had the opportunity to develop a parent-child relationship with the baby whose birth may have triggered the gestational carrier's decision to renounce the surrogacy agreement. However, the intended parents may have done everything possible to become that child's functional parents. If they have done so, they should be declared the child's legal parents. Of course, the gestational carrier has her own functional argument. This argument relies on the fact that she carried the child for nine months and then went through the pains of childbirth to deliver the child. But that contention must be viewed in its proper context. The surrogate intended to form no family tie with the child. She intended to be anything but the child's legal parent. Had she not solemnly expressed her intent to *avoid* parenthood, she would never have become the gestational carrier for this child. In many of these cases, until after the birth of the child, the surrogate did not act in any way to contravene the understanding that the intended parents were the legal parents.

Katharine Baker observed that "[p]reconception intent is critical to courts' allocations of parental rights" in these cases.[90] This articulated aim of the intended parents, coupled with their behavior demonstrating furtherance of their goal to create new life with the help of a gestational surrogate, establishes that the intended parents are the baby's functional and real parents. They should be declared the legal parents.

Preconception intent plus consistent behavior is key. An unusual case from California shows how this principle applies even when one of the intended parents tried to avoid responsibility for the child. In *Marriage of Buzzanca*, a heterosexual married couple, John and Luanne Buzzanca, arranged for a gestational surrogate to bring to term an embryo genetically unrelated to either spouse.[91] After fertilization, implantation, and pregnancy, John filed for divorce. The gestational surrogate made no parentage claim, and Luanne acknowledged that she and John were the lawful parents of Jaycee, the child who was brought to term by the surrogate. But John made two strikingly disingenuous assertions: (1) that he was not Jaycee's father and (2) that the surrogate and her husband were the child's legal parents. Even more bizarrely, the trial court concluded that Jaycee had *no legal parents*. The California Court of Appeal brought sense to the dispute by focusing on John and Luanne's joint preconception intent plus subsequent consistent behavior. Their acted-on intent meant that Jaycee had come into existence only because John and Luanne arranged for donated sperm and ova to be fertilized and implanted in a gestational surrogate who gave birth to their child. Because the intending parents had acted consistently with their purpose, the appellate court held that John and Luanne were the child's legal parents, even though Luanne had not given birth and neither parent was biologically related to Jaycee.[92]

Whatever the ultimate legal configuration of parentage for children of ART, the need to achieve a workable resolution could not be more pressing. Up to one-third of women who use ART are unmarried.[93] Chaotic and dysfunctional would accurately describe a legal system that excludes children born to unmarried couples from established parentage rules. Whether enacted by legislatures or developed through the equity power of the courts, rules based on preconception intent plus consistent behavior would serve both parents and children in these families.

In a world in which family composition increasingly depends more on function than on blood, the intended parents of a child should be deemed the legal parents, because they are the ones who have done the most to prepare a family for that child. In chapter 4, we considered *Baby M*, the seminal surrogacy case, and its progeny. The past quarter century has witnessed a series of legal, technological, and demographic upheavals yielding a bumper crop of new family forms. *Baby M* may have been correct in its time, but we must resolve a new generation of parenthood issues today. The children of *Baby M* deserve their real parents, those who assumed the responsibility for bringing them into being.

The legal status of the multitude of same-sex couples raising children is far from clear and is subject to the crosscurrents of disparate court opinions throughout the country. One way to explore the vagaries of the lived experience that these families face is to take a close look at one such couple who made substantial efforts to have a child and establish their family before a bitter breakup led to contentious litigation and the all-too-common "chutzpah argument." The next section tells this family's story.

The Story of Julia, Melissa, and Jacob

Julia Catherine Boseman is a lawyer and was the first openly gay North Carolina legislator, serving as a state senator from 2005 to 2011. Melissa Ann Jarrell was a veteran collegiate softball coach who served as the head coach at the University of North Carolina at Wilmington for seven years. In 1998, Julia and Melissa began an intimate relationship; they started living together the following year.[94] They discussed having and raising a child together and initiated that process in May 2000. They decided that Melissa would become pregnant and bear the child and that both women would otherwise jointly participate in the conception process. Together, they researched the available options, chose an anonymous sperm donor, and attended the medical appointments necessary both to impregnate Melissa and to address her prenatal care. Julia read to the minor child "in the womb and played music for him."[95] Julia also cared for Melissa during the pregnancy and was present for the delivery.

Melissa gave birth to a boy in October 2002, and she and Julia jointly selected his first name, Jacob, and gave him a hyphenated last name linking each of their last names. Julia and Melissa consistently held themselves out as the parents of Jacob Boseman-Jarrell. They "had a baptismal ceremony for the child at [Julia's] church during which they publicly presented themselves to family and friends as parents of the child."[96] Each woman integrated Jacob into her respective extended family, and each family accepted Jacob as the child of Julia and Melissa.

Within their home, the women shared equally in the tasks and joys of parenting. Julia's parenting skills were found to be "very attentive, very loving, hands on and fun." Melissa was found to be "very hands-on and patient in parenting" and to "reprimand[] [Jacob] by talking to him in a nice way." As a result of occupational responsibilities, each partner was occasionally required to be temporarily away from their home. During such an absence, the one who was staying at home would care for the child. Jacob treats each woman as his parent, calling Julia "Mom" and Melissa "Mommy." The trial court concluded that Jacob "shows lots of love and respect for both parties" and that "[e]ach party agrees that the other is and has been a good parent."[97]

In 2004, the women discussed having Julia adopt Jacob, while of course retaining Melissa as his legal natural parent. But North Carolina's adoption statute provided that a "decree of adoption severs the relationship of parent and child between the individual adopted and that individual's biological . . . parents."[98] The statute contains an exception for stepparent adoptions,[99] but Julia could not become Jacob's stepmother under North Carolina law, since Melissa and Julia were forbidden to marry in that state.[100] Nor could the women enter into a valid marriage outside North Carolina and expect that it would be recognized in their home state.[101]

What other alternatives did they have? Julia might have adopted Jacob in a jurisdiction that permits a second-parent adoption, one that would declare her a legal parent without terminating Melissa's parentage.[102] After securing such an adoption decree, they could have returned home and relied on the full faith and credit clause of the U.S. Constitution to have the other state's adoption decree accepted in North Carolina.[103] However, not only would that strategy have been cumbersome (requiring them to travel to and establish residency in another state), but its success would not have been guaranteed.[104]

Melissa and Julia instead attempted a legal maneuver within the terms of the North Carolina adoption statute, in an effort to obtain a second-parent adoption in their home state. In June 2005, they petitioned the Durham County District Court to allow the adoption, asking the court to waive the statutory provisions requiring that the biological mother terminate her parental rights. To that end, Melissa filed a pleading consenting to Julia's adoption of Jacob, stating her aim that "when this adoption is entered . . . the minor child shall have two legal parents, [herself and Julia.]"[105] In August 2005, the adoption decree was issued.

Tensions between Melissa and Julia resulted in their spending significant time apart beginning in 2005 and separating in May 2006. Julia continued to provide "most of the financial support for the partnership" and for Jacob. Melissa acknowledged that Julia "is a very good parent," that Julia "loves Jacob and that Jacob loves her," and that it is important for Julia "to be in Jacob's life." Nevertheless, Melissa began limiting Julia's contact with the child.

Julia then brought a court action asking that she and Melissa be given joint custody of Jacob.[106] Melissa countered by claiming that Julia's adoption of Jacob was void and that Julia had no parental status in the case. The trial court upheld the adoption decree and also found that Melissa had voluntarily shared with Julia the responsibilities of raising Jacob from the child's birth, that Melissa had publicly acknowledged Julia as a parent of Jacob, and that she had voluntarily joined with Julia so that she could adopt Jacob. These actions demonstrated to the court that Melissa had acted inconsistently with her constitutionally protected parental rights, in fostering Julia's parental relationship with Jacob. In short, the court concluded that Melissa and Julia had intentionally created a functioning two-parent family from preconception until the parents separated. The court then ruled that it would be in the best interest of Jacob for Melissa and Julia to have joint legal custody, with Melissa having primary residential custody.

Melissa appealed to the North Carolina Court of Appeals, which ruled unanimously in 2009 that the adoption decree was valid and, thus, that Julia was a legal parent of Jacob. Since the record established that both Melissa and Julia were legal parents and fit custodians, the appellate court affirmed the trial court's custody determination.[107] Melissa then petitioned the North Carolina Supreme Court to review the case.

The state's supreme court had a quite different view of the case. A majority of the court held that the adoption decree was void ab initio. The state's adoption statutes simply did not permit a second-parent adoption. Melissa and Julia could not legally obtain an adoption decree that would establish that Julia was Jacob's legal parent without simultaneously severing Melissa's status as a legal parent. Nor was Melissa statutorily barred from challenging the adoption she had labored so hard to achieve. A void adoption is no adoption at all, and Julia "is not legally recognized as the minor child's parent."[108]

Having disallowed the adoption of Jacob, the North Carolina Supreme Court turned to the issue of custody, viewing it as a "dispute between a parent and a third party."[109] The court began by observing that every parent has an "interest in the companionship, custody, care, and control of [his or her children that] is protected by the United States Constitution."[110] A nonparent may not interpose a custody claim as long as the child's parent continues to have this "paramount interest in the custody of his or her children."[111] But a parent can lose this paramount interest by acting inconsistently "with his or her constitutionally protected status."[112]

Had Melissa acted inconsistently with her constitutionally protected status as the child's parent? The supreme court found ample evidence that she "intentionally and voluntarily created a family unit in which [Julia] was intended to act—and acted—as a parent." The court pointed to a myriad of factors: the women's joint decision to bring a child into their relationship, working together to conceive the child, choosing the child's first name together and deciding on a last name hyphenating their two last names, and publicly holding themselves out as the child's parents. The court concluded that Melissa allowed Julia and Jacob to develop a "parental relationship," pointedly adding that Melissa even "agrees that [Julia] . . . is and has been a good parent."[113]

Although the court had invalidated the adoption, it referred to those proceedings as further evidence that Melissa had intended for Julia to assume full parental status. In asking for an adoption so that Jacob would have "two legal parents," Melissa stated that she and Julia "have raised [Jacob] since his birth and have jointly and equally provide[d] [him] with care, support and nurturing throughout his life." Melissa had further affirmed that she "intends and desires to co-parent with another adult who has agreed to adopt a child and share parental responsibilities."[114] The supreme court concluded that Melissa had shared parental responsibilities with Julia without any expectation of termination and thus "acted inconsistently with her paramount parental status."[115] The high court therefore affirmed the trial judge's determination that Julia and Melissa would exercise joint custody of Jacob.

What does this resolution mean for Melissa, Julia, and Jacob? Although Melissa and Julia have joint legal custody, the court's voiding of Julia's adoption of Jacob means that Melissa is apparently Jacob's only legal parent.[116] In the absence of a statutory definition of the term *legal custody,* North Carolina case law has construed it as "the right and responsibility to make decisions with important and long-term implications for a child's best interest and welfare."[117] Joint legal custody thus involves shared parental decision-making authority. Indeed, in a joint custody decision, a trial court may specifically allocate "certain decision-making authority that would normally fall within the ambit of joint legal custody to one party rather than another" only upon making "sufficient findings of fact to show that such a decision was warranted."[118] Thus, the manner in which the couple shares parental decision making is generally left to them, as it was in this case. Melissa was given primary physical custody, which means that Jacob will be living with her. Julia will exercise visitation; thus, she and Jacob will have the time together that Melissa and Julia can agree on or that a court will order if the former domestic partners cannot agree on a visitation schedule.

How will Julia be able to exercise her custodial rights with Jacob, who turned ten years old in 2012? The adoption decree naming her as a legal parent is no more. What documentation can she present to show her authority to exercise her parenting rights at Jacob's school or to access his medical records? Must she carry with her the trial court order, supplemented by the supreme court opinion? Will the school officials and health care providers be expected to parse these complex judicial texts to glean the scope of Julia's parental rights? There are no clear answers to these questions.[119] Moreover, given the prolonged and contentious litigation in which the former domestic partners engaged over the right to parent Jacob, it may not be easy for them now to cooperate on jointly making the major decisions about Jacob's health, education, religion, and welfare.

What does the *Boseman v. Jarrell* ruling voiding the adoption mean for same-sex couples in North Carolina? As of 2010, some 27,250 same-sex couples lived in North Carolina.[120] Twenty-three percent of these same-sex couples (6,290) were raising children.[121] According to one report, state courts had allowed over 200 second-parent adoptions involving same-sex couples.[122] Now the state supreme court has declared all such adoptions invalid. Unless the state legislature amends the adoption statute to allow second-parent adoptions, there is no legally sanctioned method for same-sex couples to securely create a family with children in North Carolina. In May 2012, a ballot referendum amended the state constitution to provide that "marriage between one man and one woman is the only domestic legal union that shall be valid or recognized in this state."[123] While this amendment constitutionalizes the state's ban on same-sex marriage, its broader adverse effect on couples such as Melissa and Julia is as yet unknown.

Both same-sex and opposite-sex couples often turn to ART to enable them to achieve parenthood. Legal standards governing family composition are evolving, and couples often find that a seemingly straightforward plan can encounter significant hurdles, especially when the members of the couple later find themselves at odds. The following story recounts one heterosexual couple's tortuous journey.

The Story of Cindy, Charles, and the Triplets

Cindy Lee Culpepper met Charles Kenneth Galiwango in 1993, when both were working at Vanderbilt University Medical Center in Nashville, Tennessee.[124] Cindy was a nurse-practitioner and managed a department through which Charles, then a medical resident, rotated. They started dating in 1994. After several years of an on-again, off-again relationship, Charles and Cindy reunited in 1999 and began discussing having a child together. Both were then in their mid-40s. Charles was childless, and after a visit that year to Uganda, where he had been born and had received his medical education, he decided that he wanted to be a father. Cindy already had two adult children from prior marriages as well as grandchildren, but she agreed to start a family with Charles. Given her age, however, Cindy was concerned about the viability of her ova. The couple decided to pursue in vitro fertilization through the Nashville Fertility Center. Their goal was to have Charles's sperm injected into ova from an anonymous donor, with the resulting embryo implanted in Cindy's uterus so she could give birth to their child.

On May 2, 2000, they jointly executed several agreements with the fertility center. Although Cindy and Charles were unmarried, they did not alter the center's boilerplate language describing them as husband and wife. The agreement they signed indicated that even though any resulting children would have the genetic material of only Charles and the anonymous donor, Cindy would be the mother, and she would "accept all the legal responsibilities required of such a parent."[125] This document was witnessed and signed by a physician who represented that he had fully explained the procedure to Charles and Cindy and had answered all their questions.

Soon afterward, Charles paid the fertility center $10,000 for the procedure of having two anonymously donated eggs fertilized with his sperm and inserted in Cindy's uterus. Charles intended for them to conceive only one child (two eggs were probably used to increase the procedure's odds of success). After fertilization, one of the eggs divided, resulting in the development of three embryos, all of which flourished. Cindy had become pregnant with triplets.

During Cindy's pregnancy, Charles began residing consistently at her home. Due to pregnancy complications, Cindy took an early leave from her job and was placed on bed rest, and Charles maintained the household. On February 21, 2001, Cindy gave birth to three children.[126] Each of their birth certificates identify Charles as the father and Cindy as the mother.

Although Charles had never promised to marry Cindy, he made it known that he desired permanence and stability with her. In turn, Cindy understood and expected that they would raise the children together as mother and father. Cindy even sought assurance from Charles that she would not have to rear the children by herself. Cindy stayed home with the triplets on maternity leave until June 2001, when she returned to work four days per week. Having set aside money in anticipation of becoming a father, Charles took a one-year leave of absence (from February 2001 to January 2002) from his position as an emergency physician. For several months after the triplets' birth, Charles and Cindy lived together and shared both parenting responsibilities and the children's financial needs. Having for some time discussed the need for a larger home because of the children, they jointly purchased a house with the understanding that they would bear the cost equally. Cindy sold her prior residence, and she, Charles, and the triplets moved into the new house in August 2001.

Soon after they hired a nanny, Charles and Cindy's relationship fell apart. Cindy accused Charles of having affairs, and Charles admitted having sex with another woman during a December 2001 trip to London, England. Cindy also claimed that once their relationship started to deteriorate, Charles not only became markedly less involved with the children but also began to withhold financial support for them and for her. In April 2002, after utility service to their home had been cut off, Cindy filed a petition in juvenile court to establish parentage and obtain custody and child support.

Charles responded to Cindy's petition by arguing that since she had no genetic connection to the children, she was not the children's mother. He demanded sole custody of the triplets, asserting that the children have no mother. The juvenile court held that Cindy "is the birth mother and always had the intent to birth these children for herself and [Charles]."[127] The court then decided that the parents would have joint custody of the children, with Cindy designated as the primary custodial parent. Charles was given visitation with the triplets, and he was required to continue to pay Cindy child support in the amount of $3,000 per month.

Charles appealed. The Tennessee Court of Appeals held that Cindy was legally the children's mother, since she was the intended mother and since no one else claimed maternal status.[128] It also affirmed the juvenile court's rulings on custody, visitation, and child support.[129] Charles appealed again, to the Tennessee Supreme Court.

The majority opinion for the state's high court first distinguished Charles and Cindy's case from other types of maternity/surrogacy disputes. This case was not like traditional surrogacy à la *Baby M*, since Cindy was not the children's genetic progenitor. Nor did this case fit the ordinary gestational surrogacy model, in which the intended mother's egg is implanted for gestation purposes in a genetically unrelated surrogate. The anonymous donor of the ova implanted in Cindy was certainly not the intended mother. The court concluded that the case resembled "gestational surrogacy with egg donation," in which a woman carries and gives birth to a child as a result of fertilization and implantation of a third-party donor's egg.[130]

What was Cindy's legal status? Cindy claimed that she gestated and birthed the triplets on behalf of both Charles as father and herself as mother. Charles entirely disagreed, contending that Cindy was merely a gestational surrogate acting for Charles and that he was the sole legal parent. In facing this issue, the state supreme court began by confessing that the "technological fragmentation of the procreative process... has engendered a bewildering variety of possibilities which are not easily reconciled with our traditional definitions of 'mother,' 'father,' and 'parent.'"[131] As is so often the case with the rapidly changing contours of family life, the court also acknowledged that the legislature had failed to provide guidance for court resolution.[132] The court reviewed tests based on the parties' intent or a genetic tie that other jurisdictions had developed for determining maternity. But the court declined to adopt either test, finding them both problematic and inconsistent with Tennessee's statutory framework.

Instead, the court decided the case on what it termed "particularly narrow grounds,"[133] leaving to the Tennessee General Assembly the formulation of a general rule to deal with the "far-reaching, profoundly complex, and competing public policy considerations"[134] of this area. Even though the court disclaimed reliance on any general test in resolving this case, it stressed the importance of the parties' preconception intent and subsequent behavior. The court emphasized that Cindy and Charles had from the outset "voluntarily demonstrated the bona fide intent that Cindy would be the children's legal mother."[135] Moreover, the couple had "agreed that Cindy would accept all the legal responsibility as well as the legal rights of parenthood."[136] While Cindy had not contributed any genetic material to the triplets, she had gestated them, and the court considered that factor significant in the circumstances of this case.[137] Concluding that Cindy was the triplets' legal mother, the court affirmed the lower court orders regarding custody, visitation, and child support. In other words, Cindy was the gestational carrier, but she was nobody's surrogate.

The court's majority opinion also thoroughly rejected the notion that the anonymous egg donor could rationally be considered the legal mother. Although the donor was a genetic progenitor of the triplets, she had fully waived her parental rights and remained anonymous. The court stated that to deem the anonymous egg donor as the triplets' legal mother "would result in the absurdity of children having, for all practical purposes, no legal mother."[138] For a child to know "that he or she has an anonymous and inaccessible mother somewhere in the world would provide only cold comfort, and demanding such a result in cases like this one could hardly promote the best interests of children."[139] In dissent, Justice Adolpho A. Birch criticized the majority for suggesting that the children would have no mother if not for Cindy. Instead, the dissent made the astounding assertion that the legal mother of the triplets was not Cindy but, rather, the anonymous egg donor.[140] How this unknown, unintended, and unavailable "mother" would care for "her" triplets was left unexplained by the dissent.

In the end, this custody battle ended as many others do, with the parents given joint legal custody, the father allowed visitation, and the mother receiving both primary residential custody and child support. But the voyage toward that resolution was distinctly untraditional. "I admit," said Charles, "all of this may not sound very classical. But I always wanted to have a child."[141] As a reporter narrated the events leading up to the triplets' birth, Charles found himself, in his mid-40s, "[u]nmarried and with no immediate prospects for a wife."[142] Despite all the evidence in the case, Charles told the reporter that he "expected [Cindy] to relinquish the triplets as they had agreed informally ahead of time."[143] "I know in my heart how I feel," Cindy said, adding, "I know in my heart I'm my children's mother."[144]

Charles's lawyer claimed that Cindy was only a surrogate mother and "not the legal mother," because she has no genetic connection to the children and did not adopt them.[145] Cindy's lawyer argued that Charles's position would "leave the children without a mother, which the courts are likely not to do."[146] This dilemma brings into play the fundamental connection between parent and child. Is that linkage "the strand of DNA" or the decision "of an individual or a couple to undergo what is one of the most profound experiences of a human being, which is to have and nurture a child?"[147]

Unlike Julia Boseman in relation to Jacob,[148] Cindy is both a legal parent and a joint legal custodian of her children. But how effectively will Cindy and Charles be able to exercise joint legal decision making for the children after Charles spent several years vigorously contending in three different courts that Cindy was not the triplets' legal mother? How will future cases be decided, in view of, first, the Tennessee Supreme Court's disavowal of a general test to resolve these cases and, second, the state legislature's reluctance to legislate in this area? The state's highest court left the issue in limbo in 2005, with a call for legislative resolution. In 2010, the Tennessee Legislature passed a law defining a surrogate birth but declining to either validate or invalidate it.[149] As described in a 2013 appellate court opinion, the legislative action resulted in "a curious provision by which the General Assembly 'kicked the can down the road' by leaving it to a later general assembly or the courts to authorize surrogacy birth contracts."[150] The status of ART families is not especially secure.

CHAPTER 6

Unsafe Havens, Unplanned Children, and Future Generations

Our last few decades of experience have urged acceptance and appreciation of alternative family forms. To a fair extent, Americans have cooperated, although to celebrate diversity simply for its own sake wears out credulity. Nontraditional families are here to stay. To deny them legal and social recognition merely because they are unconventional would be to discount and disenfranchise a sizable portion of the population. However, among the current profusion of alternative family forms—driven by ART, same-sex unions, cohabitation, stepparenting, nonmarital childbearing, and single parenting—are some that are inherently unstable and prone to recklessness or negligence in childbearing. Our current dilemma resides in how to support and strengthen alternative families without sanctioning and perpetuating dysfunctional practices that undermine family structure. We wish to acknowledge family diversity, but not at the expense of endangering the viability of family as an institution. Many nontraditional families have proved admirably resourceful in their determination to survive and prosper. Others, plagued by instability and irresponsible childbearing, have plunged countless children into poverty.

In chapter 3, we noted that economics plays a major role in family formation. The presence or absence of steady, adequate income likely determines whether or not a couple will marry. Unfortunately, unmarried couples and individuals do not always apply the same fiscal foresight to childbearing. This chapter further explores the connection between financial and relationship stability. Since the last decade, marriage promotion initiatives have targeted low-income couples, hoping to bring them into the marital fold and thereby bolster and solidify their unions. Although valid in theory, these programs often disregard economic realities that make permanence untenable. We also here discuss the continuing rise of nonmarital childbearing, its possible causes, and why the problem merits close and immediate attention. In a world of growing economic inequality, where the affluent are increasingly segregated from the rest, children born into poverty have even further to go to overcome their circumstances. The implications for posterity are enormous. If each generation's wealth is the gift of good fortune to the next, we may be dividing our descendants into rich and poor well into the future.

Marriage, in a Larger Sense

According to a well-worn adage, the more things change, the more they stay the same. Each generation views its particular round of social crises as unprecedented, just as each new crop of adolescents believes that it alone has invented the art of rebellion. Perhaps, in the structure and culture of families, there are only a limited number of ways that things can change. In the final analysis, the social ebb and flow either promotes family stability or does not.

By the 20th century, we grew accustomed to the notion of marrying for love. Then, amid a drenching cascade of divorce, we paused to rethink the purpose of marriage and the cost of upholding romantic idealism as its pretext. This was not the first time that the love-and-marriage connection had been questioned. More than four hundred years ago, Michel de Montaigne chided those "who think they honor marriage by joining love to it."[1] Montaigne regarded transitory passions as inimical to secure, fruitful unions.

> I see no marriages where the conjugal intelligence sooner fails, than those that we contract upon the account of beauty and amorous desires; there should be more solid and constant foundation, and they should proceed with greater circumspection; this frivolous ardor is worth nothing.[2]

The value of marriage, observed Montaigne, exceeds the needs and wants of the two individuals engaged in it. People "marry as much for their posterity and family," he wrote, adding, "[T]he custom and interest of marriage concern our race much more than us."[3]

That marriage is not solely a private arrangement but also a "core social institution"[4] serves to magnify its burdens and benefits, extending them beyond the personal. Marriage formalizes family relationships, defines the parameters of parenthood, and forges chains of ancestry. Family is "the chief agency of socialization," where two parents create a "union of love and discipline" in which children receive their earliest lessons in ethical norms and permissible social behavior.[5] Married life increases the prospect of economic mobility, a boon to succeeding generations. It has even been known to exert a "civilizing power"[6] over the conduct of young men.

Our current era is notable for its paradoxical marital trends. While the less affluent classes in America are beating a retreat from matrimony, same-sex partners eagerly aspire to fill the vacancies left at the altar. Gay and lesbian couples desiring the right to marry are not simply seeking a show of legitimacy. They want to be part of the communal endeavor, to collaborate with other members of society who have signed on for a shared future. In the recent past, when we talked about marriage, we talked about relationships. Today's discussions are not so myopic and are more apt to encompass legal, economic, cultural, and even political issues. Montaigne was right to conjoin marriage, social obligation, and posterity, although marrying for love will probably never quite go out of style.

The diminishing allure of marriage instills a longing to revive and reinstate the institution to its former prominence. In devising social policy, however, we must be careful to distinguish between nostalgia and common sense. Matrimony has never been for everyone. It is not unusual to question whether a particular couple is marrying for the right reasons. Today, with fewer weddings to attend, we are just as apt to wonder if there is a defensible basis for so frequently rejecting marriage. But wherever we turn for clarity, we come up against the forces of economics.

Get Them Married

By way of the Healthy Marriage Initiative of the Administration for Children and Families, the U.S. government's Deficit Reducation Act of 2005 channels $150 million a year into programs promoting marriage and responsible fatherhood.[7] On the state level, attempts to encourage marriage have included "campaigns and proclamations, covenant marriage, different divorce laws for parents, marriage education, incentives for marriage preparation, reducing [the] marriage tax penalty, marriage support, fatherhood programs,"[8] and relationship and financial counseling. Whether these programs actually work is debatable, since "they may be more effective at persuading high-risk couples not to tie the knot at all than changing the behavior of those who do."[9]

James Q. Wilson has attributed the source of our present cultural problems—namely, crime, drug abuse, and out-of-wedlock births—to "the failure of marriage to hold its ground among many poor people."[10] In his view, employment programs and financial assistance for the lower classes "will not change matters nearly as much as *getting them married.*"[11] There is at least some reason to suppose that marriage can ameliorate the effects of material hardship—by reliance on safety nets furnished by friends, family, and community; by promoting better budgeting and financial planning; and by the sheer advantage of pooling resources to weather a crisis.[12] Marriage rates have also been linked to indicators of wealth that are more universal. Median household income, which more than doubled between 1947 and 1977, has grown more slowly of late. One major factor, cited by the National Marriage Project, is that married couples, which are more financially prosperous than single people, have declined in proportion to total families.[13] Given the association between marriage and increased wealth and well-being, it is not difficult to grasp the rationale behind marriage promotion programs: "that if low-income parents can be encouraged to form strong and healthy marriages, we will ultimately reduce poverty and improve child well-being."[14]

The problem with this mode of thinking is that it ignores the extent to which economic stability is a prerequisite for marriage. In the absence of sufficient, consistent financial contributions from their partners, women will often opt for cohabitation and single parenthood.[15] That poverty rates among children in cohabitating households are higher than those in married families owes more to their parents' earning capacities than to their marital status. The economic welfare of the male partner, measured by education, earnings, or employment, often determines whether a cohabiting couple will transition to marriage. The optimum economic benefits of marriage accrue when two people with good educations and earnings potential marry each other. Thus, it is not marriage per se that engenders financial security, and policies that simply funnel cohabiting couples into marriage will not improve their economic circumstances.[16]

Between 1975 and 2000, the economic divide between rich and poor increased substantially. U.S. tax policies were modified to benefit the affluent, while the minimum wage and government programs for the less well-off were reduced or left to stagnate. As the focus of the American economy turned to technology, information, and financial services, unionized manufacturing jobs began to disappear. Working-class whites, who previously relied heavily on the availability of unionized work to support their families, were especially disadvantaged.[17] Along with the decline in union jobs came loss of health insurance, decreased work hours, and a shift from direct hiring to the subcontracting of labor.[18] In the "new political economy of affluence,"[19] class divisions deepened, while ethnic and racial distinctions in family structure became less pronounced.[20]

Trends in income inequality in the late 20th century may appear less racially and ethnically discriminatory, but they disproportionately target low-income minorities, especially those "living in concentrated poverty."[21] The crisis of black male unemployment, ongoing since the 1970s, parallels black male incarceration rates that have soared even as the crime rate has plummeted. For a young black man who has dropped out of high school, "the lifetime odds of going to prison vastly exceed those of getting married, joining a union, attending college, or maintaining a career."[22] The stigma of a criminal record further diminishes one's education and employment prospects. As a result, black women in the marriage market find "far fewer marriageable partners within their race group from which to choose."[23]

Urging matrimony on those who lack the educational and economic wherewithal to maintain their unions creates an unintended risk of more breakups. Marriage promotion strategies may be especially maladapted to "high rates of incarceration, unemployment, substance abuse, and domestic violence among low-income men and with high rates of early unwed childbearing among low-income women."[24] According to a recent estimate, women without high school degrees are nearly twice as likely as college-educated women to see their marriages end in separation or divorce.[25] In the aggregate, divorces create prohibitive public expense, with each one costing state and federal governments as much as $30,000 in increased use of food stamps and public housing, as well as leading to more bankruptcies and higher rates of juvenile delinquency.[26] On an individual level, women who have a nonmarital birth and then go on to marry and divorce are "economically worse off than those who never married."[27] Births out of wedlock reduce a woman's marriage prospects, curtailing her likelihood of finding a partner with sufficient income to propel her family out of poverty. To complicate matters even further, research published in 2011 states that 59 percent of unwed parents have children with multiple partners. These numbers are bound to increase as some of these unwed mothers and fathers continue to have children with multiple partners throughout their childbearing years.[28]

Among all classes, poor women have the highest rates of accidental pregnancy, unintended births, and abortions.[29] But as the moderately and least educated come to resemble each other in rates of unwed childbearing, worries increase about the stability and economic security of working-class and middle-income families.[30] In this sense, differentiating family-strengthening strategies by class seems less important. As a matter of public policy, the current emphasis on fortifying fragile relationships and promoting marriage between nonmarital partners with children may not be nearly as effective as making the reduction of unwed childbearing the primary goal.[31]

Begetting and Bearing

Nowadays, if only the married bore children, our schoolyards and playgrounds would seem eerily quiet. Four in 10 American children are born out of wedlock,[32] and today's young adults increasingly view marriage and childbearing as "largely independent events."[33] Few of us, if any, would wish to return to an era when unmarried mothers were cast out and punished as sinners. Morality's relativism, we have learned, is its most constant feature. But as it turns out, the surge in unmarried births sets millions of children adrift on very thin ice. The mere absence of wedlock is not, in and of itself, to blame, since "families that would be unstable anyway are just skipping marriage."[34] It is the haphazard way in which these families are built that poses the greatest future risk. Unmarried, unplanned births carry little or no provision for bringing a baby out of infancy, much less through childhood and adolescence and into adulthood. Childbirth preceded by marriage presents at least the hope of a communal future, propped up by shared material and emotional resources. While marriage rarely strengthens an unstable union, having children threatens to obliterate it altogether. Childbearing within transient, insecure relationships is, at best, thoughtless and shortsighted. At its worst, irresponsible, unplanned childbearing is a matter of willful blindness.

Nonmarital births occur in a variety of circumstances. They can be first births, second births, or higher-order births. They can precede a first marriage, can come to an unmarried parent who never marries afterward or to a parent whose marriage has terminated, or can occur within a cohabiting relationship.[35] Although unwed childbearing has long been associated with teenage parenthood, 63 percent of births to unmarried women in 2010 occurred within the 20–24 age group.[36] Teenage mothers account for 50 percent of all first nonmarital births.[37]

Babies born out of wedlock are more likely to result from unplanned pregnancies. From 2006 to 2010, 62 percent of unintended births were to unmarried women.[38] Among cohabiting women in particular, the rate of unintended births is more than twice that of married women.[39] Overall, half of all yearly pregnancies in the United States are unintended, with roughly an equal number ending in birth or abortion and the remainder resulting in fetal losses.[40] Women whose pregnancies are unplanned, unwanted, or mistimed are at greater risk of depression, both during pregnancy and postpartum. Unintended births are also linked to higher incidences of domestic violence and physical abuse.[41] Further, women undergoing unplanned pregnancies are more likely to forgo prenatal care, to continue to use alcohol and tobacco, and to have maternal and infant outcomes that are generally more adverse.[42] As for the children produced by unplanned birth, they are "less likely to succeed in school and are more likely to live in poverty, claim public assistance and engage in delinquent and criminal behavior later in life."[43]

U.S. efforts at pregnancy prevention have principally focused on teens, which is understandable given the enormous social and economic costs of children having children. The price of teenage parenthood is an estimated $9.1 billion annually, based on increased public expenditures in connection with health care, child welfare, criminal justice, and lost tax revenue.[44] For a young person enrolled in school, pregnancy and childbirth serve to "truncate education."[45] Moreover, hastening adulthood by an unintended pregnancy compresses the developmental stages of adolescence and young adulthood. The failure to achieve developmental proficiency at each stage creates an ongoing risk of future developmental deficits.[46] Less well publicized than the teen pregnancy problem is the crisis unfolding among America's so-called emerging adults, aged 18 to 24. Along with high rates of unmarried childbearing, these young people suffer elevated risks of "poverty, accidental injury, violence, death, substance abuse, sexually transmitted diseases and HIV."[47] Although considerably more vulnerable than teens, this age-group has been largely overlooked by government ad campaigns and public service providers.

Fertility patterns among the disadvantaged are often viewed in terms of "opportunity costs." With fewer venues available for educational and economic advancement, the poor believe they are sacrificing no "compelling opportunities" by having a child.[48] As explained by one young woman who chose to delay childbearing, "if I didn't have any ambition I would probably have children right now."[49] Poorly educated women, however, do not value childbearing solely by default and merely because they lack the means to garner self-esteem through professional titles and rewarding careers. According to Edin and Kefalas, lower-income women regard motherhood as "one of life's most fulfilling roles" and see childlessness as one of life's "great tragedies."[50] At the lower rungs of the economic ladder, the association between childbearing and opportunity costs is at its most tenuous. It is, for example, commonly assumed that early childbearing among poor inner-city girls is chiefly responsible for their failure to complete their educations, obtain job skills, and earn a decent income. But it is equally plausible that "early childbearing is highly selective of girls whose other characteristics—family background, cognitive ability, school performance, mental health status and so on—have already diminished their life chances so much that an early birth does little to reduce them much further."[51] At its most intransigent, this population is immune to exhortations about contraception and the value of an education. Opportunity costs are only relevant when viewed through a prism of meaningful, tangible possibilities.

Young women with the highest educational and career aspirations tend to use birth control consistently and effectively.[52] Beyond this rather obvious assertion, it is extremely difficult to draw a straight line between fertility intentions and actual birth outcomes among today's young adults, particularly those who are cohabiting. The fertility intentions of married couples and cohabitants differ dramatically, with cohabitants being far less likely than married couples to expect to bear children within an immediate two- to five-year window.[53] Despite their stated childbearing preferences, however, cohabitants' use of contraceptives bears only a weak connection to their intentions regarding pregnancy. Sharon Sassler and her colleagues studied a group of 30 cohabiting couples, nearly one-third of whom became pregnant during their relationships, some of them twice. Of a total of 12 reported pregnancies, 6 of which were carried to term, none was intended.[54] The rate of unplanned pregnancies among cohabiting women has been estimated at 70 percent and even as high as 80 percent.[55]

There are four criteria for planned pregnancy, identified as "intention to become pregnant, cessation of contraception, partner agreement, and attainment of a desired lifestyle and stage."[56] With so many cohabiting couples failing to meet the first of these criteria, their chances of reaching the other three are dismayingly slim. As it is, cohabiting couples accounted for more than half (52 percent) of all U.S. births occurring outside of marriage in 2001.[57] Contraceptive failure is rife among cohabiting women, with those under age 30 experiencing a higher failure rate than either married or single women, no matter what type of contraception used.[58] Among young unmarried women in general, contraceptive use can be woefully inconsistent, and pregnancy risks can be poorly understood.

In an illuminating study, Joanna Reed and her colleagues surveyed a racially diverse group of 51 never-married women aged 20 to 29 who attended community colleges in the San Francisco area. Those who were "always consistent" in their use of birth control (37 percent) were, not surprisingly, strongly education minded and career oriented. As a group, they demonstrated high levels of efficacy, assuming control over contraception within the relationship and refusing to relent when partners urged engaging in unprotected or inadequately protected sex. The "mostly consistent" group (also 37 percent) used contraception only slightly more than half the time, relied more heavily on use of the Plan B morning-after pill as a primary mode of birth control, and had considerably more pregnancies, births, and abortions than the previous group. Among these women, 60 percent (compared to 95 percent in the "always consistent" group) planned to obtain a four-year college degree, 30 percent sought certification in nonprofessional or semiprofessional careers, and 10 percent reported no specific educational or career goals. Due to perceived side effects, these women often engaged in switching between different contraceptive methods. Frequently, they underestimated their risk of getting pregnant while between methods. As a group, they tended to defer to their partners in decisions about birth control, even if doing so resulted in the use of inadequate measures, like withdrawal or no protection at all. Drug and alcohol intoxication during sexual encounters was more common among these women than in the "always consistent" group.[59]

About a quarter of the women in this study fell within the "sometimes or rarely consistent" group. Unlike the second group, where the intent to prevent conception was more often present though not always practiced, these women were far less definite about their desire to avoid pregnancy. Some of them wanted to have children with a particular partner, while others were ambivalent or blatantly indifferent about getting pregnant. As with the second group and unlike the first group, there was a likelihood of drug or alcohol intoxication during sexual encounters. Several of these women had enrolled in school to satisfy state public assistance requirements and were vague about their educational and career goals. These women were poorer than those in the other groups and led lives that were seemingly more chaotic and difficult. They were also far more likely to be misinformed about various contraceptive methods and to rely on erroneous assumptions about pregnancy risks. Further, they lacked a sense of control over their lives and were more prone to give in to their own and their partner's impulses to indulge in unprotected sex.[60]

Reed and her coauthors cited four determining factors in achieving avoidance of unplanned pregnancy. The first, efficacy, was strongly characteristic of motivated, self-disciplined women able to exert control over contraceptive practices within their relationships. The second, the behavior of male partners, makes a substantial difference, especially for those women less than consistent in their own birth control practices. In decisions about whether or not to proceed with a pregnancy, men are apt to feel powerless at affecting the outcome. They therefore tend to view contraception as their partner's responsibility. Meaningful male participation goes well beyond the willingness to use a condom, extending to providing a partner with transportation to clinic appointments and reminding her to take her pill. As scientific research expands the range of available male contraceptives, sexual partners may achieve contraceptive decision making that is more equitable.[61] The third element, side effects, pertains to hormonal methods in the form of pill or injection. Due to physical discomforts arising from these methods, many women lapse, discontinue use, or switch to another hormonal method. In the interim, they go unprotected or rely on withdrawal or inconsistent condom use. Despite its potential for misuse, the pill is the most widely employed method among women in their teens and 20s, cohabiting women, those who are childless, and those with at least a college degree.[62] The fourth factor, incorrect information, often misleads women into underestimating their risk of becoming pregnant. They may believe, for example, that several months of unprotected sex without a resulting pregnancy means that they are infertile and not in need of contraception.

The establishment of consistent, effective, and informed family planning, especially among young adults, is imperative and long overdue.

Some Remedial Suggestions

Births arising from unintended pregnancies are increasingly concentrated among poor and low-income women.[63] Nationally, there were 1.6 million births resulting from unplanned pregnancies in 2006, 64 percent of which were financed by public insurance programs.[64] At the rate of $11.1 billion in a single year, the cost to state and federal budgets is staggering.[65] If not for publicly funded family planning programs, expenses would be even higher. According to the Guttmacher Institute, publicly provided contraceptive services help to avert 1.5 unintended pregnancies per year, 650,000 that might result in births and 600,000 that might result in abortions.[66] Without public programs, the overall U.S. rate of unplanned pregnancy in 2008 would have been 47 percent higher, and the abortion rate would have been 50 percent higher.[67] The average annual cost per client in publicly funded family planning clinics is $257, compared to $576 for a government-funded abortion and $12,613 for one Medicaid-covered birth.[68] In 2008, an estimated $2 billion expended on publicly funded family planning services yielded $7 billion in gross savings from helping women avoid unintended pregnancies and the succeeding births.[69]

In 2011, the Obama administration issued new standards requiring health insurance plans to cover all government-approved contraceptives for women while eliminating copayments and other charges.[70] The 2010 Patient Protection and Affordable Care Act included a broad array of reproductive health initiatives, among them state and community-based grants for adolescent pregnancy prevention.[71] Fortunately, proposals directed at teens provide contraceptive guidance and are not limited to abstinence-only philosophies.

It is absolutely essential that programs for teen pregnancy prevention be comprehensive. Abstinence-only measures have produced no demonstrably beneficial effect on the sexual behavior of young people.[72] Research shows that 95 percent of Americans have had sex before marriage, a practice that "has been the norm for *at least four or five decades.*"[73] Ignoring the near inevitability of adolescent sexual encounters leaves teenagers entirely unprepared for their first sexual experiences. The good news is that frequency of sexual activity among male and female teenagers aged 15 to 19 steadily decreased from 1988 to 2010. In fact, the teen birthrate declined by 37 percent between 1991 and 2009. These numbers represent a historic low for the United States, although the rate is still higher than in a number of other developed countries, such as Canada and Germany.[74] The drop in teenage births is largely due to increased use of contraceptive methods that are more effective, like the pill and the patch.[75] Doctors now appear more comfortable prescribing hormonal birth control methods to teenagers than in the past.[76]

If only these teens would sit down and have a talk with their older brothers and sisters. Just as important as teen pregnancy prevention are programs and services aimed at young adults in their 20s. Unplanned pregnancies abound within this age-group, principally due to misinformation and improper or inconsistent use of contraception. Since these young adults are no longer in the educational system, efforts to reach them pose particular challenges. Intensive information campaigns with expansive and popular appeal may go a long way toward reducing abortions and unplanned births, especially among young cohabiting couples.[77]

The removal of cost as a barrier to effective family planning will undoubtedly benefit all individuals of reproductive age. But it cannot ensure the intelligent, diligent, and consistent use of contraception. Even more obstructive than cost is the "hassle factor,"[78] the lack of sufficient motivation and organization to schedule a medical appointment, travel to a clinic, obtain a prescription, and use it appropriately and effectively. Working adults, even those adversely affected by a worsening economy, are not immune to misplaced priorities. As a result of the recession, birth rates have been declining since 2007.[79] Although a majority of women agree that it would be unwise to have a baby they cannot afford, many of them report lapses or discontinued use of contraceptives as a cost-saving measure.[80] Oral contraceptives range in cost from $3.20 per month for the least expensive to $14.70 per month for the most costly.[81] One need not be an economist to balance this expense against that for an abortion or for carrying a pregnancy to term and raising a child to adulthood.

Contraceptive failures and unplanned births occur to women of various ages, but they are especially prevalent in younger, cohabiting couples, especially those "in low-quality or unstable unions."[82] These individuals do not always profit by experience. Research by Huang and Tanfer on multiple unplanned pregnancies shows that "those who are unable to avoid having a first birth are equally unable to avoid having a subsequent one."[83] According to official statistics, 16.4 million children lived in poverty in 2010, the most since 1962.[84] Child poverty rates in 2010 stood at 22 percent, the highest percentage since 1993.[85] Many of these children owe their existence to forgetfulness, lack of foresight, or misinformation. No-cost contraception and an onslaught of media-based educational strategies may help young people to avert early, unplanned childbearing. But they have to want to do so, and the incentive is strangely lacking for many.

The Marriage Question, Again

Unintended and mistimed births do not occur nearly as often among married couples as they do among cohabitants.[86] Marital notions of a shared future and mutual goals provide a more or less predictable and harmonious context for decision making about childbearing. Cohabitants, in contrast, do not necessarily gravitate toward each other because they crave permanency or joint planning or because they view their partners as potentially good parents. If they are not cohabiting with a view toward marriage, they tend to be vague about whether and when they desire children. Discussions about childbearing are not a priority among cohabitants, and when the subject does arise, couples are not always in agreement. Most do not intend to become pregnant, but many do. Even those most averse to having children are not exempt from contraceptive lapses.[87] Moreover, an "unintended pregnancy resulting in a live birth does not necessarily indicate consonance in the desires of partners, nor does it indicate a resolution of conflicting birth intentions."[88] Such discord and uncertainty do not bode well for the future of these mothers and children, whatever their economic status. Many working-class women who dissolve their cohabiting unions after childbirth will likely end up courting poverty.[89]

A large majority of poor unmarried parents are romantically involved at the time of their child's birth.[90] Long-term survival of these relationships, however, "seems particularly uncommon."[91] Once the romantic relationship between parents terminates, a father's involvement with his child drops precipitously.[92] During this century's first decade, marriage promotion initiatives zeroed in on new unmarried parents, hoping to nudge them toward unions that are more permanent and stable. Despite the warmest of intentions and a five-year budget of $1.5 billion, these programs demand too much too late of their intended participants.[93] Generally, if cohabitants have not married prior to the birth of their child, few are inclined to do so afterward.[94] Fewer than 30 percent of white and Hispanic cohabiting and/or romantically involved couples marry within 30 months of their child's birth, and only 10 percent of African American couples do.[95] Among those parents who remained unmarried 30 months after a child's birth, a diminishing proportion maintained their cohabiting relationship or romantic involvement.[96]

For marriage promotion advocates, the moment a cohabiting couple has a baby is "the magic moment for policy intervention—a time when couples redefine their relationships."[97] Unfortunately, the arrival of newborn children, especially if they are unintended and not biologically related to both parents, can subvert relationship stability. As a potential source of financial worry and emotional conflict in fragile unions, childbirth undermines, rather than strengthens, these dyads.

The assumption that new unmarried parents will eagerly embrace matrimony ignores the extent to which marriage has faded as a pretext for childbearing. In their study of young, working-class cohabiting couples, Sassler and her colleagues noted a "common refrain" among both men and women that "a child is not an adequate reason for marriage."[98] Of those couples who said they would have the child should they become pregnant, only a third expressed definite intentions to marry before the birth.[99] Couples who fail to see marriage as advantageous to their own relationships are unlikely to be swayed by the presence of children. Courtship rituals have changed so radically that the "once normative sequences of adulthood have been upended."[100] If parenthood precedes marriage for many young adults, the impetus to marry must reside elsewhere. Finishing school, establishing a career, accumulating some savings, and, perhaps, buying a house are today's principal prerequisites for marriage but not for having children.[101] At the same time, less economically advantaged cohabiting couples may find their schooling prolonged by their having to work and attend school part-time or interrupted by childbearing.

In their study of young working and middle-class cohabiting couples attending an urban university, Sassler and Cunningham remarked on the "increasingly protracted nature of postsecondary education."[102] Nationally, although college enrollment rates have been steadily climbing, graduation rates have not kept pace. Students in both two- and four-year colleges often fail to complete their degrees on time and sometimes do not complete them within eight years.[103] Of older students, black and Hispanic students, and those requiring financial aid, fewer than one in five earn a degree within six years. Four in 10 students at public colleges attend part-time, and no more than a quarter of them will ever graduate. "Time is the enemy of completion," said a report by Complete College America.[104] The longer schooling takes, "the more life gets in the way of success."[105] For many couples, delaying marriage until the completion of school may put it off indefinitely. Meanwhile, children are likely to arrive well in advance of the time when many young adults can attain their educational and career objectives.

Cohabitation has its risks and limitations, but it is only one facet, albeit a conspicuous one, of contemporary intimate associations. Young adults are marrying later but engaging in sexual contacts earlier, exposing a highly varied landscape of romantic relationships.[106] They may engage in sex without emotional intimacy (hookups), have friends with whom they engage in sex with no expectation of long-term romantic involvement (friends with benefits), or take part in the practice of spending several nights a week together without actually living together (stayovers). The stayover, in particular, demonstrates the extent to which ambivalence is integral to emerging adulthood.

Developmentally, these young people are exploring their identities and negotiating entry into roles that are more adult. The resolution of ambivalence "either creates movement toward increased commitment or encourages the dissolution of the relationship."[107] As a "transitional state between dating and cohabitation,"[108] the stayover offers convenience as well as physical and emotional closeness, while avoiding the need for shared finances and living quarters. In fact, college students who act as stayover partners evince a strong desire for control over their personal space and belongings and are actively hindering the progress of their relationships. They are extremely focused on their educational goals and highly averse to entering into commitments that might limit their personal freedom. At present, little is known about the risk of unintended pregnancy within these relationships. College students who act as stayover partners do appear to be quite goal-directed and quite vocal about their lack of readiness for arrangements that are more formal and constraining.[109] Their ambivalence about long-term emotional commitment may serve to delay marriage, but it may also save them from further, ill-advised entanglements. Stayover patterns "that precede full-time cohabitation may play a part in couples sliding into poorly planned unions"[110] and, possibly, into poorly planned parenthood.

Commitment is a fairly monolithic concept, but today's young adults are finding ways to mime certain aspects of it without wholly endorsing it. That marriage is now so often postponed is perhaps understandable—the road to adulthood seems to lengthen with each generation. If ambivalence is a normal state of mind for many 20-somethings, circumspection about full commitment is probably commendable. The problem with cohabiting without a view toward marriage, however, is that it concretizes ambivalence. Rather than fostering the means to resolve contradictory feelings, cohabitation invites them to make themselves at home. Childbearing within these unions, especially if it is unplanned or mistimed, can agitate mixed emotions to untenable levels, producing breakups as well as poverty and instability for children. In marriage, there is, at the very least, an expectation that children might result. In cohabitation, childbearing wishes and intentions are too often vague, unexplored, or left to the vagaries of chance.

Maybe the Problem Really Is the Economy

Fifty years ago, the idea of vigorously promoting marriage might have seemed puzzling. Marriage used to be self-promoting, sought after on its own terms as the most auspicious way to raise a family and to build and preserve personal wealth. That marriage has to be touted as something good for us reveals how tempted we are by options less wholesome yet more accessible and immediately gratifying. Cohabitation and other forms of nonmarital intimacy appeal to many, not because they are as good as marriage but because they are easier to enter and exit. Earlier in this chapter, we noted that limited or poor economic prospects militate against the drive for permanent relationships. If financial conditions suddenly improved, would marriage rates soar? The answer depends in part on the degree to which commitment shyness has rooted itself within our culture. By the 1990s, in a more favorable economic climate than the decades following, cohabitation was already a thriving social trend. Its prominence among Americans who are less wealthy certainly implicates financial considerations. But to be fearful of or averse to enduring relationships is an emotional response. Economic factors may provoke, sustain, or create a convenient rationale for commitment avoidance. It seems a matter of the heart as well as of the purse. Undeniably, money plays a major role in relationship stability, but if the spirit is unwilling, a person simply will not marry.

The economic downturn is expected to continue well into the second decade of the current century. In 2010, the poverty rate had risen to 15.1

percent, its third consecutive annual increase.[111] Unemployment, the prime mover of the latest crisis, has hit young, working-age Americans especially hard, particularly those without college degrees. With their median incomes sharply dropping, "[y]oung, less-educated adults, mainly men, can't support their children and form stable families because they are jobless."[112] Many of those aged 25 to 34 cannot maintain their own households and have been forced by the recession to move in with friends or family.[113] Marriage rates will not be rising anytime soon.

It appears, then, that James Q. Wilson was mistaken to insist that marriage, more than money and jobs, was the best way to fix dysfunctional poor families.[114] At least one study, part of the Minnesota Family Investment Program (MFIP), demonstrates the impact of income on intimate relationships. A group of welfare recipients received "treatment" in the form of child care and enhanced benefits and were permitted to keep more of their work earnings. As a result, "MFIP increased marriage rates among single parents and reduced instability among two-parent families, with these effects driven largely by the increase in families' incomes."[115] The study's focus was welfare, not marriage promotion, and though the outcomes were modest, they are notable. Welfare reform in the 1990s emphasized work over cash assistance. The strategy may have been theoretically sound, but increasing the supply of workers who are less educated and less skilled puts even greater pressure on a faltering job market. Young families with children now live in poverty at a rate of 37 percent.[116] Since growing up poor interferes with social and educational advancement, this is a trend that "handicaps the next generation of American workers."[117]

Paul Amato and his colleagues define a "pro-marriage policy" as "any initiative that improves the financial security and well-being of married couples."[118] In a similar vein, proponents of a more liberal, nontraditional social order assert that "a promising future is the best contraceptive."[119] Delaying childbearing in favor of financial independence seems like impeccable advice. Still, for those whose economic outlook is dreary and unlikely to improve, the message just "does not resonate."[120] In the current era, love and money are so entwined that relationship security displays a price tag. For lower-class wedded couples, an adequate income and the stability it brings are "important protectors of marriage."[121] As for wealthy couples ensconced in acquisitive, hedonic matrimony, money makes their world go round as well.

Cohabitants who are less affluent wait for that defining, monetary moment—the house, the savings, the career, the church wedding—to signal their preparedness for marriage. Yet at least some of them are no economically worse off than young, aspiring couples who previously might have married and taken up the struggle together. Income is meant to bolster relationship stability, not serve as the sine qua non of emotional commitment. Nowadays, if couples—even the able-bodied and employed—wish to steer clear of deep intimacy and permanence, they have only to claim that they cannot afford them. This overwhelming sense of insufficiency pervades the outlook of many young adults—a deficit of faith in the future and in one's own capacity to carve out a place in it.

In the midst of last century's divorce boom, Christopher Lasch derided what he called "the ideology of nonbinding commitments."[122] Such thinking "radiates pessimism," he said, "a growing distrust of the future and a reluctance to make provisions for it—to lay up goods and experience for the use of the next generation."[123] Among that "next generation" are the current purveyors of nonbinding commitment. Arguably, they have even greater cause for future dread and pessimism than their forebears. As for how they address the good of posterity, irresponsible childbearing promotes little in the way of intergenerational wealth and wisdom. In fact, the contraceptive practices of many of today's cohabitants reflect an insouciance bordering on fatalism. It *is* the economy, but it is something else too.

If, as Montaigne suggested, marriage and family are tightly woven into the cloth of civilization, our legacy looks alarmingly frayed. Current social science research warns us that "the rise of cohabiting households is the largest unrecognized threat to the quality and stability of children's family lives."[124] Fluid, multilayered family arrangements repeatedly test children's capacities to adjust to new rules, expectations, and alliances. All signs point to the declining preeminence of marriage, not just in America, but throughout the industrial world.[125] Stephanie Coontz maintained that marriage will never regain its former supremacy, because "the state's coercive power over personal life" has steadily eroded.[126] Shifting gender roles, the rise of women's economic independence, the fading stigma of illegitimacy, delayed marriage and nonmarriage, the expanded use of reproductive technology—all these factors combine to create a "recipe for a world where the social weight of marriage has been fundamentally and irreversibly reduced."[127] Yet even as we consign it to irrelevancy, if not extinction, marriage's halo seems to glow ever more golden. The drive to legitimate same-sex unions has made the act of marrying seem prized and fashionable again. Social scientists continue to extol the state of wedlock as the highest form of family life. Even those cohabitants who dare not risk it regard marriage as the lodestar to a happier, richer level of existence.

What the marriage promoters really want is for people to grow up, educate themselves, get jobs, settle down, take care of each other, and support their children. Once, the pathway to maturity and self-sufficiency was clearly marked—finish school, leave home, find work, and marry. Nowadays, "fewer young people accomplish the tasks that have traditionally signaled that transition" from adolescence to adulthood.[128] They prolong their schooling or fail to complete it, and many remain at home well into their 20s. With the highest unemployment rate now since World War II, jobs for emerging adults are terribly hard to come by. One in five young people risks living in poverty,[129] and long-term commitment is out of the question.

Still, a majority of Americans, 67 percent, remains optimistic about the future of marriage and family.[130] Americans are far more confident about our domestic unions than about the education system (50 percent), the economy over the long run (46 percent), or moral and ethical standards (40 percent).[131] Perhaps succeeding generations of Americans will find new and better ways to grow up, fall in love, form personal attachments, and care for their families. Perhaps this current generation of young adults is breaking ground for roadways to the next juncture of intimate relationships. Ultimately, family stability is not a matter of which relationship ideal we choose to uphold or promote. The more pertinent question is how to help all families maximize their strengths, address their vulnerabilities, and raise their children responsibly.

CHAPTER 7

The Uses of the Law for Contemporary Families

In a 2004 episode of the television series *ER*, Dr. Kerry Weaver's cohabiting partner, Sandy Lopez, is mortally injured in an accident.[1] At the hospital, Dr. Weaver's colleagues gently urge her to wait outside the operating room. Determined to remain at Sandy's side, Kerry answers, "She's my wife." Together for three years, the couple is raising a son, Henry, borne by Sandy through artificial insemination and now about six months old. Kerry has no other family, while Sandy's is numerous and close-knit, often providing child care for Henry during his parents' work hours. Although Sandy's relatives do not appear overtly hostile to Kerry, it is clear that they regard Sandy, not Kerry, as the child's mother. At the time of Sandy's death, Henry is at the home of his maternal uncle.

Numb with grief, Kerry goes to pick up Henry, fully anticipating that he, her only surviving family member, will go home with her. Barring entrance to his house, Sandy's brother flatly refuses to surrender the child. Henry is also his family's only direct and living link to Sandy. As he begins to shut the door in Kerry's face, his simple, bald assertion "We are blood" is all the justification he requires. Kerry protests frantically, clawing at the door that closes, seemingly inexorably, on her life's expectations.

That door is a metaphor for a number of things—prejudice, preconceptions based on social and cultural norms, judgments founded on truths believed to be universal. It is also a metaphor for the law that swings open or shut, usually only by inches, depending on the weight of reasoning on either side of it. Family law has evolved not in a gradual, orderly progression but more in the manner of what paleontologist Stephen Jay Gould referred to as "punctuated equilibrium," periods of stasis suddenly disrupted by episodes of rapid change.[2] In the mid-20th century, the divorce revolution triggered swift and sweeping legal innovations. In the current era, the dynamic duo of ART and same-sex unions provides the impetus for redefining and expanding the scope of family law.

Across the United States, nontraditional family disputes inspire a patchwork of judicial responses, from willingness to treat these families as legitimate entities with recognizable parental roles to an outright rejection of unions and parent-child relationships that fail to approach the norm. In the absence of marriage and biological ties, at least as we used to understand them, parent-child relationships are no longer self-evident. In nontraditional custody and visitation disputes, courts must sometimes trace the thread of parentage before they can even reach issues concerned with best interests. Further, judges are repeatedly called on to examine each particular family's habits and interactions and accord a value to each internal relationship. The need to sift through facts and weigh their relevance, to invent and articulate case-specific legal standards, makes each new bout of litigation a matter of first impression.

We will return to Kerry Weaver's dilemma shortly. For the moment, we note that her nonmarital relationship with Sandy and her nonbiological tie to Henry substantially imperil her parental claim. With the benefit of hindsight, we can see that there are steps the couple might have taken to safeguard Kerry's parental relationship in the event of Sandy's death. Had they made use of existing legal remedies, Sandy and Kerry would have made it less necessary for a court to later substitute its own judgment about their parental intentions. Judicial reluctance to treat all families as equal under the law is not simply a matter of bias, homophobia, or resistance to social change. Courts have an obligation to uphold certain standards unless and until they are proven unworkable, irrational, or discriminatory. Moreover, American legal traditions are justly famous for insulating the rights of individuals from undue state intrusion. The current constellation of family forms includes those that wish to be let alone, those that clamor for legitimacy, and others that, it seems, want it both ways. To be sure, some aspects of family law are more than ripe for change. At the same time, individuals who knowingly create families outside of legal confines bear some responsibility for protecting and furthering their own interests. This chapter describes what these families can do to make the law serve their interests, as well as how our legal system has sometimes incorporated these changes and at other times mightily resisted them.

In chapters 3 and 6, we described how spikes in cohabitation and nonmarital childbearing have worked to the detriment of family well-being. Cohabiting parents who could have married but chose not to have made a conscious decision to conduct their family lives outside of the law. They have and should have access to legal remedies for issues such as child support, paternity, and family violence. But the many legal protections and presumptions accorded to married couples are largely unavailable to them. The state cannot force unwed couples to marry, nor should it deem them married against their express wishes. Although traditional families no longer predominate in this century, their success at promoting family stability justifies pro-marriage policies and preferential legal treatment for these relationships. But deeply meaningful parent-child bonds are often forged outside of traditional unions. Although a biological or other legally recognized tie might be lacking, all the indicia of loving, responsible parenting are present. To exclude these relationships from the law's consideration creates an indefensible hardship for children. As in Kerry Weaver's case, it may even render children parentless. How to accommodate nontraditional parent-child bonds while sacrificing none of the rights and privileges earned by traditional families is one of the principal dilemmas of 21st-century family law.

In chapter 1, we noted how courts are loath to intervene in the day-to-day internal workings of families. As we explain shortly, this reticence is firmly rooted in American legal tradition, especially at the federal level. This conformist streak imbues the states as well: only a minority of them recognize common-law marriage, and a mere handful allow same-sex couples to wed. But while courts may reasonably decline to treat unwed couples as married, they owe deference to parent-child bonds formed within unconventional unions. This is particularly true when these relationships dissolve and the fate of the children rests on obsolete notions of what constitutes parenthood. For the good of children born by ART or for those whose parent figures are unrelated to them by operation of marriage or biology, it is imperative that we set criteria for normalizing these relationships. Furthermore, in view of the states' disparate legal treatment of families, we must weigh the merits of striving for uniformity in family law standards against respecting and preserving the regional beliefs and differences of the various states.

Kerry Weaver's Options

The setting for *ER* is Chicago. So, to evaluate Dr. Weaver's custody case, we apply the law of Illinois. Since the child was conceived via an anonymous sperm donor, we need not consider a natural father's rights in this matter. For this discussion, we rely solely on the facts presented in the episode previously described, rather than taking into consideration what transpired later in the series.

Kerry and Sandy may have loved each other as spouses, but they were not married. This makes a great deal of difference to Kerry and Henry's parent-child relationship. Marriage confers a presumption deeming both partners as legal parents of children born during that union. In 2011, more than seven years too late for Kerry and Sandy, their home state enacted the Illinois Religious Freedom Protection and Civil Union Act.[3] Had Kerry and Sandy entered into a civil union under that law, each would have the same presumptive rights to children born during their union as married persons have. That Kerry is biologically unrelated to Henry would in no way have precluded her parental status. In 2000, shortly before Kerry and Sandy began their relationship, Vermont enacted its civil union statute, the first of its kind in the United States to offer same-sex partners the same legal rights and responsibilities as married couples. Unfortunately, even if Kerry and Sandy had traveled to Vermont to obtain a civil union, their home state of Illinois would have been under no obligation to recognize it. It was not until 2011 that the Illinois legislature deemed that same-sex marriages or civil unions lawfully entered into in other jurisdictions would be recognized as civil unions in Illinois.[4]

Kerry and Sandy jointly planned for Henry's birth and loved and co-parented him throughout his young life. Under Illinois law, when the episode aired as well as today, Kerry is not entitled to call herself Henry's mother. The Illinois Parentage Act of 1984 defined a parent-child relationship as "a legal relationship existing between a child and his natural or adoptive parents incident to which the law confers or imposes rights, privileges, duties and obligations."[5] With no presumptive or statutory basis to support her parental claim, Kerry's rights to Henry are no greater than those of the child's maternal uncle who barred Kerry at the door. Notwithstanding his assertion of a blood tie, however, Henry's uncle also has no presumptive legal right to custody of Henry without a court order.

How might this case arrive in court—in 2004 as well as in the present day? With Sandy's death and no legal father existing, the state would almost certainly file a proceeding to declare Henry a dependent child, one who is without a parent, guardian, or legal custodian.[6] While the case is pending, the court would place Henry in temporary custody, most likely with his uncle. Assuming that Henry is residing with his uncle when the proceeding is filed and that child welfare investigators find the home adequate, the court would be unlikely to remove him and place him in foster care. Kerry would, no doubt, have petitioned for temporary custody, but the court would have weighed the fact that she now lives alone and has no family support system, as well as her long and demanding work hours. Both she and Sandy previously relied on Sandy's relatives, principally Henry's maternal grandmother, to provide backup care for the child. As a practical matter, the court would likely view Sandy's family as better equipped to provide for Henry's needs, at least on a temporary basis. In view of Kerry's prior relationship with the child, however, it is probable that she would be granted visitation.

Upon making a finding of dependency, the court would proceed to a hearing on permanent guardianship. In making that determination, the court's guiding principle must be Henry's best interests.[7] Although a temporary custody order is not meant to be dispositive of the entire case, it does disadvantage Kerry that Henry has been placed with his maternal uncle. Henry may have bonded with Kerry during the time she coparented him, but he is very young and able to bond with other parent figures, particularly those with whom he has already become familiar. Further, he cannot speak for himself and express his own preferences. In his current placement, Henry is surrounded by members of his biological extended family, many of whom have the flexibility to care for him day and night. Kerry, by contrast, has a rigorous work schedule and would have to hire child care providers. On the positive side, as a respected physician and well-educated individual, Kerry presents as an excellent role model for Henry, with the personal and material resources to help him succeed in life. To aid in its determination, the court might order social work assessments and psychological evaluations of Kerry, the uncle, and all extended family members involved in Henry's care (a possible liability for Kerry, as she has a rather difficult, uncompromising personality). Both Kerry and Henry's uncle might also be permitted to present their own expert witness testimony on the issue of best interests.

The "best interests of the child" standard is, by necessity, fairly pliable. In applying it to the matters before them, courts have to consider cultural, religious, and behavioral patterns unique to each family. To the best of their ability, judges have to accommodate family customs and idiosyncrasies while protecting and furthering the child's welfare. Despite their appearance of impartiality, however, judges are subject to their own personal biases and preferences. These biases often dictate how flexible and innovative courts will be in recognizing social realities when interpreting the law.

In support of her position, Kerry's most compelling argument would be that she functioned, for all intents and purposes, as Henry's parent from the moment of his birth. As we described in chapter 5, courts have sometimes used this common-law doctrine of de facto parenthood to accommodate the needs and wishes of nontraditional families when statutes would otherwise exclude them. But appellate courts in Illinois were unwilling to consider de facto parenthood when analyzing nonbiological parent-child relationships. In 1999, an Illinois appellate court decided whether a nonbiological lesbian coparent had standing to petition for visitation when the birth mother refused to allow her to see the child after their relationship had ended.[8] The lesbian coparent had been "dutifully involved in all the preparations prior to" the child's birth and "equally involved in the care of [the child] for the next year-and-a-half."[9] But the relevant statutes allowed a petition for visitation to be filed only by the child's legal or adoptive parent, stepparent, grandparent, great-grandparent, or sibling.[10] The lesbian coparent argued that her undisputed parent-child relationship should provide her with standing as a common-law de facto parent. The court denied her claim. Although "not unmindful of the fact that our evolving social structures have created non-traditional relationships," the court refused to substitute its own judgment for that of the legislature and expand on its stated requirements.[11] Under this reasoning, Kerry Weaver would not even have been able to file a visitation petition.[12]

Appellate courts in several other jurisdictions have admitted that "statutes often fail to contemplate all potential scenarios which may arise in the ever-changing and evolving notion of familial relations."[13] Rather than wait for the legislature to act on these blossoming realities, these courts hold that "[r]eason and common sense support recognizing the existence of *de facto* parents and according them the rights and responsibilities which attach to parents in this state."[14] The Illinois decision previously cited was not a ruling on the merits of de facto parenthood but, rather, one limiting the court's sights to the words of the statute and refusing to make room for nontraditional litigants seeking access to the court in family disputes. This aversion to common-law decision making bespeaks a certain rigidity when the choice is between conventional and unconventional family options. In most respects, Henry's uncle and Kerry appear as equally loving and capable potential guardians. The court must decide between a traditional family with a biological connection to Henry and a single woman who has no legal or biological ties to the child but who helped bring him into the world and coparented him until his biological mother's death.

Could Kerry and Sandy have anticipated this problem and dealt with it beforehand? There are two ways in which Kerry and Sandy could have safeguarded Kerry's parental relationship to Henry and avoided the acrimonious litigation that followed Sandy's death. Illinois law permits a parent, adoptive parent, adjudicated parent, or guardian of a minor child to designate, in writing or in a will, a guardian for that child should the parent or original guardian die or become incapacitated.[15] Known as standby guardianship, the procedure is especially applicable to Henry, who has no other living parent. Had Sandy executed a standby guardianship document shortly before or after Henry's birth, Kerry could have appeared in court and been appointed Henry's standby guardian. The guardianship would have been activated by Sandy's death, and Kerry could have assumed her duties immediately. Within 60 days, Kerry could have filed a petition to become Henry's permanent guardian and, barring a finding that it was no longer in Henry's best interests, would have been so appointed.[16]

A second way that Kerry and Sandy could have forestalled a court battle over their son would have been for Kerry to adopt Henry. Second-parent adoptions were first authorized in Illinois in 1995.[17] Under the Illinois Adoption Act, reputable persons of legal age and of either sex may adopt, and they need not be married.[18] The Illinois appellate court construed the language of the statute to permit a biological or adoptive parent to preserve his or her parental rights while consenting to an adoption by another person.[19] Kerry would most likely not have had time to complete a second-parent adoption prior to Sandy's death. Had the process been initiated and had it substantially progressed, however, it might have provided valuable evidence of Sandy's wishes for Henry and Kerry's clear intentions as to parenthood.

Had Kerry and Sandy's drama been played out in 2011 or later, the couple could have entered into an Illinois civil union, which would have legitimized the parent-child relationship between Kerry and Henry. Even so, however, Kerry and Sandy would have been advised by a competent lawyer to have Henry adopted by Kerry and to draw up wills and powers of attorney. Were they to relocate to or even travel through another state, they could not be certain that their state's presumptions regarding civil union parentage would be recognized in that jurisdiction.

Especially poignant about Kerry Weaver's case is her necessity to prove the existence of a bond that is so real and so obvious to her and that would have been to Henry as well had he been older. Couples as relatively young and healthy as Sandy and Kerry often either fail to see the urgency for legal precautions like adoption or standby guardianship or delay in initiating them. Given their clear intention to function as parents, the penalty for their procrastination or lack of foresight seems unduly harsh. Nontraditional parent-child relationships are here to stay, and their numbers are growing. The legislative and judicial systems bear some responsibility for the legal ambiguity that obstructs and destroys these relationships and for the bitter and protracted litigation that often arises from nontraditional family disputes. Social reality has arrived at the legal system's doorstep, and it is demanding entrance into the law and policy of families.

Legal Recognition for Nontraditional Parent-Child Relationships

In chapter 5, we explored the evolution of the functional norms of parenthood and their legal implications. Here we present some proposals for giving those norms a more secure place in the legal system. The emerging nontraditional family forms could achieve legal recognition in one of two principal ways. Reform could take the path of statutory change, with legislatures enacting provisions validating de facto or psychological parenthood. Legislatures have the capacity to conduct sustained fact-finding and to view the issues in a broad context, not simply as they concern one particular set of litigants. Comprehensive revision may be best in determining the direction of significant changes in social policy, particularly as legislative preeminence in lawmaking assures our legal system's "democratic pedigree."[20]

At the same time, however, courts continue to carry out their long-established common-law role, one that "relies on precedent while gradually updating it to take account of new conditions and to embody new insights."[21] The heritage of equity jurisprudence, by which family courts decided questions of law as well as factual issues, has imbued these judges with a great deal of discretion.[22] Moreover, most family law statutes are written in broad terms, such as prescribing the "best interests of the child" standard or listing—but not prioritizing—a large number of factors for the court to consider in allocating marital property or spousal support.

In an important sense, courts are the ultimate *functional* legal institutions—they must resolve the cases that come to them. Legislatures take up whatever matters they choose and have no institutional obligation to decide any particular issue. The U.S. Supreme Court enjoys a virtually complete discretionary review power, but all other federal and most state judges must consider and determine the outcome of every dispute that legitimately comes their way. Both trial and appellate courts are also expected to articulate intellectually justifiable reasons for their holdings. Legislatures, by contrast, often enact statutes with little or no legislative history, findings, or other sources reflecting legislative intent, leaving courts to discern all meaning from the bare words of the statute.[23]

Courts also have the flexibility to deal with unanticipated changes in social conditions in a way that promotes justice while preserving, to the greatest extent possible, the certainty, uniformity, and predictability essential to a working legal system. Especially in the arena of developments relating to the family, society is evolving faster than the legislatures can track and respond. Former New York State chief judge Judith S. Kaye noted that "the inability of legislatures to react immediately to the many changes in society," combined with the "unending array of novel fact patterns" that courts must sort out on a daily basis, had led her to the conclusion "that common-law courts interpreting statutes and filling the gaps have no choice but to 'make law' in circumstances where neither the statutory text nor the 'legislative will' provides a single clear answer."[24]

Although fictional, the previously discussed dilemma of Kerry Weaver presents the core issues of a nontraditional parent seeking recognition in a society in transition. Her "case" also illustrates the paradox that as statutory reform seeks to extend protections, it sometimes excludes those who might have qualified had the legislature left the development to the common law. Prior to the 1977 passage of the Illinois Marriage and Dissolution of Marriage Act, the state courts had carried out their common-law function of crafting equitable remedies. For example, Illinois courts had grafted grandparent visitation into the law with no statutory warrant.[25] But then the state legislature began its process of "general and comprehensive legislation," which the courts saw as shutting the door to further common-law expansion.[26] The resulting legislation was indeed far-reaching and represented what the court considered an all-inclusive law, granting standing to petition for visitation to parents, stepparents, grandparents, great-grandparents, and siblings.[27]

The statute's thoroughness is both its strength and its weakness. By defining and regulating eligibility for visitation, the statute extended access to those family members, such as stepparents, who had been previously excluded. But the statute also suggested a finis to the common-law expansion of visitation rights. Under its terms, Kerry Weaver would never qualify to petition for visitation with her son, as the statute made no provision for a functional or de facto parent.

Of course, we do not know if, unencumbered by the statutory revision, Illinois courts would have developed a common-law right of visitation for de facto parents. But nationally, a consensus is emerging on functional parenthood, based on the evolving jurisprudence in the states, the overwhelming weight of scholarly literature, and the American Law Institute's *Principles of the Law of Family Dissolution*.[28] While formulations differ, the three prevalent factors common to these sources are the (1) legal parent's consent, (2) the functional parent's intent, and (3) the formation of a parent-child bond.[29] When those three factors have been established, it is extremely difficult to argue sensibly that the legal parent's rights have been infringed, that the other parent is being dragooned into an unwanted relationship, or that a determination for a functional parent signifies an intrusion into the family, particularly when the facts show the vitality of the child's bond with that functional parent. In fact, demonstrating the existence of those three factors leads to the conclusion that both the child and the functional parent would be harmed by the failure of the courts to confirm their relationship.[30]

Acknowledging the power of common-law expansion to adjust the legal rules to social reality does not imply that statutory remedies should be minimized or shunted aside. To the contrary, sometimes—when courts are unwilling to extend relief to functional parents—legislative initiatives prove quite salutary. Every real-life couple in a relationship resembling that of Kerry Weaver and Sandy Lopez may today enter into a civil union in Illinois, thereby legitimizing the parental status of the nonbiological mother (at least in that state). The opportunity to formalize their family ties comes courtesy of a legislative enactment, one that establishes a reciprocal legal relationship analogous to marriage. The statute affords persons entering a civil union "the obligations, responsibilities, protections, and benefits afforded or recognized by the law of Illinois to spouses."[31]

Contracts for Couples

Disputes arising from heterosexual cohabiting relationships have elicited their own array of judicial and statutory responses.[32] But unlike the parent-child quandaries posed within same-sex unions and by ART, they seem less urgent and more limited in their legal and cultural impact. To be sure, the headline "palimony" case of the 1970s, *Marvin v. Marvin,* produced widespread publicity and vigorous social commentary.[33] The issue seemed new and refreshingly relevant: in this lawsuit for "palimony," a woman sought financial remuneration after the breakup of a nonmarital intimate relationship. That the defendant was a prominent Academy Award–winning movie star and that the subject matter was titillating and illicit fanned the journalistic flames.[34] In reality, the notion of legally enforceable contracts between unmarried persons was not all that novel.[35] Moreover, the holdings in *Marvin* and its progeny have not been explicitly incorporated into statutory frameworks governing domestic arrangements. Contemporary legalized "domestic partnerships," discussed shortly, vary significantly among the states and municipalities in terms of availability and the number and type of benefits offered.

Michelle Marvin, actor Lee Marvin's longtime paramour, claimed that she and Lee had lived together pursuant to an oral agreement to hold themselves out publicly as husband and wife and to share equally in all earnings and property accrued by their joint efforts. In return, Michelle would give up her career as an entertainer and render him services as housewife, homemaker, cook, and companion. When the six-year relationship ended, Michelle sued to enforce the contract, asserting that she had kept her part of the bargain and was thus entitled to half the property as well as to support payments. The trial court held the contract unenforceable, immoral, and against public policy, deeming it akin to prostitution in that it rested on payment for sexual services. The California Supreme Court reversed that finding, ruling that while sexual services may have formed part of the agreement, any economic portions of the contract were separate and enforceable. The court based its reasoning "on the principle that adults who voluntarily live together and engage in sexual relations are nonetheless as competent as any other persons to contract respecting their earnings and property rights."[36]

At the eventual trial of this case, the court found that Michelle had proven none of her claims.[37] Rather than a spousal-type contract, the parties began their cohabitation based on an agreement "to live together as unmarried persons so long as they both enjoyed their mutual companionship and affection."[38] No support or other obligation could be premised on such a transient arrangement.[39]

The California Supreme Court's acceptance of both express and implied agreements relied on established common-law contract principles. Agreements can be founded on the parties' spoken or written words and can also be interpreted in light of the parties' actual conduct.[40] In the *Marvin* court's view, to allow for enforcement of one type of contract but not the other would result in "a schizophrenic inconsistency."[41] In a similar vein, the New Jersey Supreme Court observed that unmarried partners "usually do not record their understanding in specific legalese."[42]

Palimony claims à la *Marvin* are not welcome in all jurisdictions, and states vary widely in their interpretations of contracts between unmarried cohabitants.[43] In 1980, New York's highest court noted that express contracts between unmarried persons living together, whether oral or in writing, had long been recognized in New York. Implied contracts, however, were deemed "conceptually so amorphous as to practically defy equitable enforcement."[44] As the court reasoned, two people living together often exchange personal services because they find it enjoyable, convenient, or rewarding. Without express contracts to guide them in nonmarital cohabitant disputes, judges are forced to use hindsight to discern the parties' intentions, by weighing their past conduct. Distinguishing between services rendered out of affection and those for which there was an expectation of payment invites a risk of "emotion-laden afterthought" as well as fraud.[45]

In *Marvin*, the California Supreme Court did not intend to denigrate the marital institution. In fact, the opinion contains a paean to the state of matrimony as "the most socially productive and individually fulfilling relationship that one can enjoy in the course of a lifetime."[46] Even when a court enforces an express nonmarital contract, it states its determination to uphold the institution of marriage and "distinguish its contractual consequences from less formal and less permanent living arrangements."[47] Marriage is far more than a contractual arrangement. Married persons render services to each other, often in self-sacrifice, out of mutual devotion and to strengthen and enhance their union. The balance is not always equal, as evidenced by Lydia McGuire and her skinflint husband, who denied her even the smallest of luxuries, a story we told in chapter 1. In cohabitation, with its greater allowance for contract, parties can define their interests and expectations with some specificity. In comparison, a marriage ruled by strict quid pro quo is probably in trouble.

Cohabitation agreements and contract forms are within easy reach on any home computer. Rather than rely on courts to sort matters out retrospectively, unmarried persons should protect their economic interests at the outset. But the concerns of cohabiting couples often go well beyond issues of money, property, and personal possessions. Those in nonmarital relationships also want to be able to visit each other in the hospital, participate in medical decision making, and have standing to sue for wrongful death and inheritance. These vital family understandings are not within the scope of private contracts and require state implementation.

Civil Unions and Domestic Partnerships

Civil unions provide all or nearly all of the specific rights and responsibilities provided to married persons under state law, but they do not provide any of the federal benefits of marriage.[48] As of 2013, New Jersey, Illinois, Rhode Island, Hawaii, and Delaware have passed civil union statutes.[49] Several states also recognize comprehensive domestic partnerships substantially similar in scope and effect to civil unions. For example, Oregon's domestic partnership statute expresses the state's "strong interest in promoting stable and lasting families, including the families of same-sex couples and their children."[50] The law provides that all rights, benefits, and responsibilities that state law accords individuals in marriage shall be granted "on equivalent terms, substantive and procedural," to persons in a domestic partnership.[51]

More typically, a domestic partnership is a city-, county-, state-, or employer-recognized status that affords a relatively small number of rights to same-sex couples and, less commonly, opposite-sex couples.[52] For example, Colorado provides a range of benefits to unmarried same-sex or opposite-sex couples who register as "designated beneficiaries."[53] A designated beneficiary agreement can bestow a number of rights and responsibilities, including hospital visitation, medical decision making, recognition as beneficiaries of certain state employee pensions, standing to sue for wrongful death, and inheritance.[54] In the private sector, the number of employers offering domestic partner benefits has increased substantially in recent years, as employers have come to recognize that "to remain competitive in attracting and retaining top talent," they need to accommodate workers whose family relationships are nontraditional.[55]

A domestic partnership is sometimes enacted as a symbolic gesture by a municipality, in the hope that provisions of substance will follow. Cleveland's domestic partner registry illustrates this pattern. When enacted in 2008, the city registry merely compiled a list of "non-marital committed relationships of two adults of the same or different sex who share a common residence and affirm that they share responsibility for each other's common welfare."[56] The registry had no legal effect, but supporters hoped that it "could prompt employers, hospitals and other organizations to grant privileges typically reserved for married couples."[57] In 2011, the city itself decided to extend health care benefits to the domestic partners of city employees who had signed up in the registry.[58] The chief sponsor of the measure indicated that "[t]he goal is to keep opening the door."[59] But the problem with all such state and municipal measures is that the door will only be as open as the federal government and the next state allow.[60]

The Cost of Federalism in Family Law

The oft-repeated principle of American federalism holds that "families are a matter for local rather than national control."[61] But this prime directive is generally honored only in the abstract. In the concrete world of families and their interactions with the legal system, federal "intrusion" into matters of local domestic relations has long been the norm. Many state policies, from child support guidelines to gender neutrality in alimony to interstate enforcement of child custody orders, bear the footprints of their genesis in federal mandates. As Professor Ann Estin phrased the point, family law in the states "is extensively shaped by national law, with both Congress and the Supreme Court deeply engaged in setting policies, defining norms, and harmonizing the competing laws of different states."[62]

States have retained important decision-making authority, particularly with regard to the status of marriage, the legality of marital alternatives, and the definition of parenthood. A half century ago, most Americans agreed on all three: marriage should be limited to heterosexual couples, marital alternatives were taboo, and parenthood meant a biological or adoptive tie. Today, these basic propositions are vigorously contested, and widely dissimilar state laws regulate families as they take shape, try to resolve disputes, or seek dissolution. The result is legal cacophony, a discordant battle among the states concerning which legal rules govern a family when it relocates or simply travels across state lines. Known legally as a conflict-of-laws or choice-of-law problem, the rapid changes in contemporary family composition have turned this dilemma from a minor legal squabble into one of enormous proportions.[63]

It is difficult to resolve the conflict-of-laws problem without infringing on one or another set of cardinal principles and strongly held values. The millions of citizens in the 30 states who have voted to enact constitutional provisions banning same-sex marriage have voiced their opinions in a definitive fashion.[64] The 7 other states whose legislatures have enacted statutes barring same-sex marriage have similarly acted in a democratic manner.[65] But honoring those states and the majority of their citizens comes at a steep cost in individual liberty and in the right of Americans to equal treatment under the law.[66]

Following the Obama administration's decision to no longer support it, a crucial component of the Federal Defense of Marriage Act (DOMA) failed to survive a 2013 equal protection challenge in the U.S. Supreme Court.[67] But while the federal government must now recognize same-sex marriage for the purpose of access to federal entitlements and tax benefits, DOMA continues to allow—and has served in encouraging—states to refuse to recognize each other's same-sex marriages. Moreover, until the issue is resolved by federal statute, same-sex couples duly married in one state may not be eligible to apply for federal benefits if they then move to a state that declines to recognize their union.

Same-sex marriages, civil unions, and domestic partnerships are subject to bewildering differences in treatment as they cross state lines. Some jurisdictions recognize all three institutions even when they originate out-of-state. Others extend recognition to none or only some of these marital and quasi-marital arrangements.[68] The same couple may be legally married in one state and unmarried a mile away in the next state. Registered domestic partners may enjoy a cornucopia of rights in one jurisdiction and none in the adjoining one. Children of a civil union may have two legal parents in one state and only one in another. In light of these vertiginous twists, our present system of family law may well be regarded as dysfunctional, supporting the contention of at least one scholar that "U.S. family law is in chaos."[69]

Absent Fathers

One of family law's main functions is to create minimally acceptable standards for parental behavior. Most often, however, judges enact this role by determining what parents cannot do rather than what they should be doing. Courts, for instance, cannot order a nonresident father to play a meaningful, caring, and supportive part in a child's upbringing. As adult relationships become more friable, fathers are slowly but surely removing themselves from the center of family life. Historically, absent fatherhood began with desertion, intensified with divorce, and became rampant with unmarried childbearing.

Unlike marriage, cohabitation carries no presumption of paternity. Unmarried childbearing often occurs within cohabitation, a nonlegal arrangement where father-child relationships are not always formalized. Unwed fathers can establish paternity either by court order or by signing certain documents acknowledging their parental rights and obligations. A declaration of paternity allows a biological father to, for example, petition a court for custody or visitation. On the flip side, he also incurs parental obligations such as child support. With the exception of child protective proceedings, unless unwed couples actively seek assistance from the courts, the legal system has limited effect on the behavior and functioning of nonmarital families. When a marriage dissolves, judges have a role in structuring parenting and support plans. Further, in order to mitigate the impact of divorce on children, judges can direct the parties to participate in court-supervised programs of parent education. When cohabiting couples with children separate, courts are largely oblivious to the event. Since no formal process for disuniting a cohabiting couple exists, formal recognition is unavailable. Thus, in unmarried families, the barriers to asserting and maintaining meaningful, long-term father-child relationships are not legal but social.

When adult relationships end, the vast majority of children continue to live with their mothers. Divorce, as well as the frailty and mutability of cohabiting unions, makes absent fatherhood a grim reality. In the 1980s, most nonresident fathers of children born inside or outside of marriage paid no or very little child support.[70] Frequency of visitation varied, but there was generally no evidence that father-child contact benefited child well-being.[71] Payment of child support, by contrast, was positively associated with better academic performance and higher math and reading scores.[72]

More recently, a younger cohort of fathers has somewhat increased its parental involvement, resulting in 35 to 40 percent of nonresident children having at least weekly contact.[73] But as noted by Amato and Gilbreth, not sharing a residence with children makes effective parenting difficult.[74] Absent fathers tend to focus on recreational activities during visitation, in an effort to ensure that time spent together is enjoyable. Rather than practicing "authoritative parenting"—setting limits, helping with homework, discussing problems—they are reluctant to impose discipline and function more as adult companions.[75] Regardless of its frequency, contact lacking in competent parenting contributes little to a child's development.

Even more than parental contact, the payment of support has great potential to promote child well-being.[76] Financial contributions by nonresident fathers help to provide "wholesome food, adequate shelter in safe neighborhoods, commodities (such as books, computers, and private lessons) that facilitate children's academic success and support for college attendance."[77] Among the factors preventing payment of adequate child support are the "intricate webs of parenting and family obligations"[78] formed when absent fathers remarry or enter new cohabiting relationships. Of all nonresident fathers, about half "have parenting responsibilities beyond a single set of nonresident children," and "nearly three-quarters of those who are remarried or cohabiting face potential obligations to other children."[79] This "crowding-out effect"[80] does not necessarily result in diminished contact. The presence of resident stepchildren negatively affects child support payment but not visitation with nonresident children.[81] However, fathers who have biological children with their current partners are significantly less likely to visit or support their previous set(s) of nonresident children.[82]

At a total of $84 billion, the amount of child support arrearages owed in the United States exceeds the gross national product of Ireland.[83] The most commonly used enforcement mechanisms—drivers' license suspensions, booting (attaching a steel 50-pound clamp to an automobile tire), and incarceration—have proved moderately effective.[84] For men with the lowest incomes, however, formal enforcement methods have been counterproductive, alienating fathers and reducing their involvement in their children's lives.[85] Programs that encourage young parents to stay together and preserve the family unit, as well as those that promote the voluntary acknowledgment of paternity and responsible fatherhood, may benefit poor young families more than have coercive enforcement measures.[86]

Complex parenting relationships are rarely taken into account by programs that promote marriage among the disadvantaged.[87] Cooksey and Craig observed that cohabiting fathers are less likely to visit their children than married ones, suggesting that "men who are most linked to traditional family life . . . are most likely to maintain contact with their previous offspring."[88]

Children born out of wedlock have less contact with nonresident fathers than those born within marriage.[89] Further, low levels of income and education among fathers generally result in decreased parental involvement.[90]

The diminished role of fathers in their children's lives is one of the unintended consequences of nontraditional family formation. In an era when marriage rates are falling and unstable cohabiting unions are on the rise, actively engaging in fatherhood seems less and less a male priority.[91] The law can only go so far in formalizing father-child relationships and in enforcing orders of support. In light of the complexity of current family arrangements, child support systems can hardly avoid "pitting the interests of one group of children [against] another."[92] Social policies can simplify family relationships by fostering and rewarding planned, responsible childbearing. Educating potential parents about the vital importance of each of their respective roles is also essential. For too many families, the place of fatherhood is quickly sliding toward irrelevance.

What to Keep

"Legal marriage," wrote Nancy Cott, "remains a privileged public status, buttressed by government policies that allow and inspire people to have confidence in it."[93] In 2004, the General Accounting Office identified 1,138 federal statutory provisions "in which marital status is a factor in determining or receiving benefits, rights, and privileges."[94] In New York, same-sex couples who marry will have access to "hundreds of different protections and benefits" under state law.[95] Although marriage itself is not founded on contract, it does have a give-and-take relationship with society. In exchange for its privileged status, marriage provides the optimum context for fostering family health and stability. The marriage-like benefits available through civil unions and, to a lesser extent, domestic partnerships are not equal to the "public acknowledgment and respect for personal bonds" accorded wedded couples.[96] In deciding which protections to reserve for marriage only and which should be shared with couples in unions that are less formal, the state exerts great power over family security and legitimacy. Behind these choices is a thinly veiled intention to reward commitment and to be less magnanimous to those who fall short of it.

Cohabitation, declared Waite and Gallagher, is not "the functional equivalent of marriage," and "[g]iving the benefits of marriage to people who have refused its responsibilities is neither fair nor wise."[97] Marriage is self-legitimating and self-explanatory, equipped with "all the presumptions that a cohabiting couple has to prove, in court or out."[98] But while the state might not wish to indulge the whims of couples who can but will not marry, it has a general interest in promoting stability in all families, no matter what their composition. Framing the issue as one of family well-being rather than morality helps to clarify the options somewhat. More heat than light has been generated by debate on what family forms are sanctioned by the Bible or natural law or were contemplated by our nation's Founding Fathers.[99] We propose to ask instead whether, for instance, a cohabiting couple with children would be better off if one partner's health insurance could cover the other partner and the children? If the answer is yes, then making this legally possible seems a worthy civic goal, one consistent with the aims of family promotion. Caring for nontraditional families does not disrespect those who have chosen marriage but, to the contrary, strengthens communities in which all types of families live, work, go to school, and play.

State efforts to uphold the primacy of marriage are defensible in most ways but blindly irrational in others. Prohibitions against same-sex marriage are plainly inconsistent with support for permanent, well-functioning domestic relationships. Gay couples are raising children in at least 96 percent of all U.S. counties.[100] More than a quarter century of research has concluded that "there is no relationship between parents' sexual orientation and any measure of a child's emotional, psychosocial and behavioral adjustment."[101] All children, regardless of their parents' sexual preferences, profit by the rights and privileges that flow from legally recognized commitment.

The greatest strength and weakness of our governmental system of federalism is its sensitivity to regional differences and beliefs. States control modern-day intimate attachments by taking positions for or against same-sex marriage and adoptions, by their willingness to codify principles of de facto parenting, by their acceptance or rejection of parent-child bonds created by ART, and by the degree to which they hew to the biological model of parenthood. Although local customs and preferences are relevant to good state governance, they are no substitute for rationality in lawmaking. As Judge Brooke Murdock of the Circuit Court for Baltimore City in Maryland explained, "When tradition is the guise under which prejudice or animosity hides, it is not a legitimate state interest."[102]

Tradition, like permanence and continuity, is good for families, except when it is arbitrary to the point of injury. Nontraditional families suffer social, economic, and legal insecurity when formal recognition of their bonds is withheld.[103] Amid the tumult of evolving domestic arrangements, it is hard to be certain which forms are destined to flourish and which ones are transitory and maladaptive. Some forms will be awarded rights and privileges, while others will either opt out of consideration or be discredited. Perhaps only in retrospect will we understand the implications of our choices and the logic that compelled them. Not all innovation is worth preserving. What to keep is our devotion to the ideal of family as refuge, a shelter from outside hazards where each of its members is intrinsically valued.

Conclusion

Echoes in a Canyon

The fallacy of predicting the future based solely on current events is well illustrated by Andrew Cherlin. In the cash-strapped, low-birthrate era of the 1930s, no one could have anticipated the baby boom.[1] In 1955, Paul H. Landis affirmed what he saw as a time-honored truth, that marriage is "the *natural state* for adults."[2] By 2011, barely half of all American adults were married, a record low down from 72 percent in 1960.[3] Now "less dominant and more distinctive,"[4] marriage has changed from a badge of conformity to one of prestige, high in symbolic value yet waning in practical significance. In one view, marriage has become a kind of cultural phantom limb—because the institution was so socially preeminent 50 years ago, people continue to marry, as yet unaware that to do so "is no longer important."[5] As the 21st century advances, the aura of marriage is fading, "diminishing, like an echo in a canyon."[6]

According to recent research by Kelly Musick and Larry Bumpass, marriage and cohabitation were found to be statistically indistinguishable on measures of psychological well-being, health, and social ties.[7] The authors acknowledge their study's modest sample size, the short duration of the period measured (six years), and the fact that the underlying data is more than 10 years old.[8] Furthermore, relative to staying single, moving into any union tends to increase happiness,[9] and these gains diminish over time for both marriage and cohabitation.[10] In light of the study's findings, however, it may well be that today's young adults are guided by increasingly flexible norms and expectations, leading them to feel more comfortable in privately ordered domestic arrangements. Perhaps these preferences will ultimately spill over into marriage, making it a suppler, more democratic institution.

But it is far too soon to agree with Musick and Bumpass's conclusion that the relative merits of marriage may have been overstated.[11] Subjective well-being is important, but it is only one potential marker of relationship stability. The commonly noted prerogatives of marriage—legal recognition, social roles, and supports and commitment—operate on a continuum rather than as discrete variables.[12] These benefits may be less observable and more difficult to quantify in short-range studies.

It is entirely possible that, in time, cohabitation will mature, developing its own rules and vocabulary, even its own myths. In an increasingly atomistic culture, intimate associations based on private, quasi-contractual agreements seem more fitting and relevant than public pledges of long-term, possibly lifetime commitment. Societal recognition of marital vows is highly significant to many same-sex partners but less so to great numbers of heterosexual couples. With the growth of laws sanctioning domestic partnerships, cohabitation may yet become "institutionalized." But there is still the issue of durability, of how and why a relationship was formed and what ultimate purpose it will serve. Couples who slide into live-in relationships bypass the crucial step of discussing the advantages and implications of living together. If and when they do marry, they discover that bonds born of ambiguity or convenience "can interfere with the process of claiming the people [they] love."[13] Whatever level of legitimacy cohabitation achieves, it is only when marriage and cohabitation come to mirror each other in trust and commitment that we will see them "on an equal footing."[14] Until then, cohabitation remains an alternative to singlehood, not marriage.

On the whole, it seems reasonable to expect that family diversity will continue to thrive well into the coming decades. Same-sex couples are firmly entrenched in the cultural mainstream, despite persistent state efforts to prohibit them from marrying or entering into civil unions and domestic partnerships. Across the United States, "legal conveyor belts"[15] are carrying cases challenging restrictions on same-sex marriage toward the Supreme Court. In 2013, a key portion of DOMA was invalidated on equal protection grounds.[16] It remains to be seen whether a future U.S. Supreme Court decision on the magnitude of *Loving v. Virginia* will sweep away all gender-based restrictions on marriage just as it invalidated antimiscegenation laws.[17] The next few years will determine the fate of both federal and state efforts to oppose this more liberalized view of marriage.

As long as there are same-sex and infertile couples who desire children, ART will retain a vital role in family formation. Unless it is found to be medically or scientifically unsound and unless all would-be parents suddenly revert to starting families in their peak childbearing years, ART will become an integral part of the law of parentage and parenthood. The expanding use of these technologies and the proliferation of families based on nonbiological or quasi-biological ties may be far more momentous events than we realize. In less than a century, we have mounted a challenge to beliefs and practices that have lasted many thousands of years.

In her carefully researched yet beautifully imagined *Earth's Children* series, Jean M. Auel depicted the day-to-day existence of Ice Age prehistoric man. She posited that a pivotal stage in our development occurred when we discovered that human agency, not supernatural forces, supplied the means by which our species propagates.[18] From this revelation flowed notions of relatedness and responsibility, the implications of kinship and ancestral origins—the connections underlying the formation of social, cultural, and even political identity. As the human line progresses, these ancient and long-validated bonds may be loosening, slated for extinction in a future world where biology is readily manipulated and where the concept of family is reinvented and transformed. In some ways, the revolution has already begun.

For now, however, there are children to raise. What remains impossible to forecast is whether stability and commitment will ever return to American family life. Given our recent history of turbulent domestic relationships, the practice of "cohabitation as prophylaxis"[19] seems understandable, if not always effective. Children of divorce and broken families are prone to worry about their capacity to be steadfast and trusting in their own personal relationships. The "dialectic between belonging and dread of separation in childhood"[20] plays out in adult romantic attachments. The resulting cycle of failed marriages and fragile unions, remarriage and serial cohabitation, replicates itself in the behavior of children of these alliances. Too often, they grow to adulthood without ever having witnessed a secure, continuous bond between their parents. As a nation, "the U.S. is accumulating a deep psychological national deficit for many of our children and their children."[21]

One generation's devotion to forging safe havens for children may be all it takes—to restore family stability and a sense of security and permanence, to halt the succession of frail and emotionally compromised relationships.[22] As a wise and near-immortal duo once wrote, all you really need is love—and the courage to commit.

NOTES

Chapter 1: American Marriages Yesterday

1. PAUL H. LANDIS, MAKING THE MOST OF MARRIAGE 13 (1955); *see also* ROBIN M. WILLIAMS JR., AMERICAN SOCIETY: A SOCIOLOGICAL INTERPRETATION 76–77 (1951) (contrasting the modern family, "an almost purely consuming and affectional unit," with the "old-style 'trustee family'—practically a self-contained social system"). In 1960, the U.S. Department of Health, Education, and Welfare acknowledged changing family roles in noting that the family had shifted from a "patriarchal" to a "companionship" unit. U.S. DEP'T OF HEALTH, EDUC., & WELFARE, ILLEGITIMACY AND ITS IMPACT ON THE AID TO DEPENDENT CHILDREN PROGRAM 5, 18 (1960) (noting that families were no longer the nerve center of such life activities as "work, education, religion, recreation, and security," that parents were becoming less authoritative and that wives and children were being given more decision-making power, and that household chores were being shared in a more democratic way).

2. "Family in transition" is a much-abused trope in sociological literature. *See, e.g.,* ERNEST W. BURGESS & HARVEY J. LOCKE, *The American Family in Transition, in* THE FAMILY: FROM INSTITUTION TO COMPANIONSHIP (1945); RAY E. BABER, *The Family in Transition, in* MARRIAGE AND THE FAMILY (2d ed. 1953); Ruth Nanda Anshen, *The Family in Transition, in* THE FAMILY: ITS FUNCTION AND DESTINY 3–19 (Ruth Nanda Anshen ed., rev. ed. 1959). When Arlene Skolnick and Jerome Skolnick began editing their popular series of sociological readings for college students in the 1970s, they chose the title *Family in Transition*. The series has now reached 16 editions. *See* FAMILY IN TRANSITION (Arlene S. Skolnick & Jerome H. Skolnick eds., 16th ed. 2010).

3. ELAINE TYLER MAY, HOMEWARD BOUND: AMERICAN FAMILIES IN THE COLD WAR ERA 11 (1988). *See also* STEPHANIE COONTZ, THE WAY WE NEVER WERE: AMERICAN FAMILIES AND THE NOSTALGIA TRAP 25 (1992) (describing the 1950s family as "a qualitatively new phenomenon"; *id.* at 25); CHRISTOPHER LASCH,

WOMEN AND THE COMMON LIFE: LOVE, MARRIAGE, AND FEMINISM 104–5 (1997) ("The traditional family, so called, where the husband goes out to work and the wife stays home with the children, was not traditional at all. It was a mid-twentieth-century innovation, the product of a growing impatience with external obligations and constraints, of the equation of freedom with choice, and of tumultuous world events that made the dream of a private refuge in the suburbs more and more appealing.")

4. Christopher Lasch noted that the prototypical 1950s suburban culture was "founded on the separation of the home not merely from the workplace but from outside influences of any kind." LASCH, *supra* note 3, at 105.

5. LANDIS, *supra* note 1, at 21.

6. *Id.* Landis's text equated marriage with the drive to establish family life. Several headings in the book's chapter titled "Needs Fulfilled by Marriage" reflect the era's rock-solid perception that true love and family life always commenced at the altar: "Marriage Meets the Need for Love and Emotional Security"; "Marriage Meets the Need for Status and Appreciation for Personal Worth"; "Marriage Answers the Need for Companionship"; and "Marriage Meets the Physiosexual Need for Response." *Id.* at 15–26. The final heading in this chapter is the admission "Marriage Is Not a Perfect Institution." *Id.* at 32. While insisting that "marriage is designed to meet more human needs than is any other institution," Landis acknowledged that the high expectations that often accompany marriage can be frustrated by human frailty, rendering marriage "more capable of producing misery, human suffering, and personal torture than any other relationship." *Id.; see also* J. HERBIE DIFONZO, BENEATH THE FAULT LINE: THE POPULAR AND LEGAL CULTURE OF DIVORCE IN TWENTIETH-CENTURY AMERICA 14 (1997) (noting that "the greater emotional content of family relations elevated the stakes in marriage, making domestic life delightful when it succeeded and devastating when it failed").

7. ROBERT F. WINCH, THE MODERN FAMILY 323 tbl.10.2 (rev. ed. 1963).

8. *See generally* MAY, *supra* note 3; JESSICA WEISS, TO HAVE AND TO HOLD: MARRIAGE, THE BABY BOOM, AND SOCIAL CHANGE (2000). *See also* Paul H. Landis, *Divorce in Our Time*, 105 FORUM 865 (1946) (observing that the "companionship family," which "prizes romance and its ethereal happiness," was replacing the "institutional family rooted in the traditions of child-bearing, joint economic activity and filial duty").

9. *See* ERIC BURNS, INVASION OF THE MIND SNATCHERS: TELEVISION'S CONQUEST OF AMERICA IN THE FIFTIES 106 (2010). ("Most of these shows featured mother, father, a kid or two or more, and at least one complication per thirty minutes. They were set in the living rooms and kitchens of middle-class suburban homes, and all of them ended happily, if not ever after, at least until next week, when a complication very similar to that of the previous week would bedevil the cast yet again.")

10. *See* WEISS, *supra* note 8, at 1 ("Regardless of the speaker and whatever the target—the divorce rate, deadbeat dads, teen pregnancy, or working mothers—American family life in the 1950s is the standard that critics use to judge family life today."); STEPHANIE COONTZ, MARRIAGE, A HISTORY: FROM OBEDIENCE TO INTIMACY, OR HOW LOVE CONQUERED MARRIAGE 229 (2005) (suggesting that the 1950s constituted "a unique moment in the history of marriage"); BURNS, *supra* note 9, at 32–51

(describing the role television played in creating the "New American Family"); Ellen Goodman, *So Dies the "Father Knows Best" Charade*, BOSTON GLOBE, July 28, 1998, reprinted as Father Who Knew Best, *in* PAPER TRAIL: COMMON SENSE IN UNCOMMON TIMES 71 (2004). ("To the Baby Boomers, all history begins with television. The Andersons, like the Nelsons and Cleavers, form the collective myth of our origins. Their middle-class subdivisions are our Eden, their nuclear families the cultural baseline against which we judge all other families, especially our own.")

11. *See generally* Talcott Parsons, *The American Family: Its Relations to Personality and to the Social Structure*, *in* FAMILY, SOCIALIZATION, AND INTERACTION PROCESS 3–33 (Talcott Parsons & Robert F. Bales eds., 1955).

12. William E. Nelson, *Patriarchy or Equality: Family Values or Individuality*, 70 ST. JOHN'S L. REV. 435, 481 (1996) (noting that "judges in the 1940's perceived an increase in 'marriage[s] torn asunder by a disordered society under the stress and strain of war'" (quoting Clair v. Clair, 64 N.Y.S.2d 889, 890 (Sup. Ct. Albany County 1946))).

13. STEPHANIE COONTZ, THE WAY WE REALLY ARE: COMING TO TERMS WITH AMERICA'S CHANGING FAMILIES 35 (1997). For a poignant and Oscar-winning cinematographic depiction of the difficulties veterans had in elbowing back, see THE BEST YEARS OF OUR LIVES (Samuel Goldwyn Productions 1946).

14. *See* JAMES GILBERT, ANOTHER CHANCE: POSTWAR AMERICA, 1945–1985, at 57 (2d ed. 1986). Within two years after war's end, two million women had lost their jobs. DAVID HALBERSTAM, THE FIFTIES 589 (1993).

15. COONTZ, *supra* note 13, at 35.

16. ARLENE SKOLNICK, EMBATTLED PARADISE 54 (1991). *See* Nelson, *supra* note 12, at 437 ("[T]he two decades after World War II were . . . decades of extraordinary optimism, when it seemed that all Americans who made the necessary effort could achieve their goals and obtain happiness.").

17. COONTZ, *supra* note 13, at 35.

18. MAY, *supra* note 3, at 14. *See* HALBERSTAM, *supra* note 14, at 591 ("A family was a single perfect universe—instead of a complicated, fragile mechanism of conflicting political and emotional pulls.").

19. MAY, *supra* note 3, at 24.

20. NANCY F. COTT, PUBLIC VOWS: A HISTORY OF MARRIAGE AND THE NATION 197 (2000).

21. MAY, *supra* note 3, at 16.

22. *Id.* at 20. To a majority of Americans, an unmarried life was unthinkable. Fifty-three percent of respondents to a 1957 survey expressed the belief that anyone preferring bachelorhood to marriage was "sick or immoral, too selfish or too neurotic to marry." JOSEPH VEROFF ET AL., THE INNER AMERICAN: A SELF-PORTRAIT FROM 1957 TO 1976, at 147 (1981). By 1976, the percentage expressing a negative attitude toward a nonmarrying person had shrunk to 34 percent. *Id.*

23. MAY, *supra* note 3, at 21 tbl.6. Census Bureau tabulations for 1950, 1960, and 1970 report the adult married population rising from 66 percent to 68 percent and then falling to 63 percent. Conversely, the percentage of single adults decreased from 23 per-

cent to 21 percent before rising to 25 percent. In all three census tallies, the percentage of divorced and widowed adults held steady at 8 and 3 percent, respectively. U.S. CENSUS BUREAU, HISTORICAL STATISTICS OF THE UNITED STATES, COLONIAL TIMES TO 1970, Series A, 160–71, *Marital Status of the Population, by Age and Sex: 1890 to 1970* (1970), *available at* http://www2.census.gov/prod2/statcomp/documents/CT1970 p1-02.pdf.

24. Paul C. Glick, *American Families: As They Are and Were*, *in* FAMILY IN TRANSITION 93 (Arlene S. Skolnick & Jerome H. Skolnick eds., 8th ed. 1994).

25. *Id.* at 94.

26. COONTZ, *supra* note 13, at 36. Spacing children so closely together resulted in an early ending of the couple's child-rearing years. WEISS, *supra* note 8, at 4.

27. WINCH, *supra* note 7, at 662; *see also* WILLIAMS, *supra* note 1, at 47 (accurately predicting in 1951 that the "extraordinary emphasis in modern, urban, middle-class America upon the marriage pair is bound to result . . . in a greatly simplified kinship structure of isolated families").

28. MAY, *supra* note 3, at 25. *See* MICHAEL J. ROSENFELD, THE AGE OF INDEPENDENCE: INTERRACIAL UNIONS, SAME-SEX UNIONS, AND THE CHANGING AMERICAN FAMILY 95 (2007) ("The suburban dream of the 1950s was created as a retreat from everything the city had come to stand for: racial diversity, the presence of artists, bohemians, homosexuals, voyeurs, immigrants, the red-light districts, disorder, political corruption, crime, and a general lack of social control.").

29. WILLIAMS, *supra* note 1, at 48. *See* JOANNA L. GROSSMAN & LAWRENCE M. FRIEDMAN, INSIDE THE CASTLE: LAW AND THE FAMILY IN 20TH CENTURY AMERICA 7 (2011) (observing that the development and expansion of suburbs "helped accelerate the flight away from the so-called extended family"). Few critics at the time questioned the merit of the newly isolated nuclear family. *Cf., e.g.*, ROBERT A. NISBET, THE QUEST FOR COMMUNITY 62 (1953) (contending that the family in isolation had "a structure that has become fragile and an institutional importance that is almost totally unrelated to the economic and political realities of our society").

30. Talcott Parsons, *The Normal American Family*, *in* MAN AND CIVILIZATION 31–50 (S. Farber, P. Mustacchi, & R. H. L. Wilson eds., 1965).

31. *See* John Scanzoni, *Household Diversity: The Starting Point for Healthy Families in the New Century*, *in* HANDBOOK OF CONTEMPORARY FAMILIES: CONSIDERING THE PAST, CONTEMPLATING THE FUTURE 3 (Marvin Coleman & Lawrence H. Ganong eds., 2004).

32. *Id.*

33. *Id.*

34. GILBERT, *supra* note 14, at 62

35. SKOLNICK, *supra* note 16, at 52.

36. GILBERT, *supra* note 14, at 68.

37. SKOLNICK, *supra* note 16, at 52.

38. MAY, *supra* note 3, at 13.

39. *Id.*

40. *Id.* at 28.

41. *See* Talcott Parsons, *The Social Structure of the Family, in* THE FAMILY: ITS FUNCTION AND DESTINY, *supra* note 2, at 262–72.

42. BETTY FRIEDAN, THE FEMININE MYSTIQUE, ch. 12, *Progressive Dehumanization: The Comfortable Concentration Camp* (1963).

43. WEISS, *supra* note 8, at 16. For contemporary affirmations of this gender conflict, see Therese Benedek, *The Emotional Structure of the Family, in* THE FAMILY: ITS FUNCTION AND DESTINY, *supra* note 2, at 365 ("[T]he modern [1950s] marriage—in each of its partners—manifests the conflict between the passing patriarchal and the present individualistic society. . . . We speak about 'working out the marriage,' so aware are we of the problems involved and of the amount of good will necessary to solve them. The axis of the emotional structure of the modern family is this conflict-laden interpersonal relationship between husband and wife."); and Parsons, *supra* note 41, at 274 ("It seems quite clear . . . that the sources of ambivalence concerning the feminine role go so deep that any attempt to force or persuade an overwhelming majority of American women to accept a role of pure and virtuous domesticity alone is probably doomed to failure.").

44. Similarly, Alfred Kinsey's startling revelations about extramarital and "deviant" sexual practices revealed a dissonance between the theory and practice of monogamy. See his SEXUAL BEHAVIOR IN THE HUMAN MALE (1948) and SEXUAL BEHAVIOR IN THE HUMAN FEMALE (1953).

45. Instead of seeking careers, these women generally worked in part-time clerical or service jobs to supplement the family income. They did, however, help to eradicate stigmatizing notions that only lower-class married women or women with husbands in "dire financial straits" worked. SKOLNICK, *supra* note 16, at 53.

46. Howard N. Fullerton Jr., *Labor Force Participation: 75 Years of Change, 1950–98 and 1998–2025,* MONTHLY LABOR REVIEW, Dec. 1999, 4 tbl.1, *available at* http://www.bls.gov/opub/mlr/1999/12/art1full.pdf. By contrast, the percentage of adult males in the labor force slowly diminished over those same decades, at 86.4 percent in 1950, 83.3 percent in 1960, 79.7 percent in 1970, 77.4 percent in 1980, and 76.1 percent in 1990. *Id.* Accordingly, the difference between men's and women's rates of participation in the labor force has sharply diminished, from 52.5 percent in 1950 to 18.6 percent in 1990. *Id.* at 5 tbl.1. Another way to view this phenomenon is to consider the change in percent distribution of the labor force by gender. In 1950, 70.4 percent of the workforce was male, and 29.6 percent was female. In 2000, men comprised 53.4 percent of the labor force, and women comprised 46.6 percent. Mitra Toossi, *A Century of Change: The U.S. Labor Force, 1950–2050,* MONTHLY LABOR REVIEW, May 2002, 16 tbl.1, *available at* http://www.bls.gov/opub/mlr/2002/05/art2full.pdf.

47. Fullerton, *supra* note 46, at 3.

48. *Id.*

49. U.S. CENSUS BUREAU, STATISTICAL ABSTRACT OF THE UNITED STATES: 2003, tbl.HS-30, *Marital Status of Women in the Civilian Labor Force: 1900 to 2002* (2003), *available at* http://www.census.gov/statab/hist/HS-30.pdf (Current Population Survey data).

50. Id.

51. MAY, *supra* note 3, at 26.

52. BENJAMIN SPOCK, THE COMMON SENSE BOOK OF BABY AND CHILD CARE (1946); NORMAN VINCENT PEALE, THE POWER OF POSITIVE THINKING (1952). *See* Rosenfeld, *supra* note 28, at 130 (noting that the seven editions of Dr. Spock's book "sold more than 50 million copies, making it by far the most influential child-care manual of the post–World War II era").

53. GILBERT, *supra* note 14, at 62. One writer of the period even proposed that differential functioning of the endocrine system might contribute to marital disharmony. Irritation and incompatibility with the spouse's level of excitability could be glandular in origin and best approached from a medical perspective. *See* BABER, *supra* note 2, at 235–37.

54. COONTZ, *supra* note 3, at 9.

55. Frank F. Furstenberg Jr., *Good Dads–Bad Dads: Two Faces of Fatherhood, in* FAMILY IN TRANSITION, *supra* note 2, at 352.

56. MAY, *supra* note 3, at 185.

57. *Id.* at 187; JOSEPH VEROFF ET AL., MENTAL HEALTH IN AMERICA: PATTERNS OF HELP-SEEKING FROM 1957 TO 1976, at 7–8, 10 (1981).

58. MAY, *supra* note 3, at 187.

59. *Id.* at 36.

60. WILLIAMS, *supra* note 1, at 77.

61. MAY, *supra* note 3, at 36.

62. *Id.* at 203–4. Concern about divorce rates in the aftermath of World War II may have had a significant impact on some contemporary observers' conclusion that marriages of the 1950s were fragile, even as other indicators denoted marital stability. *See, e.g.,* BABER, *supra* note 2, at 173 ("Few will dispute the claim that the marriage relationship is becoming more difficult."); WILLIAMS, *supra* note 1, at 75 ("In spite of many cultural prescriptions nominally supporting the permanence of the marriage tie and the solidity of the nuclear family, American society is characterized by high rates of divorce and other forms of family dissolution.").

63. GILBERT, *supra* note 14, at 62.

64. ANDREW CHERLIN, MARRIAGE, DIVORCE, REMARRIAGE 25 (1981).

65. *See generally* DIFONZO, *supra* note 6; Lawrence M. Friedman, *A Dead Language: Divorce Law and Practice Before No-Fault,* 86 VA. L. REV. 1497 (2000). New York, one of the most restrictive states, permitted divorce only on the ground of adultery from 1787 until 1967. J. Herbie DiFonzo and Ruth C. Stern, *Addicted To Fault: Why Divorce Reform Has Lagged in New York,* 27 PACE L. REV. 559, 559 (2007).

66. HARRIET F. PILPEL & THEODORA ZAVIN, YOUR MARRIAGE AND THE LAW 39 (1952).

67. *Id.* at 36–39.

68. *Id.* at 43–44.

69. *Id.* at 40. On the history of common-law marriage, see generally HENDRIK HAR-

TOG, MAN AND WIFE IN AMERICA: A HISTORY (2000); and Ariela R. Dubler, *Wifely Behavior: A Legal History of Acting Married*, 100 COLUM. L. REV. 957 (2000).

70. PILPEL & ZAVIN, *supra* note 66, at 40.

71. Nelson, *supra* note 12, at 444.

72. PILPEL & ZAVIN, *supra*, note 66, at 26.

73. *Id.* at 26–28. Pilpel and Zavin noted that Arizona, "apparently concerned with the possibility of having the ranges overrun by turbaned riders, prohibits the marriage of whites with Hindus." *Id.* at 27.

74. Joseph Carroll, *Most Americans Approve of Interracial Marriages*, Gallup News Service, Aug. 16, 2007, *available at* http://www.gallup.com/poll/28417/Most-Americans-Approve-Interracial-Marriages.aspx (reporting the 1958 poll results).

75. *Id.* By 2010, almost two-thirds (63 percent) of Americans would approve if someone in their family married a person of a different race or ethnicity. PEW RESEARCH CENTER, THE RISE OF INTERMARRIAGE 36 (2012), *available at* http://www.pewsocialtrends.org/files/2012/02/SDT-Intermarriage-II.pdf.

76. COTT, *supra* note 20, at 184. The California statute banned marriage of a white person "with a Negro, mulatto, Mongolian, or member of the Malay race." *Id.*

77. Perez v. Sharp, 32 Cal. 2d 711 (1948).

78. COTT, *supra* note 20, at 185.

79. *Id.* In 1967, the U.S. Supreme Court declared that state statutes barring interracial marriage violated the federal constitution. Loving v. Virginia, 388 U.S. 1 (1967). In 1980, interracial marriages constituted 6.7 percent of new marriages. By 2010, the percentage of marriages between spouses of a different race or ethnicity had more than doubled, to 15 percent. PEW RESEARCH CENTER, *supra* note 75, at 1.

80. PILPEL & ZAVIN, *supra* note 66, at 29.

81. In Baker v. Nelson, 191 N.W.2d 185 (Minn. 1971), the Minnesota Supreme Court considered the first same-sex marriage case, rejecting the plaintiffs' statutory and constitutional claims in a brief opinion.

82. HARTOG, *supra* note 69, at 306. The limits of this doctrine are discussed shortly in text.

83. HARTOG, *supra* note 69, at 306. *See* COTT, *supra* note 20, at 174–79 (discussing how the structure and implementation of social insurance and welfare programs dating from the New Deal economically reinforced the subservience of the dependent wife/mother to the wage-earning husband/father).

84. Anastasiadis v. Anastasiadis, 279 N.Y.S.2d 936, 937 (Sup. Ct. N.Y. County 1967). In 1979, the U.S. Supreme Court declared unconstitutional a spousal support statute that imposed alimony obligations on husbands but not on wives. Orr v. Orr, 440 U.S. 268 (1979).

85. HARTOG, *supra* note 69, at 306.

86. *See generally* HOMER H. CLARK JR., THE LAW OF DOMESTIC RELATIONS IN THE UNITED STATES 286–308 (2d ed. 1988).

87. JOHN DEWITT GREGORY ET AL., UNDERSTANDING FAMILY LAW § 7.02[A], at

206 (3d ed. 2005); PILPAL & ZAVIN, *supra* note 66, at 55. Tort suits by wives against husbands for harm to their property interests were allowable under the Married Women's Property Acts, which all states had adopted by the end of the 19th century. But interspousal suits for personal injuries were barred for two reasons born of somewhat contradictory policy concerns: (1) such actions might encourage fraud on insurers through collusion between the spouses, and (2) such suits would destroy the "peace and harmony" of the marital home. GREGORY ET AL., *supra*. Interspousal tort immunity has been subjected to prolonged and acerbic criticism. *See, e.g.,* CLARK, *supra* note 86, at 371 ("[T]he kindest thing to be said about . . . these policy arguments is that they are frivolous."). Since 1970, the immunity rule "has been transformed dramatically from a majority to a minority rule." Carl Tobias, *Interspousal Tort Immunity in America*, 23 GA. L. REV. 359, 359 (1989).

88. HARTOG, *supra* note 69, at 306–7.

89. *Id.* The prevalent view in the 1950s was that a husband who coerced his wife into sexual intercourse was not committing rape, since the element of unlawfulness was missing. *Id.* at 307. Only in the 1980s did scholars and courts engage in serious reconsideration of this view. Today, while most states allow for rape prosecutions in cases in which husbands and wives were estranged, many states still bar the prosecution of husbands for raping their wives if they were living together at the time of the forcible sex act. GREGORY ET AL., *supra* note 87, § 7.08[C], at 230.

90. Nelson, *supra* note 12, at 517.

91. *Id.* (citing cases).

92. *See* Axelrod v. Axelrod, 150 N.Y.S.2d 633 (Sup. Ct. Kings County 1956).

93. Nelson, *supra* note 12, at 514. In one case, an appellate court reversed the grant of a judicial separation to the wife based on cruelty. The appellate court admitted that the trial court "was entitled to conclude that the beatings concerning which the wife testified occurred, it was also evident that the husband was provoked by the wife's neglect of her conjugal relationships and her frustration of her husband in his effort to establish a normal marital relationship." Petrella v. Petrella, 255 N.Y.S.2d 962, 963 (App. Div. 1st Dep't 1965).

94. *See* Baker v. Baker, 228 N.Y.S.2d 470, 472 (App. Div. 1st Dep't 1962).

95. *See* Reese v. Reese, 185 N.Y.S. 110, 111 (App. Div. 2nd Dep't 1920).

96. Nelson, *supra* note 12, at 518. Annulment rulings in this era manifested the same gender bias. New York cases declared a man entitled to an annulment if his wife had failed to disclose a previous illegitimate pregnancy or even if "she turned out not to be the virgin he had expected her to be." *Id.* at 514 (citing cases). But a wife who proved prior undisclosed sexual activity on the part of her husband—impregnating an unwed girl who bore him a child—was denied an annulment. Pankiw v. Pankiw, 256 N.Y.S.2d 448 (Sup. Ct. Monroe County 1965). A husband was granted an annulment when his wife told him after the wedding that she would decide when to have a child, a proposition that violated "the usual implications" of marriage. Schulman v. Schulman, 46 N.Y.S.2d 158, 159 (Sup. Ct. Kings County 1943).

NOTES TO PAGES 16–17   159

97. McGuire v. McGuire, 59 N.W.2d 336 (Neb. 1953).
98. HARTOG, *supra* note 69, at 9.
99. *Id.*
100. *Id.* at 6–7 (summarizing the trial transcript).
101. *Id.* at 7.
102. HARTOG, *supra* note 69, at 8. *See* McGuire v. McGuire, 59 N.W.2d at 342 ("As long as the home is maintained and the parties are living as husband and wife it may be said that the husband is legally supporting his wife and the purpose of the marriage relation is being carried out. Public policy requires such a holding.").
103. HARTOG, *supra* note 69, at 10. Whether Lydia McGuire could have left the marriage is problematic, as she did not appear to have grounds to seek separation or divorce. A woman who moved out without adequate grounds would be deemed to have abandoned her marriage and thus as entitled to no support whatever. GREGORY ET AL., *supra* note 87, § 9.03, at 312.
104. *See* Martha Albertson Fineman, *What Place for Family Privacy?*, 67 GEORGE WASH. L. REV. 1207, 1214 (1999) (observing that the McGuire case "illustrate[s] the contours of the common law doctrine of family privacy"); Eric Rasmusen and Jeffrey Evans Stake, *Lifting the Veil of Ignorance: Personalizing the Marriage Contract*, 73 IND. L.J. 453, 456 (1998) (noting that "courts have traditionally abstained from intervening in conduct during marriage and this has not changed with the no-fault revolution"); U.S. v. Chestman, 947 F.2d 551, 580 (2d Cir. 1991) (Winter, J., concurring and dissenting) (noting that the law's reluctance to recognize family obligations "as legal obligations is in large part derived from a concern that intra-family litigation would exacerbate strained relationships and weaken rather than strengthen the sense of mutual obligation underlying family relationships"; *id.*, citing McGuire).
105. HARTOG, *supra* note 69, at 320 n. 7 (quoting the trial transcript).
106. *Id.*
107. McGuire v. McGuire, 59 N.W.2d at 338. That the McGuire court interpreted the requirement of discontinuing cohabitation both literally and narrowly may be inferred from its favorable reference to cases from other states in which a wife had successfully obtained spousal maintenance even though she continued to live in the marital home. *Id.* at 340–42. The distinction was subtle but key: the parties in those cases were living apart, even within the marital domicile, while the McGuires were still cohabiting. *Id.*
108. Another view of the case suggests that the trial court simply intruded too far into the domestic arrangements.

> The district court decreed that the plaintiff was legally entitled to use the credit of the defendant and obligate him to pay for certain items in the nature of improvements and repairs, furniture, and appliances for the household in the amount of several thousand dollars; required the defendant to purchase a new automobile with an effective heater within 30 days; ordered him to pay travel expenses of the plaintiff for a visit to each of her daughters at least once a year; that the plaintiff

be entitled in the future to pledge the credit of the defendant for what may constitute necessaries of life; awarded a personal allowance to the plaintiff in the sum of $50 a month; awarded $800 for services for the plaintiff's attorney; and as an alternative to part of the award to made, defendant was permitted, in agreement with plaintiff, to purchase a modern home elsewhere.

McGuire v. McGuire, 59 N.W.2d at 336. Even the dissenting justice, who maintained that the equitable power of a trial court did extend to the relief sought by Lydia McGuire, would have limited the award to a modest cash amount. *Id.* at 345 (Yeager, J., dissenting).

109. *See, e.g.,* Vetrano v. Vetrano, 54 N.Y.S.2d 537, 538 (Sup. Ct. Queens County 1945) (noting "the well-settled principle of law that the domicile of the wife is the place where the husband has his domicile").

110. *Id.,* quoting Downes v. Downes, 225 App. Div. 886, 233 N.Y.S. 39, 40 (2d Dep't 1929).

111. *See* Bennett v. Bennett, 79 A.2d 513, 515 (Md. 1951) ("The doctrine is well established that the husband, being the head of the family and legally responsible for its support, has the right to choose and establish the domicile for himself and his wife, and when he provides a new domicile, his wife's refusal to follow him constitutes desertion, unless the change is plainly unreasonable."). This rule that a married woman's domicile was ordinarily that of her husband was abrogated in Maryland in 1972 by an amendment to the state constitution. *See* Blount v. Boston, 718 A.2d 1111, 1124 n.5 (Md. 1998) (explaining the impact of the state equal rights amendment). In New York, the Domestic Relations Law was amended in 1976 to provide that the "domicile of a married man or woman shall be established for all purposes without regard to sex." L. 1976, ch. 62, § 2. The modern view on whether desertion has occurred depends on the justification for one spouse's decision to establish a new marital residence and the other's justification for refusing to follow. *See* Kerr v. Kerr, 371 S.E.2d 30 (Va. App. 1988).

112. Eftimiou v. Eftimiou, 204 N.Y.S.2d 785 (Sup. Ct. Kings County 1960).

113. *Id.* at 786.

114. *Id.* at 789.

115. *Id.* at 790.

116. *Id.* As late as 1974, a court declared that it was "still a wife's burden to move with her husband to a location selected by him in good faith." Cavallo v. Cavallo, 359 N.Y.S.2d 628, 629 (Sup. Ct. Suffolk County 1974). Acknowledging that "the winds of change may shortly impose new strictures" upon this legal rule, the court insisted that the principle remained "reasonable if it relates to the husband's employment as the sole support of the family." *Id.*

117. Rosner v. Rosner, 108 N.Y.S.2d 196, 200 (Dom. Rel. Ct. Queens County 1951).

118. *Id.* at 201.

119. *Id.* The same gendered norms underlay the "tender years" presumption, by which the custody of young children was typically awarded to their mothers on grounds of natural fitness. *See* GREGORY ET AL., *supra* note 87, § 11.03[B][1], at 461. This presumption gradually yielded to facially gender-neutral custody rules in the 1970s. *Id.*

120. Mary Ann Glendon, *The New Marriage and the New Property, in* MARRIAGE AND COHABITATION IN CONTEMPORARY SOCIETIES: AREAS OF LEGAL, SOCIAL, AND ETHICAL CHANGE 59, 63 (John M. Eekelaar & Sanford N. Fetz eds., 1980).

121. Katharine Fullerton Gerould, *Romantic Divorce,* 88 SCRIBNER'S MAG. 485, 485 (1930).

122. *Id.*

123. Brown v. Brown, 281 S.W.2d 492, 498 (Tenn. 1955) (citation omitted). Note that only a wife could be the "unfortunate person" who could be deprived of alimony. Wives who sinned against their marriage vows risked divorce and loss of alimony; husbands who did the same risked only divorce.

124. *Id.*

125. Lawrence M. Friedman & Robert V. Percival, *Who Sues for Divorce? From Fault through Fiction to Freedom,* 5 J. LEGAL STUD. 61, 79–80 (1976).

126. *See* PAUL H. JACOBSON, AMERICAN MARRIAGE AND DIVORCE 122 (1959).

127. *Id.* at 121 tbl.58.

128. *See* ALBERT C. JACOBS & JULIUS GOEBEL JR., CASES AND OTHER MATERIALS ON DOMESTIC RELATIONS 428–37 (4th ed. 1961); MAX RHEINSTEIN, MARRIAGE STABILITY, DIVORCE, AND THE LAW 101–5 (1972).

129. IOWA CODE 1939, § 10475. A husband could proffer similar grounds. IOWA CODE 1939, § 10477. This divorce ground remained intact until Iowa converted to a no-fault standard in which breakdown of the marriage relationship became the sole basis for termination of the marriage. IOWA CODE 1971, § 598.17.

130. DIFONZO, *supra* note 6, at 43–75, 91–106 (describing the radical transition in the legal understanding of marital cruelty). The authors of the famous Middletown study noted that the cruelty divorce ground "may cover almost any variety of marital maladjustment" and that "the increase in divorces on this charge probably indicates chiefly a growing flexibility which allows divorces on other than specific charges such as 'adultery' and 'abandonment.'" ROBERT S. LYND & HELEN MERRELL LYND, MIDDLETOWN: A STUDY IN CONTEMPORARY AMERICAN CULTURE 122–23 (1929). The allegation of cruelty in a divorce case frequently constituted a strategic choice rather than an allegation of beastliness. Roscoe Pound exposed the farce at the heart of this divorce ground when he asked his readers to "consider what any American community would think of a man convicted of extreme physical cruelty to his wife if those words were taken seriously." Roscoe Pound, *Foreword to A Symposium in the Law of Divorce,* 28 IOWA L. REV. 179, 184 (1943).

131. PROCEEDINGS OF THE INSTITUTE OF FAMILY LAW 179 (John S. Bradway ed., 1959) (quoting Judge Paul W. Alexander).

132. *See* MAXINE B. VIRTUE, FAMILY CASES IN COURT 86–87 (1956) (noting that the majority of couples in divorce court in Illinois agreed on the dissolution, so "uncontested" cases were the norm, with the defendant either absent or appearing "only to be sure that financial and custody matters are handled as previously agreed upon").

Divorce-minded New York couples were statutorily barred from devising fables of matrimonial cruelty, since their state only allowed divorces on the ground of adultery until 1967. They became versed in three alternative strategies: (1) migratory divorces for those able to afford six weeks in Nevada or some other divorce-friendly venue; (2) annulments for those wishing to engage in the fiction that their marriages never legally occurred; and (3) staged hotel adultery. *See generally* DiFonzo & Stern, *supra* note 65; Richard H. Wels, *New York: The Poor Man's Reno,* 35 CORNELL L.Q. 303 (1950). The option of staged hotel adultery consisted of nothing less than routinized off-Broadway productions calling for "the husband to be caught in the act of sitting beside a scantily clad correspondent when the wife, a process server, and a private detective . . . burst into the hotel room." DIFONZO, *supra* note 6, at 89. Indeed, so endemic was this procedure that the rare judge who refused to accept the faked hotel evidence would "not be long hearing divorce cases." Max Rheinstein, *Our Dual Law of Divorce: The Law in Action versus the Law of the Books, in* THE LAW SCHOOL, THE UNIVERSITY OF CHICAGO, CONFERENCE ON DIVORCE 41 (1952).

133. Homer H. Clark Jr., *Divorce Policy and Divorce Reform,* 42 U. COLO. L. REV. 403, 407 (1971). On the disingenuous nature of divorce litigation in this period, see NELSON MANFRED BLAKE, THE ROAD TO RENO: A HISTORY OF DIVORCE IN THE UNITED STATES 1–8 (1962) (observing that under a fault-based system of divorce, thousands have had to "resort to some type of make-believe" in order to have the sour marriage dissolved); and Paul Sayre, *Divorce for the Unworthy: Specific Grounds for Divorce,* 18 LAW & CONTEMP. PROBS. 26, 27 (1953) (stating that divorce litigation provides a striking exception to the rule that the defendant tries to prevent the plaintiff from succeeding).

134. In a 1947 essay, David L. Cohn connected the dots that linked marriage to happiness and happiness to divorce.

> We teach our young that to be married is automatically to be happy. We believe that everybody is, ought to be, or can be made happy; that all are "entitled" to happiness as to fresh air. . . . But simultaneously, in our anarchy of impermanence, we believe that if we are not happy in one marriage we shall surely be happy in another.

David L. Cohn, *Are Americans Polygamous?,* ATLANTIC MONTHLY, Aug. 1947, at 30, 32. *See also* Christopher Lasch, *Divorce American Style,* N.Y. REV. BOOKS, Feb. 17, 1966, at 3, 4 ("Easy divorce is a form of social insurance that has to be paid by a society which holds up domesticity as a universally desirable condition . . . .").

135. *See generally* DIFONZO, *supra* note 6, ch. 4, *The Case of the All-Too-Consenting Adults* (describing the widely acknowledged failures of the fault system to preserve marriages); *see also* COTT, *supra* note 20, at 195–96 ("It was well known by the 1950s . . . that couples colluded to present divorce suits as the fault of one, rather than the wish of both, to terminate their marriages."); Katherine L. Caldwell, *Not Ozzie and Harriet: Postwar Divorce and the American Liberal Welfare State,* 23 LAW AND SOC. INQUIRY 1, 2 (1998) (arguing that by the middle of the 20th century, "the ever-increasing number of divorcing spouses and the greater cultural acceptance of divorce already confirmed for many

the legal system's lack of control over marital dissolution"). As early as 1948, the American Bar Association's divorce section recommended a form of no-fault divorce, pointing out that the fact that 85 to 90 percent of all divorces were uncontested suggested that the primary cause of divorce was marital breakdown on both sides. Paul W. Alexander, *Family Life Conference Suggests New Judicial Procedures and Attitudes toward Marriage and Divorce*, 32 J. AM. JUDICATURE SOC. 38–47 (1948).

136. Charlton Ogburn, *The Role of Legal Services in Family Stability*, 272 ANNALS AM. ACAD. POL. & SOC. SCI. 127 (1950).

137. VIRTUE, *supra* note 132, at 229–30.

138. U.S. CENSUS BUREAU, STATISTICAL ABSTRACT OF THE UNITED STATES: 2012, tbl.78, *Live Births, Deaths, Marriages, and Divorces: 1960 to 2008* (2012), *available at* http://www.census.gov/compedia/statab/2012/tables/12s0078.pdf.

139. *Id.* California's Family Law Act of 1969 (ch. 1608, § 8, 1969 Cal. Stat. 3314, 3324) (codified as amended at CAL. FAM. CODE § 2310 (West, Westlaw through ch. 20 of 2011 Reg. Sess.)) was the nation's first true no-fault divorce law and constituted "the most radical transformation of divorce law in America history." James Herbie DiFonzo, *Customized Marriage*, 75 IND. L.J. 875, 884 (2000).

140. War has had a significant impact on the divorce rate, which rises sharply at the end of a conflict and then decreases in succeeding years. During the 20th century, World War II triggered the largest postwar divorce boom. In 1946, the divorce rate reached 4.4 per thousand, a rate double that of 1960. *See* JACOBSON, *supra* note 126, at 90 tbl.42.

141. Although skeptics remain, Cherlin demonstrated that the surge in national divorce rates began in the early 1960s, prior to the liberalization of divorce law in the 1970s. *See generally* ANDREW J. CHERLIN, MARRIAGE, DIVORCE, REMARRIAGE (rev. ed. 1992).

142. U.S. CENSUS BUREAU, *supra* note 138, tbl.78.

143. The increase in the divorce rate in the 1970s (41 percent) was just over two-thirds (69 percent) of the increase in the 1960s (59 percent). References suggesting that the 1970s spawned the "greatest divorcing generation" thus need to be understood within the larger context of marital dissolution rates, which peaked in the 1970s after rapidly rising the previous decade. Tara Parker-Pope, *What Brain Scans Can Tell Us about Marriage*, N.Y. TIMES, June 6, 2010, *available at* http://www.nytimes.com/2010/06/06/fashion/06gore.html (quoting economist Betsey Stevenson).

144. U.S. CENSUS BUREAU, STATISTICAL ABSTRACT OF THE UNITED STATES: 2012, tbl.133, *Marriages and Divorces—Number and Rate by State: 1990 to 2009* (2012), *available at* http://www.census.gov/compedia/statab/2012/tables/12s0133.pdf.

145. Katherine Caldwell is largely correct in maintaining that the "'divorce revolution' of the 1970s was . . . less a revolution than a continuation and expansion of postwar divorce patterns." Caldwell, *supra* note 135, at 47. In 2012, the U.S. Department of Health and Human Services reported that the probability that the first marriages of women and men will survive 20 years was 52 percent for women and 56 percent for men in 2006–10. CASEY E. COPEN ET AL., FIRST MARRIAGES IN THE UNITED STATES: DATA FROM THE 2006–2010 NATIONAL SURVEY OF FAMILY GROWTH 7 (Nat'l Health Stat. Rep.

No. 49, 2012, *available at* http://www.cdc.gov/nchs/data/nhsr/nhsr049.pdf. These levels, the report noted, were virtually identical to estimates based on vital statistics from the early 1970s. *Id.*

146. In California, the Governor's Commission on the Family, which devised the nation's first modern no-fault divorce law, was appointed in 1966 to mount a "concerted assault on the high incidence of divorce in our society and its often tragic consequences." REPORT OF THE GOVERNOR'S COMMISSION ON THE FAMILY 1 (1966) (quoting Governor Edmund G. Brown, Charge to the Commission, May 11, 1966). *See* DiFonzo, *supra* note 139, at 885 ("[T]he history of no-fault divorce illustrates the gulf between founding intentions and achieved effects: the major family law reforms . . . in the 1960s and 1970s were carefully considered efforts aimed at reinforcing the family and lowering the rate of divorce. They largely failed."); Caldwell, *supra* note 135, at 47 (arguing that "the 'no-fault revolution' was unintentionally instigated by conservatives hoping that without the formalism of fault-based legal grounds, judges could deny divorces more frequently"); HERBERT JACOB, SILENT REVOLUTION: THE TRANSFORMATION OF DIVORCE LAW IN THE UNITED STATES 60–61, 78–79, 101–3, 162–73 (1988) (arguing that no-fault divorce law reforms were not widely intended or expected to radically alter either marriage or divorce).

147. DiFonzo, *supra* note 139, at 887.

148. Family Law Act of 1969, ch. 1608, 1969 Cal. Stat. 3312, 3314–51 (*effective* 1970; *repealed* 1994).

149. Unif. Marriage and Divorce Act, 9A (Pt. I) U.L.A. 159 (1998) (*originally proposed* 1970).

150. No-fault divorce statutes proliferated rapidly. By 1977, only three states—Pennsylvania, Illinois, and South Dakota—remained wedded to purely fault concepts for divorce. *See* Doris J. Freed & Henry H. Foster Jr., *Divorce in the Fifty States: An Overview*, 11 FAM. L.Q. 297, 298 (1977). Pennsylvania adopted no-fault divorce in 1980, Illinois did in 1983, and South Dakota was the 50th state to do so, in 1985. *See* Ira M. Ellman & Sharon L. Lohr, *Dissolving the Relationship between Divorce Laws and Divorce Rates*, 18 INT'L REV. L. & ECON. 341, 347–48 (1998). New York's history is unusual. Even though the Empire State had adopted a form of no-fault divorce in 1967, its procedure proved so cumbersome that the vast majority of divorces continued to be granted on fault grounds until the state finally adopted a true no-fault divorce law in 2010. *See* New York Laws 2010, ch. 384, § 1 (providing a divorce ground when the "relationship between husband and wife has broken down irretrievably for a period of at least six months"). On the tortuous history of New York divorce, see J. Herbie DiFonzo & Ruth C. Stern, *Addicted to Fault: Why Divorce Reform Has Lagged in New York*, 27 PACE. L. REV. 559 (2007).

151. *See* GREGORY ET AL., *supra* note 87, § 8.01[C], at 238.

152. As the Colorado Supreme Court admitted, the necessity to prove fault "'permits the parties to obtain divorces by consent, but subjects them to [the] humiliation, hypocrisy, sometimes perjury, and needless hostility of having to testify to one of the pre-

scribed grounds.'" *In re* Marriage of Franks, 542 P.2d 845, 849 (Colo. 1975) (omission in original) (quoting Clark, *supra* note 133, at 407).

153. *See* J. Herbie DiFonzo, *No-Fault Marital Dissolution: The Bitter Triumph of Naked Divorce*, 31 SAN DIEGO L. REV. 519 (1994).

154. MARY ANN GLENDON, ABORTION AND DIVORCE IN WESTERN LAW: AMERICAN FAILURES, EUROPEAN CHALLENGES 81 (1987); *see also* BARBARA DAFOE WHITEHEAD, THE DIVORCE CULTURE 68 (1997) (no-fault divorce "established a disaffected spouse's right unilaterally to dissolve a marriage simply by declaring that the relationship was over").

155. Twila L. Perry, *No-Fault Divorce and Liability without Fault: Can Family Law Learn from Torts?*, 52 OHIO ST. L.J. 55, 62 (1991).

156. Robert T. Michael, *Why Did the U.S. Divorce Rate Double within a Decade?*, in 6 RES. POPULATION ECON. 367–99 (T. Paul Schultz ed., 1988).

157. JOSEPH VEROFF ET AL., THE INNER AMERICAN: A SELF-PORTRAIT FROM 1957 TO 1976, at 191 (1981).

158. ROBERT BELLAH ET AL., HABITS OF THE HEART: INDIVIDUALISM AND COMMITMENT IN AMERICAN LIFE 6 (1985). *See generally* ANDREW CHERLIN, THE MARRIAGE-GO-ROUND: MARRIAGE AND THE STATE OF THE FAMILY IN AMERICA TODAY 87–115 (2009). Unsurprisingly, the spread of no-fault divorce was accompanied by critiques that the post–World War II nuclear family had focused too much on parenting and not enough on the marital dyad. *See* Scanzoni, *supra* note 31, at 6. In 1967, Margaret Mead had tossed an early volley in this direction, calling the nuclear family "a massive failure" and advocating changes to facilitate the development of family members as individuals. Quoted in *id.* at 5.

159. GROSSMAN & FRIEDMAN, *supra* note 29, at 12. The prime expositor of companionate marriage early in the 20th century was Judge Ben B. Lindsey. *See* BEN B. LINDSEY & WAINWRIGHT EVANS, THE COMPANIONATE MARRIAGE (1927).

160. Bruce C. Hafen, *Individualism and Autonomy in Family Law: The Waning of Belonging*, 1991 BYU L. REV. 1, 3. *But see* Naomi R. Cahn, *The Moral Complexities of Family Law*, 50 STANFORD L. REV. 225, 270 ("Individuals continue to want a familial relationship; they simply want more control over the terms of that relationship. This movement toward personal autonomy is nonetheless a movement toward relationships, not away from them.").

161. ERICH SEGAL, LOVE STORY 131 (1970).

Chapter 2: How Marriage Became Optional

1. RAY E. BABER, MARRIAGE AND THE FAMILY 163 (2d ed. 1953).
2. PAUL H. LANDIS, MAKING THE MOST OF MARRIAGE 8 (1955).
3. LANDIS, *supra* note 2, at 10 fig.3. Since grooms are typically older than brides (*see id.* at 9), the percentages for men married at those ages were lower: 17.7 percent by age 20 and 66.1 percent by age 25. *Id.* at 10 fig.3.

4. PEW RESEARCH CENTER, THE DECLINE OF MARRIAGE AND RISE OF NEW FAMILIES i (2010), *available at* http://pewsocialtrends.org/files/2010/11/pew-social-trends-2010-families.pdf.

5. *Id.* The overall numbers are not as stark but reflect the same trend. In 1960, 72 percent of American adults were married; by 2008, only 52 percent were married. *Id.* at 1.

6. U.S. CENSUS BUREAU, 2005–2009 COMMUNITY SURVEY 5-YEAR ESTIMATES, tbl.S1101, *Households and Families* (2009), *available at* http://factfinder2.census.gov/rest/dnldController/deliver?_ts=380802032791 (reporting that of 112,611,029 households in 2009, 55,974,600 were headed by married couples).

7. Press Release, U.S. Census Bureau, Unmarried and Single Americans Week, Sept. 16–22, 2012 (July 31, 2012), *available at* http://www.census.gov/newsroom/releases/pdf/cb12ff-18_unmarried.pdf.

8. *See* Jana B. Singer, *The Privatization of Family Law,* 1992 WIS. L. REV. 1443, 1453 (stating that marriage is "just one of several permissible choices for individuals who wish to pursue an intimate relationship within the framework of the law").

9. *See* Rose M. Kreider & Diana B. Elliott, The Complex Living Arrangements of Children and Their Unmarried Parents, Poster Presentation to the Population Assoc. of Am. (May 2, 2009), *available at* http://www.census.gov/population/www/socdemo/complex-abstract.pdf; Press Release, U.S. Census Bureau, U.S. Census Bureau Reports Men and Women Wait Longer to Marry (Nov. 10, 2010), *available at* http://www.census.gov/newsroom/releases/archives/families_households/cb10-174.html.

10. U.S. Census Bureau, Living Arrangements of Children Under 18 Years Old: 1960 to Present, tbl.CH-1, *available at* http://www.census.gov/hhes/families/data/children.html (last visited May 7, 2011).

11. *Id.*

12. Common-law parentage principles aimed to reinforce the central role of marriage. Children born to a married woman were legally the offspring of their biological mother and her husband. *See* Theresa Glennon, *Somebody's Child: Evaluating the Erosion of the Marital Presumption of Paternity,* 102 W. VA. L. REV. 547, 562–65 (2000) (describing the foundations and evolution of paternity determinations at common law). If the child's mother was unmarried, only she was considered the child's legal parent. The term applied to an "illegitimate" child, *filius nullius* (literally "son of no one"), suggested the law's disdain for—and simultaneous fear of—these progeny. Acknowledging these children risked upending the regime of marriage, viewed as society's bedrock. The same five decades that washed away the distinction between legitimate offspring and those born out of wedlock saw the percentage of children born to unmarried mothers skyrocket—from 5 percent in 1960 to 41 percent in 2008. PEW RESEARCH CENTER, *supra* note 4, at 2.

13. *See* Janet Radcliffe Richards, *The Meaning of Marriage: Metaphysics for the Marriage Debate,* 42 SAN DIEGO L. REV. 1125, 1135 (2005) ("Sex before marriage is normal, childbearing by single women and unmarried couples is no longer much condemned,

men can be held responsible for the support of their children irrespective of whether they are married, and married couples can deal with their tax and incomes separately.").

14. NANCY F. COTT, PUBLIC VOWS: A HISTORY OF MARRIAGE AND THE NATION (2000), 212 n.120. *See* June Carbone, FROM PARTNERS TO PARENTS: THE SECOND REVOLUTION IN FAMILY LAW 227 (2000) (noting that "the dismantling of marriage as the exclusive determinant of family connections . . . [has been] well documented in every discipline that has undertaken the task").

15. GARY J. GATES & ABIGAIL M. COOKE, UNITED STATES CENSUS SNAPSHOT: 2010 (2011), *available at* http://williamsinstitute.law.ucla.edu/wp-content/uploads/Census2010Snapshot-US-v2.pdf.

16. Social science findings confirm that same-sex and heterosexual relationships do not differ in their essential psychosocial dimensions and that a parent's sexual orientation is unrelated to her or his ability to provide a healthy and nurturing family environment. *See* Gregory M. Herek, *Legal Recognition of Same-Sex Relationships in the United States: A Social Science Perspective,* 61 AMERICAN PSYCHOLOGIST 607–21 (2006).

17. Pew Research Center, *Less Opposition to Gay Marriage, Adoption, and Military Service* (Mar. 22, 2006), http://people-press.org/report/273/less-opposition-to-gay-marriage-adoption-and-military-service (data for 1999 and 2006); Press Release, Quinnipiac University, Gays in the Military Should Be Allowed to Come Out, U.S. Voters Tell Quinnipiac University National Poll; Key Is Belief That Being Gay Is By Choice or By Birth (Apr. 30, 2009), *available at* http://www.quinnipiac.edu/x1295.xml?ReleaseID=1292 (data for 2009).

18. Jeffrey M. Jones, *Majority of Americans Continue to Oppose Gay Marriage,* Gallup.com (May 27, 2009), http://www.gallup.com/poll/118378/majority-americans-continue-oppose-gay-marriage.aspx.

19. Fifty-four percent of Americans polled in 2009 opposed the federal law denying same-sex couples access to federal benefits; 39 percent supported their exclusion. Press Release, Quinnipiac University, *supra* note 17.

20. *See* Sheryl Gay Stolberg, *Obama Signs Away "Don't Ask, Don't Tell,"* N.Y. TIMES, Dec. 22, 2010, *available at* http://www.nytimes.com/2010/12/23/us/politics/23military.html.

21. *See* JUDITH STACEY, IN THE NAME OF THE FAMILY: RETHINKING FAMILY VALUES IN THE POSTMODERN AGE 6–7 (1996) ("[T]he term postmodern family . . . signal[s] the contested, ambivalent, and undecided character of our contemporary family cultures."); Barbara Stark, *Marriage Proposals: From One-Size Fits-All to Postmodern Marriage Law,* 89 CALIF. L. REV. 1479, 1481 n.1 (2001) ("[T]here is a widespread perception that 'anything goes' with respect to contemporary marriage.").

22. JANE LAWLER DYE, FERTILITY OF AMERICAN WOMEN: 2008, at 1 (U.S. Census Bureau ed., 2010), *available at* http://www.census.gov/prod/2010pubs/p20-563.pdf.

23. GRETCHEN LIVINGSTON & D'VERA COHN, THE NEW DEMOGRAPHY OF AMERICAN MOTHERHOOD 1 (Pew Research Center ed., 2010), *available at* http://pewsocialtrends.org/assets/pdf/754-new-demography-of-motherhood.pdf. In 1990, only

28 percent of births were to unmarried women. *Id.* The substantial rise in births to unmarried women "reflects both their rising birth rates and the shrinking share of adults who are married." *Id.* Significantly, the rate of births to unmarried women varies greatly by race and ethnicity. The proportions of births to unmarried women in 2008 included 72 percent of black births, 53 percent of Hispanic births, 29 percent of white births, and 17 percent of Asian births. *Id.* at 11–12.

24. DYE, *supra* note 22, at 1.

25. Press Release, U.S. Census Bureau, Unmarried and Single Americans Week, Sept. 20–26, 2009 (July 29, 2009), *available at* http://www.census.gov/newsroom/releases/pdf/cb09-ff18.pdf.

26. Illinois Religious Freedom Protection and Civil Union Act, 2010 Ill. Legis. Serv. 96-1513 (West); Monique Garcia, *Illinois Civil Unions Signed into Law*, CHICAGO TRIBUNE, Jan. 31, 2011, *available at* http://articles.chicagotribune.com/2011-1-31/news/ct-met-quinn-civil-union-signing-20110131_1_civil-unions-lesbian-couples-gay-marriage. Note that under this legislation, both homosexual and heterosexual couples may form civil unions offering them the same legal rights and obligations as marriage. Almost 5,200 civil union licenses were issued in the first 18 months after the law went into effect. Press Release, 5,185 Civil Unions in Illinois Since They Began in 2011, The Civil Rights Agenda (Dec. 20, 2012), *available at* http://jointcra.org/index.php?option=com_content&view=article&id=114:press-release-5185-civil-unions-in-illinois-since-they-began-in-2011&catid=34:general-media&Itemid=18.

27. Frank Newport, *For First Time, Majority of Americans Favor Legal Gay Marriage*, Gallup.com (May 20, 2011), http://www.gallup.com/poll/147662/First-Time-Majority-Americans-Favor-Legal-Gay-Marriage.aspx.

28. DIANA B. ELLIOTT, ET AL., HISTORICAL MARRIAGE TRENDS FROM 1890–2010: A FOCUS ON RACE DIFFERENCES, SEHSD Working Paper Number 2012-12 (2012), *available at* http://www.census.gov/hhes/socdemo/marriage/data/acs/ElliottetalPAA2012paper.pdf.

29. U.S. CENSUS BUREAU, FACTS FOR FEATURES, VALENTINE'S DAY 2013: FEB. 14 (Feb. 12, 2013), *available at* http://www.census.gov/newsroom/releases/pdf/cb13-ff06_valentines.pdf.

30. Darra L. Hofman, *"Mama's Baby, Daddy's Maybe": A State-By-State Survey of Surrogacy Laws and Their Disparate Gender Impact*, 35 WM. MITCHELL L. REV. 449, 452 (2009) (quoting Jean Benward, Lecture at American Society for Reproductive Medicine 2005 Conference, Adoption and Gamete Donation: Similarities and Difference (Oct. 15–16, 2005) (internal quotations omitted)).

31. Lydia Saad, *Americans Have Complex Relationship with Marriage*, Gallup.com (May 30, 2006), http://www.gallup.com/poll/23041/Americans-Complex-Relationship-Marriage.aspx.

32. *Id.* Yet a quick glance at the recent popular bookshelf suggests a belief in marriage as dispensable or perhaps unattainable. *See, e.g.,* EMILY DUBBERLEY, I'D RATHER BE SINGLE THAN SETTLE: SATISFIED SOLITUDE AND HOW TO ACHIEVE IT (2006); ROSANNA HERTZ, SINGLE BY CHANCE, MOTHERS BY CHOICE: HOW WOMEN ARE

CHOOSING PARENTHOOD WITHOUT MARRIAGE AND CREATING THE NEW AMERICAN FAMILY (2006); JEN SCHEFFT, BETTER SINGLE THAN SORRY: A NO-REGRETS GUIDE TO LOVING YOURSELF AND NEVER SETTLING (2007); LOUISE SLOAN, KNOCK YOURSELF UP: NO MAN? NO PROBLEM; A TELL-ALL GUIDE TO BECOMING A SINGLE MOM (2007); MIKKI MORRISSETTE, CHOOSING SINGLE MOTHERHOOD: THE THINKING WOMAN'S GUIDE (2008).

33. *Marriage*, Gallup.com (May 2009), http://www.gallup.com/poll/117328/Marriage.aspx.

34. *Id.* The value placed on marital fidelity is evident in the results of a 2008 poll in which 64 percent of respondents reported that they would not forgive their spouse for having an affair. Jeffrey M. Jones, *Most Americans Not Willing to Forgive Unfaithful Spouse*, Gallup.com (Mar. 25, 2008), http://www.gallup.com/poll/105682/Most-Americans-Willing-Forgive-Unfaithful-Spouse.aspx. The stated intention not to forgive does not, of course, necessarily predict the consequences of discovering adultery. Whether forgiven or not, many marriages survive instances of cheating. *See, e.g.*, Benedict Carey & Tara Parker-Pope, *Marriage Stands Up for Itself*, N.Y. TIMES, June 28, 2009, http://www.nytimes.com/2009/06/28/fashion/28marriage.html?_r=1&emc=eta1 ("Infidelity is one of the most common reasons cited by people who divorce. But surveys find the majority of people who discover a cheating spouse remain married to that person for years afterward. Many millions more shrug off, or work through, strong suspicions or evidence of infidelity.").

35. *Marriage*, *supra* note 33. Twenty-seven percent gave their marriages a grade of B; 6 percent a C; 1 percent a D; and the remaining 1 percent either an F or "no opinion"; *see also* Carey & Parker-Pope, *supra* note 34 ("Despite strong social riptides working against it—the liberalization of divorce laws, the vanishing stigma of divorce, the continual online temptations of social sites like MySpace or Facebook—the marriage bond is far stronger in 21st-century America than many may assume.").

36. Mary Ann Glendon, *The New Marriage and the New Property*, in MARRIAGE AND COHABITATION IN CONTEMPORARY SOCIETIES: AREAS OF LEGAL, SOCIAL, AND ETHICAL CHANGE 59, 63 (John M. Eekelaar & Sanford N. Fetz eds., 1980). In the words of historian Hendrik Hartog,

> Though marriage continues to offer the fantasy of continuity and permanence (till death do us part), all sane people who enter into it know that it represents a choice to marry this person at this time and that if living with this person at a later time no longer suggests the possibility of happiness, that you are entitled (have a right) to leave and to try again.

Hendrik Hartog, *What Gay Marriage Teaches about the History of Marriage*, HNN.com (Aug. 8, 2005), http://hnn.us/articles/4400.html.

37. As chapter 1 documented, the rapid rise in divorces in the 1960s preceded the onset of no-fault divorce. *See generally* MILTON C. REGAN, ALONE TOGETHER: LAW AND THE MEANINGS OF MARRIAGE (1999) (exploring the tensions between spouses

as separate individuals with their own aims and marital partners committed to the joint goals of their union); Janet Dolgin, *The Ideological Contest of the Disability Rights Critique: Where Modernity and Tradition Meet*, 30 FLA. ST. U. L. REV. 343, 350 (2003) (describing the recent "vision of family broadly predicated on Enlightenment values, including especially equality and liberty (framed as autonomy)," and noting that adult family members "increasingly . . . view themselves as autonomous individuals free to negotiate the terms of the familial relationships").

38. PEW RESEARCH CENTER, *supra* note 4, at ii.

39. *Id.*

40. *Id.*

41. *Id.* The general public is markedly more optimistic about "[t]he institution of marriage and the family" (67 percent) than about "[o]ur ability to get along with other countries" (56 percent), "[o]ur system of education" (50 percent), "[t]he economic system over the long run" (46 percent), and "[m]oral and ethical standards" (41 percent). *Id.* at 4.

42. Lori B. Andrews & Nanette Elster, *Regulating Reproductive Technologies*, 21 J. LEGAL MED. 35, 36 (2000).

43. *See id.* at 36–40.

44. *See* Jennifer L. Rosato, *The Children of ART (Assisted Reproductive Technology): Should the Law Protect Them From Harm?*, 2004 UTAH L. REV. 57, 57–58.

45. Hofman, *supra* note 30, at 450.

46. Andrews & Elster, *supra* note 42, at 46. *See also* Michael J. Malinowski, *A Law-Policy Proposal to Know Where Babies Come From during the Reproduction Revolution*, 9 J. GENDER RACE & JUST. 549, 549–50 (2006) (noting that developments in artificial reproduction are expanding parental choice not only about whether to have children but also about their offspring's genetic characteristics). *See generally* JANET L. DOLGIN, DEFINING THE FAMILY: LAW, TECHNOLOGY AND REPRODUCTION IN AN UNEASY AGE (1997).

47. These topics are discussed more fully in chapters 4 and 5.

48. U.S. CENSUS BUREAU, STATISTICAL ABSTRACT OF THE UNITED STATES: 2003, 23 tbl.HS-14, *Birth to Teenagers and to Unmarried Women: 1940 to 2002* (2003), available at http://www.census.gov/statab/hist/HS-14.pdf. However, the birth rate per 1,000 unmarried women (15 to 44 years) increased more rapidly in those years, from 7.1 in 1940 to 19.3 in 1955. *Id.*

49. Wendy D. Manning & Pamela J. Smock, *Measuring and Modeling Cohabitation: New Perspectives from Qualitative Data*, 67 J. MARRIAGE & FAM. 989, 989 (2005).

50. TOM W. SMITH, THE EMERGING 21ST CENTURY AMERICAN FAMILY (Nat'l Op. Research Center ed., GSS Social Change Report No. 42, 1999), *available at* http://cloud9.norc.uchicago.edu/dlib/sc-42.htm.

51. CENTERS FOR DISEASE CONTROL AND PREVENTION, MARRIAGE AND COHABITATION IN THE UNITED STATES: A STATISTICAL PORTRAIT BASED ON CYCLE 6 (2002) OF THE NATIONAL SURVEY OF FAMILY GROWTH 4 (2010), *available at* http://www.cdc.gov/nchs/data/series/sr_23/sr23_028.pdf.

52. Manning & Smock, *supra* note 49, at 989.
53. PAMELA SMOCK ET AL., NONMARITAL COHABITATION: CURRENT KNOWLEDGE AND FUTURE DIRECTIONS FOR RESEARCH 5 (Population Studies Center, Inst. for Soc. Res., U. of Mich., 2008), *available at* http://www.psc.isr.umich.edu/pubs/pdf/rr08-648.pdf.
54. Sam Roberts, *Study Finds Cohabiting Doesn't Make a Union Last,* N.Y. TIMES, Mar 2, 2010, *available at* http://www.nytimes.com/2010/03/03/us/03marry.html?_r=1&hpw (quoting Pamela J. Smock).
55. Manning & Smock, *supra* note 49, at 999.
56. *Id.* at 998.
57. U.S. Census Bureau, Facts for Features, *supra* note 29.
58. PEW RESEARCH CENTER, *supra* note 4, at iii.
59. Pamela J. Smock, *The Wax and Wane of Marriage: Prospects for Marriage in the 21st Century,* 66 J. MARRIAGE & FAM. 966, 968 (2004).
60. *Id.*
61. *Id.*
62. Pamela J. Smock & Wendy D. Manning, *Living Together Unmarried in the United States: Demographic Perspectives and Implications for Family Policy,* 26 LAW & POL'Y 87, 99 (2004).
63. CENTERS FOR DISEASE CONTROL AND PREVENTION, *supra* note 51, at 2 figs.1 & 2.
64. *Id.* at 2.
65. SMOCK ET AL., *supra* note 53, at 7.
66. Smock & Manning, *supra* note 62, at 96.
67. *Id.* at 100.
68. *Id.*
69. SMOCK ET AL., *supra* note 53, at 10.
70. Smock & Manning, *supra* note 62, at 90.
71. CENTERS FOR DISEASE CONTROL AND PREVENTION, *supra* note 51, at 3.
72. SMOCK ET AL., *supra* note 53, at 12.
73. CENTERS FOR DISEASE CONTROL AND PREVENTION, *supra* note 51, at 13–14.
74. Smock & Manning, *supra* note 62, at 91–92.
75. *Id.* at 92.
76. *Id.* at 93.
77. CENTERS FOR DISEASE CONTROL AND PREVENTION, *supra* note 51, at 4.
78. SMOCK ET AL., *supra* note 53, at 7. Indeed, "35% of White cohabitors, 54% of black cohabitors and nearly 60% of Hispanic cohabitors have children present in the household." Smock & Manning, *supra* note 62, at 92.
79. Smock & Manning, *supra* note 62, at 94.
80. CENTERS FOR DISEASE CONTROL AND PREVENTION, *supra* note 51, at 5.
81. Smock & Manning, *supra* note 62, at 94.
82. Manning & Smock, *supra* note 49, at 994.
83. *Id.* at 995.

84. *Id.*
85. *Id.*
86. *Id.* at 997–8.
87. *Id.* at 996.
88. CENTERS FOR DISEASE CONTROL AND PREVENTION, *supra* note 51, at 13.
89. SMOCK ET AL., *supra* note 53, at 12.
90. Smock & Manning, *supra* note 62, at 100.
91. Smock, *supra* note 59, at 971.
92. *Id.* at 968.
93. Newport, *supra* note 27.
94. PEW RESEARCH CENTER, *supra* note 4, at i. *See also* Public Religion Research Institute, *Generations at Odds: The Millennial Generation and the Future of Gay and Lesbian Rights* (Aug. 29, 2011), http://www.publicreligion.org/research/published/?id= 677 ("There is at least a 20-point generation gap between Millennials (age 18 to 29) and seniors (age 65 and older) on every public policy measure in the survey concerning rights for gay and lesbian people.") Law professor William Eskridge predicted that "younger Americans . . . will ultimately find same-sex marriage a constitutional no-brainer." William Eskridge, *Marriage Equality State by State*, SCOTUSblog (Aug. 15, 2011), http://www.scotusblog.com/2011/08/marriage-equality-state-by-state/.

95. *See* National Conference of State Legislatures, Civil Unions & Domestic Partnership Statutes (Mar. 2013), http://www.ncsl.org/issues-research/human-services/civil-unions-and-domestic-partnership-statutes.aspx; JOANNA L. GROSSMAN & LAWRENCE M. FRIEDMAN, INSIDE THE CASTLE: LAW AND THE FAMILY IN 20TH CENTURY AMERICA 150 (2011) ("Civil unions provide meaningful rights to couples who enter them, but fall short of the substantive and symbolic advantages of marriage.") Civil union legislation continues to be controversial. *See, e.g.*, Dana Rudolph, *Governor Signs Rhode Island Civil Union Law, But Pleases No One*, Keen News Service, July 3, 2011, *available at* http://www.keennewsservice.com/2011/07/03/governor-signs-rhode-island-civil-union-law-but-pleases-no-one/ (describing the 2011 law's opposition by advocates of both LGBT civil rights and pro-traditional marriage); Zuzanna Skwiot, *Group Protesting against Civil Unions*, CHI. DAILY HERALD, Aug. 27, 2011 (describing a protest by the American Society for the Defense of Tradition, Family and Property).

96. *See* Goodridge v. Dep't of Pub. Health, 798 N.E.2d 941 (Mass. 2003).

97. *See* National Conference of State Legislatures, Defining Marriage: Defense of Marriage Acts and Same-Sex Marriage Laws (June 26, 2013), http://www.ncsl.org/issues-research/human-services/same-sex-marriage-overview.aspx. California's quite convoluted path to same-sex marriage is traced in Hollingsworth v. Perry, No. 12-144, 570 U.S. __ (June 26, 2013) (Slip Op. at 2-5).

98. GATES & COOKE, *supra* note 15.

99. After the manuscript for this book was completed, the U.S. Supreme Court ruled that the section of DOMA limiting marriage to heterosexual couples for federal law

purposes was unconstitutional as a deprivation of the Fifth Amendment's guarantee of equal liberty. U.S. v. Windsor, No. 12-307, 570 U.S. ___ (June 26, 2013). The ruling did not extend recognition of same-sex marriage to the states.

100. *See* National Conference of State Legislatures, State Laws Limiting Marriage to Opposite Sex Couples (June 26, 2013), http://www.ncsl.org/issues-research/human-services/state-doma-laws.aspx.

101. The presence of children complicates the interstate recognition issues tremendously. Unmarried same-sex couples (or married ones in states that do not accept the legality of their unions) will discover that the legal environment "is one of volatile uncertainty regarding the portability of parental rights acquired by same-sex couples and other alternative families from state to state." KAREN MOULDING, 1 SEXUAL ORIENTATION AND THE LAW § 1:24 (West 2010). The legal status of the children of gay or lesbian parents "when those families move from one state to another" is "surprisingly uncertain." Steve Sanders, *Interstate Recognition of Parent-Child Relationships: The Limits of the State Interests Paradigm and the Role of Due Process*, 2011 U. CHI. LEGAL F. 233, 233.

102. *See* Joanna Grossman, *Resurrecting Comity: Revisiting the Problem of Non-Uniform Marriage Laws*, 84 OR. L. REV. 433 (2005) (discussing the "longstanding historical tradition of comity among states," which DOMA and the mini-DOMAs have disrupted).

103. *See* Mary Patricia Byrn & Morgan L. Holcomb, *Wedlocked*, 67 U. MIAMI L. REV. 1, 2 (2012).

104. *See id.* at 4 (describing the myriad reasons for divorce, including "the pragmatic—such as distribution of property, assignment of spousal support, and division of debt, and the emotional—such as finality and repose.") (citations omitted). Nor, of course, may either party remarry absent a divorce decree.

105. The scope and dilemmas of de facto parenthood are discussed in chapter 5.

106. The irony of this situation is not lost on the attorney for J.B. in the case further discussed in the text that follows, who quipped, "If the attorney general is so against gay marriage, why is he trying to keep these guys married?" The title of the reporter's story on the case provides the answer. Robert Wilonsky, *Tomorrow, Texas AG to Make Case That Gay Divorce Is Gateway to Gay Marriage*, DALLAS OBSERVER, Apr. 20, 2010, available at http://blogs.dallasobserver.com/unfairpark/2010/04/tomorrow_texas_ag_to_make_case.php.

107. *In re* Marriage of J.B. and H.B., 326 S.W.3d 654 (Tex. App. 2010).

108. *Id.* at 664.

109. Martha Albertson Fineman, *Progress and Progression in Family Law*, 2004 U. CHI. LEGAL F. 1, 2; *see also* NANCY F. COTT, PUBLIC VOWS: A HISTORY OF MARRIAGE AND THE NATION 7 (2000) ("Marriage decisively differentiated the positions of husband and wife.").

110. *See, e.g.*, LINDA C. MCCLAIN, THE PLACE OF FAMILIES: FOSTERING CAPACITY, EQUALITY, AND RESPONSIBILITY 60–61 (2006).

111. RICHARD FRY & D'VERA COHN, WOMEN, MEN AND THE NEW ECONOMICS

OF MARRIAGE 1 (Pew Research Center ed., 2010), *available at* http://pewsocialtrends.org/files/2010/11/new-economics-of-marriage.pdf.

112. *Id.* at 1–2.

113. The evocative phrase is June Carbone's. *See* Carbone, *supra* note 14, at xiv.

114. Deborah A. Widiss, *Changing the Marriage Equation*, 89 WASH. U. L. REV. 721, 722 (2012).

115. *See* Marion Crain, *"Where Have All the Cowboys Gone?" Marriage and Breadwinning in Postindustrial Society*, 60 OHIO ST. L.J. 1877, 1878 (1999); Amanda Miller, The Gendered Work Orientations of Working and Middle Class Cohabiting Couples 6 (2010), *available at* http://paa2010.princeton.edu/papers/100122 ("Despite changing norms that allow women to participate in both the private and public realms, gendered expectations for men remain deeply entrenched and intensely rigid.") (citations omitted); Carbone, *supra* note 14, at 228 (noting the "respective strength of men and women's bargaining positions in the emerging family order").

116. *See, e.g.*, Laura A. Rosenbury, *Friends with Benefits?*, 106 MICH. L. REV. 189, 194 (2007) ("Family law scholars have praised the family law revolution that, over the past forty years, has eliminated most official gender role distinctions within the family.").

117. Crain, *supra* note 115, at 1888–89.

118. *See* Susan Frelich Appleton, *Missing in Action? Searching for Gender Talk in the Same-Sex Marriage Debate*, 16 STAN. L. & POL'Y REV. 97, 113 (2005).

119. ELLEN GALINSKY ET AL., TIMES ARE CHANGING: GENDER AND GENERATION AT WORK AND AT HOME 8 (Families & Work Inst. 2011), *available at* http://familiesandwork.org/site/research/reports/Times_Are_Changing.pdf. Significantly, the percentage of men living in dual-earner couples rose from 53 to 75 percent from 1977 to 2008. The percentage of women in dual-earner couples rose from 85 to 91 percent in the same period.

120. *See* Joanna L. Grossman, *The Lady in Red: Equal Pay Day and the Continuing Problem of Gender-Based Pay Discrimination*, Justia.com (Apr. 17, 2012), http://verdict.justia.com/2012/04/17/the-lady-in-red ("Women do not get paid less because they prefer lower-paying jobs, or because they take their work less seriously. They do get paid less because they suffer from intentional pay discrimination. Studies have shown this beyond a shadow of a doubt, and it is too late in the day to reasonably disagree.").

121. Ariane Hegewisch et al., Fact Sheet, The Gender Wage Gap: 2012 tbl.2 (Inst. for Women's Pol'y Res. 2013), *available at* http://www.iwpr.org/publications/pubs/the-gender-wage-gap-2012. *See id.* at 2 ("If the pace of change in the annual earnings ratio continued at the same rate as it has since 1960, it will take another 45 years, until 2056, for men and women to reach parity.").

122. STEPHEN J. ROSE & HEIDI I. HARTMANN, STILL A MAN'S LABOR MARKET: THE LONG-TERM EARNINGS GAP 9 (2004), *available at* http://www.iwpr.org/publications/pubs/still-a-mans-labor-market-the-long-term-earnings-gap/at_download/file. Across the decade and a half that is covered by the study, the average working woman earned only $273,592, while her male counterpart earned $722,693 (in 1999 dollars). *Id.* This

long-term calculation yields a 62 percent gender gap in earnings, far more than double the 22.2 percent gap in median annual wages that is more widely acknowledged. *Id. See also* GALINSKY ET AL., *supra* note 119, at 8 (noting the persistence of "a motherhood penalty": since women are "more likely than men to be primary caregivers," they face the economic reality "that the length of the time that mothers take out of the workforce or work reduced hours to care for their children diminishes their lifetime earnings.").

123. U.S. BUREAU OF LAB. STAT., U.S. DEP'T OF LABOR, HIGHLIGHTS OF WOMEN'S EARNINGS IN 2005, at 2 (2006), *available at* http://www.bls.gov/cps/cpswom2005.pdf. A 2011 report of the Government Accountability Office noted the persistence of the trend: "Women tended to work in industries and occupations that had lower wages than the industries and occupations in which men worked." U. S. GOVERNMENT ACCOUNTABILITY OFFICE, GENDER PAY DIFFERENCES: PROGRESS MADE, BUT WOMEN REMAIN OVERREPRESENTED AMONG LOW-WAGE WORKERS 5 (2011), *available at* http://www.gao.gov/new.items/d1210.pdf.

124. U.S. BUREAU OF LAB. STAT., U.S. DEP'T OF LABOR, HIGHLIGHTS OF WOMEN'S EARNINGS IN 2007, at 2 (2008), *available at* http://www.bls.gov/cps/cpswom2007.pdf.

125. ROSE & HARTMANN, *supra* note 122, at 18.

126. Ariane Hegewisch et al., Fact Sheet, The Gender Wage Gap by Occupation 1 (Inst. for Women's Pol'y Res. 2012), *available at* http://www.iwpr.org/initiatives/pay-equity-and-discrimination. Women are also more than twice as likely as men to have jobs with median earnings lower than the federal poverty threshold for a family of four. *Id.* at 4.

127. JUDY GOLDBERG DEY & CATHERINE HILL, BEHIND THE PAY GAP 2 (2007), *available at* http://www.aauw.org/learn/research/upload/behindPayGap.pdf. Working mothers are far more likely than working fathers to take time off from their jobs when children are ill or when arrangements for child care falter. One study found that two-thirds of "highly educated, employed" women report taking time off to take a child to a doctor, while only 7 percent of their husbands had. KARINE MOE & DIANNA SHANDY, GLASS CEILINGS & 100-HOUR COUPLES: WHAT THE OPT-OUT PHENOMENON CAN TEACH US ABOUT WORK AND FAMILY 63 (2010) (citing study).

128. *See* ROSE & HARTMANN, *supra* note 122, at 26 ("The more years that children are present the more women have: fewer years in the paid labor force, more years with low working hours, and lower annual earnings when working.").

129. *See id.* at 21 ("[B]y the time women are starting families, it often 'makes economic sense' for the woman, typically the lower paid partner, to forego work and earnings to take care of the children especially given the lack of suitable alternative care arrangements."); Allen M. Parkman, *Bargaining Over Housework: The Frustrating Situation of Secondary Wage Earners,* 63 AM. J. ECON. & SOC. 765, 773 (2004), *available at* http://findarticles.com/p/articles/mi_mo254/is_4_63/ai_n7072367 ("While both parents are responsible for the care of their children, viewed incrementally the cost of child care has to be attributed to the employment of the secondary wage earner.").

130. *See* Parkman, *supra* note 129, at 772 (describing the range of economic advantages to a family if the primary wage earners remains in the labor force, rather than the secondary wage earner).

131. Public opinion on the pay gap issue also turns on perceptions of motherhood and fatherhood. While 41 percent in a 2005 national poll stated their belief that differences in men's and women's earnings are due to employer discrimination, an identical percentage opined that the gender gap in pay was the result of women's prioritizing family over work and manifesting a lower level of commitment to their careers. CATHERINE HILL & ELENA SILVA, PUBLIC PERCEPTIONS OF THE PAY GAP 3 (Am. Ass'n of University Women Educ. Found. 2005), *available at* http://www.aauw.org/files/2013/02/public-perceptions-of-the-pay-gap-briefing-paper.pdf ("More than half (56%) of Americans include employers' unwillingness to promote young women because they may leave when they have children as either the first (29%) or second (27%) most important reason for the pay gap."). Rose and Hartmann explained that a "perverse internal logic perpetuates a system with a rigid division of labor both in the workplace and in the home." ROSE & HARTMANN, *supra* note 122, at 33. Rose and Hartmann further explained,

> Employers may feel justified in discriminating against women workers if they think they will be less devoted to their jobs because of family responsibilities. They may structure jobs as part-time and dead-end for this reason and many women may accept them because they cannot find better-paying jobs. Labor market discrimination means lower earnings for women; women's low earnings mean women spend more time in family care; women's commitments to family care contribute to discrimination against them. Single mothers especially suffer as they must attempt to support their families on women's lower wage levels.

Id.

132. DEY & HILL, *supra* note 127, at 2.

133. *Id.*

134. Press Release, U.S. Census Bureau, Census Bureau Reports Families With Children Increasingly Face Unemployment (Jan. 15, 2010), *available at* http://www.census.gov/newsroom/releases/archives/families_households/cb10-08.html.

135. LANDIS, *supra* note 2, at 4.

136. BABER, *supra* note 1, at 173.

137. *Id.* at 174; *see also* LANDIS, *supra* note 2, at 275 (observing in 1955 that the birth of children resulted in far more difficult adjustments for women than for men); ROBERT F. WINCH, THE MODERN FAMILY 411 (rev. ed. 1963) (reporting the general view in the mid-1960s that "in the American family the wife-mother fulfills the role of bandaging up the skinned knees of her children and applying balm to the scarred psyches of her husband and children," whether or not she is employed outside the home).

138. JESSICA WEISS, TO HAVE AND TO HOLD: MARRIAGE, THE BABY BOOM, AND SOCIAL CHANGE 31 (2000).

139. Hartog, *supra* note 36; *see also* Elizabeth S. Scott, *Social Norms and the Legal Regulation of Marriage*, 86 VA. L. REV. 1901, 1934 (2000) ("The legal reinforcement of spousal commitment norms was accompanied by an equally powerful validation of hierarchical gender roles and differentiated legal enforcement of commitment obligations.").

140. DEY & HILL, *supra* note 127, at 3.

141. Scott, *supra* note 139, at 1937. Professor Scott adds that the allocation of roles by gender "reinforces women's dependency and, in subtle ways, perpetuates hierarchy in marriage." *Id*; *see also* Miller, *supra* note 115, at 6 ("Women are able to choose to work, although women with children must not allow their work lives to supercede their role as 'mothers' and experience significantly more work-family conflict than do working men.") (citations omitted).

142. ARLIE HOCHSCHILD & ANNE MACHUNG, THE SECOND SHIFT: WORKING PARENTS AND THE REVOLUTION AT HOME (1989); *see* Arlie Hochschild, *The Fractured Family*, AM. PROSPECT, June 23, 1991, *available at* http://www.prospect.org/cs/articles?article=the_fractured_family ("[W]e are living in a time of a stalled revolution, a time in which women have changed much faster than the men they live with or the institutions in which both sexes work. This has indeed marginalized family life and turned it into a 'second shift.'"); *Exactly How Much Housework Does a Husband Create?*, U. Mich. News Service, Apr. 3, 2008, *available at* http://www.ns.umich.edu/htdocs/releases/story.php?id=6452 ("'There's still a significant reallocation of labor that occurs at marriage—men tend to work more outside the home, while women take on more of the household labor . . . . And the situation gets worse for women when they have children.'") (quoting Institute for Social Research economist Frank Stafford, who directed a detailed study of housework trends).

143. HOCHSCHILD & MACHUNG, *supra* note 142, at 3.

144. Scott Coltrane, *Research on Household Labor: Modeling and Measuring the Social Embeddedness of Routine Family Work*, 62 J. MARRIAGE & FAM. 1208, 1208 (2000); *see also* Jeanne A. Batalova & Philip N. Cohen, *Premarital Cohabitation and Housework: Couples in Cross-National Perspective*, 64 JOURNAL OF MARRIAGE AND FAMILY 743–55, 746 (2002), http://www.bsos.umd.edu/socy/vanneman/socy699F/BatalovaCo2.pdf (noting that "despite men's greater contribution, women still do at least twice as much routine housework as men do"); SCOTT COLTRANE, FAMILY MAN: FATHERHOOD, HOUSEWORK, AND GENDER EQUITY 53 (1996) ("[T]he majority of men still make only minimal contributions to those tasks conventionally performed by housewives, such as cooking and cleaning.").

145. Coltrane, *supra* note 144, at 1208. *See also* Parkman, *supra* note 129, at 772 (suggesting that the grossly unequal division of household tasks in two-paycheck families may stem from the recognition by wives "that they are limited in their ability to reduce

their household activities if they want to keep their spouse happy in the marriage" and that "[a]s a result, they will increase their employment more than they reduce their domestic labor"); Vicki Schultz, *Life's Work*, 100 COLUM. L. REV. 1881, 1892–1919 (2000) (arguing that mass-cultural expectations that women be nurturing wives, mothers, and daughters shape women's and society's notion of women as "inauthentic workers"). *But see* Naomi R. Cahn, *Gendered Identities: Women and Household Work*, 44 VILL. L. REV. 525, 526–28 (1999) (arguing that pursuing the domestic tasks expected of them has afforded women a "household power base").

146. Researchers have pointed to several signs of gender shift within couples since the 1960s.

> [T]here has been a growing convergence in the hours that both women and men spend in the broad categories of paid work, family work and leisure. Women's paid work time has significantly increased, while that of men has decreased. Correspondingly, women's time devoted to housework has decreased, while the time men spend in family work of all kinds has increased.

Oriel Sullivan & Scott Coltrane, Men's Changing Contribution to Housework and Childcare, Discussion Paper Prepared for the 11th Annual Conference of the Council on Contemporary Families (Apr. 2008), *available at* http://www.contemporaryfamilies.org/marriage-partnership-divorce/menchange.html (citations omitted). However, one researcher pointed to "invisible" household work as exposing the extremely uneven progress in sharing domestic labor.

> When it comes to responsibility for less "visible" aspects of housework than chores or child care, the gender divide remains large in most families. Women still tend to do the "emotional labor," noticing when things need to be discussed or resolved. They also do most of the "household management" planning, buying presents for birthday parties a child will be attending, scheduling doctor appointments, and marking things that must be done on the calendar on the refrigerator door. Finally, women still tend to do the "kin work," calling relatives, arranging for holiday gatherings, sending holiday cards and so on. Until men begin to take responsibility for invisible household work, women will continue to shoulder more family work, and therefore to face more constraints in their freedom to engage in paid work.

Id. (quoting Pamela J. Smock).

147. Sullivan & Coltrane, *supra* note 146.

148. Jennifer L. Hook, *Care in Context: Men's Unpaid Work in 20 Countries, 1965–2003*, 71 AM. SOC. REV. 639, 650 fig.1 (2006).

149. *See Exactly How Much Housework*, *supra* note 142 (reporting on research).

150. *Id.* The study also found that having a husband created an additional seven hours

a week of housework for women, while having a wife reduced men's housework by approximately one hour. *Id.*

151. *See* Benedict Carey, *Families' Every Fuss, Archived and Analyzed*, N.Y. TIMES, May 22, 2010, *available at* http://www.nytimes.com/2010/05/23/science/23family.html (describing the UCLA study).

152. *See* Crain, *supra* note 115, at 1879 ("While men and women generally agree that the trend toward sharing the breadwinner role and renegotiating caretaking roles in the family sphere has enriched both sexes, many also feel that today's gender-neutral ideal of having it all—a happy marriage, family, and a successful career—is unattainable.").

153. GALINSKY ET AL., *supra* note 119, at 9.

154. *Id.* at 11.

155. DEY & HILL, *supra* note , at 3.

156. *Id.*

157. Carey, *supra* note 151 (quoting Kathleen Christensen of the Alfred P. Sloan Foundation).

158. Batalova & Cohen, *supra* note 144, at 744 (citing studies that show that "[c]ohabitors are less likely than married people to adhere to traditional gender ideology . . . and tend to value more individual freedom within marriage"); Miller, *supra* note 115, 2 ("Cohabitors have fairly egalitarian household divisions of labor . . .").

159. Batalova & Cohen, *supra* note 144, at 746.

160. *Id.* at 753.

161. Catie Walker-O'Neal & Ted G. Futris, *Cohabiting Couples' Gender Role Attitudes, Communication, and Relationship Well-Being*, FAMILY SCIENCE REVIEW, January 2011, 42–56, at 42, *available at* http://familyscienceassociation.org/FSR16_1_2011.php.

162. Sondra E. Solomon et al., *Money, Housework, Sex, and Conflict: Same-Sex Couples in Civil Unions, Those Not in Civil Unions, and Heterosexual Married Siblings*, 52 SEX ROLES 561–75, 562 (2005), http://www.springerlink.com/content/k380613322576573/fulltext.pdf.

163. *Id.* at 566–68. A major article reviewing new scholarship on lesbian, gay, bisexual, and transgender families in 2010 found that coparenting lesbian couples have "high levels of shared employment, decision making, parenting, and family work, in part in the service of an egalitarian ideology." Timothy J. Biblarz & Evren Savci, *Lesbian, Gay, Bisexual, and Transgender Families*, 72 J. OF MARRIAGE AND FAM. 480–97, 481 (2010).

164. Solomon et al., *supra* note 162, at 562, 568–70; *see* Mally Shechory & Riva Ziv, *Relationships between Gender Role Attitudes, Role Division, and Perception of Equity among Heterosexual, Gay, and Lesbian Couples*, 56 SEX ROLES 629–38, 635 (2007), *available at* http://www.springerlink.com/content/865q4637j25346gr/fulltext.pdf (finding that "same-sex couples had more liberal attitudes toward gender roles than heterosexual couples did"); Tara Parker-Pope, *Gay Unions Shed Light on Gender in Marriage*, N.Y. TIMES, June 10, 2008, *available at* http://www.nytimes.com/2008/06/10/health/10well.html (citing studies finding that "same-sex relationships, whether between men or women, were far more egalitarian than heterosexual ones").

165. L.B. Silverstein et al., *Contemporary Fathers Reconstructing Masculinity: Clinical Implications of Gender Role Strain*, 33 PROFESSIONAL PSYCHOLOGY: RESEARCH AND PRACTICE 361–69 (2002) (noting that individual choice, aptitude, and equity, rather than gender, were the key factors in the division of labor in their sample of families with gay cofathers). Another study found that gay male couples "did not have the usual hierarchy that values paid work over homemaking; in fact, paid work was seen as a compromise that took the working partners away from spending time with their children." Biblarz & Savci, *supra* note 163, at 487 (citing Judith Stacey, *Cruising to Familyland: Gay Hypergamy and Rainbow Kinship*, 52 CURRENT SOCIOLOGY 181–97 (2004)).

166. Charlotte J. Patterson, *Family Relationships of Lesbians and Gay Men*, 62 J. MARRIAGE & FAM. 1052–69 (2000), *available at* http://people.virginia.edu/~cjp/articles/poo.pdf, at 1054. *See also* Mark Bliss, *A Look at Gender Roles in Gay Relationships*, Examiner.com (May 31, 2010), http://www.examiner.com/gay-relationship-in-baltimore/a-look-at-gender-roles-gay-relationships: "The truth is, gender roles are quite rare with homosexual couples. . . . There is a common misconception that within a gay male relationship, one of the pair is the "man", and the other is the "woman". This has a lot to do with learned gender roles among the heterosexual community that there has to be a male role and a female role to make a relationship function."

167. Patterson, *supra* note 166, at 1053. A 2010 study of Australian same-sex parents echoed the findings that these couples divided household tasks "significantly more equally than heterosexual parents." The study concluded that "[f]or many same-sex couples, major decisions around who gives up paid work and how many hours parents choose to work, as well as decisions around work/family balance, are negotiated on the basis of couple's preferences and circumstance rather than an assumption that one parent will be the primary child carer." Amaryll Perlesz et al., *Organising Work and Home in Same-Sex Parented Families: Findings from the Work Love Play Study*, 31 AUSTRALIAN & NEW ZEALAND J. FAM. THERAPY 374–91 (2010), *available at* http://www.academia.edu/1416598/Organising_work_and_home_in_same-sex_parented_families_findings_from_the_work_love_play_study.

Chapter 3: Luxury Goods

1. Paul R. Amato, *The Impact of Family Formation Change on the Cognitive, Social, and Emotional Well-Being of the Next Generation*, 15 MARRIAGE AND CHILD WELL-BEING 87 (2005).

2. STEPHANIE J. VENTURA, CHANGING PATTERNS OF NONMARITAL CHILDBEARING IN THE UNITED STATES (Centers for Disease Control and Prevention 2009), *available at* http://www.cdc.gov/nchs/data/databriefs/db18.pdf.

3. R.K. Raley, *Increasing Fertility in Cohabiting Unions: Evidence for a Second Demographic Transition in the United States?* 38 DEMOGRAPHY 59–66 (2001).

4. PAUL R. AMATO ET AL., ALONE TOGETHER 22–23 (2007).

5. Wendy D. Manning et al., *The Relative Stability of Cohabiting and Marital Unions for Children*, 23 POP. RES. & POL. REV. 137 (2004).

6. R. K. Raley & Elizabeth Wildsmith, *Cohabitation and Children's Family Instability*, 66 J. MARRIAGE & FAM. 210 (2004).

7. Jay D. Teachman, *Diversity of Family Structure: Economic and Social Influences*, in HANDBOOK OF FAMILY DIVERSITY 53 (David H. Demo et al. eds., 2000).

8. Barbara D. Whitehead, *Dan Quayle Was Right*, ATLANTIC MONTHLY, Apr. 1993, at 47.

9. *Id.*

10. ALL OUR FAMILIES 2 (Mary Ann Mason et al. eds., 1998).

11. AMATO ET AL., *supra* note 4, at 26.

12. ANDREW CHERLIN, THE MARRIAGE-GO-ROUND 9 (2009).

13. STEPHANIE COONTZ, MARRIAGE, A HISTORY: FROM OBEDIENCE TO INTIMACY, OR HOW LOVE CONQUERED MARRIAGE 23 (2005).

14. U. S. DEP'T OF LABOR, OFFICE OF THE ASSISTANT SECRETARY FOR ADMINISTRATION AND MANAGEMENT, THE NEGRO FAMILY: THE CASE FOR NATIONAL ACTION, *available at* http://www.dol.gov/oasam/programs/history/webid-meynihan.htm.

15. *Id.*

16. WILLIAM RYAN, BLAMING THE VICTIM (1971).

17. Douglas S. Massey & Robert J. Sampson, *Moynihan Redux: Legacies and Lessons*, 621 ANNALS A. ACAD. POL. & SOC. SCI. 9 (2009).

18. *Id.* at 13.

19. *Id.* at 15.

20. WHEN MARRIAGE DISAPPEARS: THE RETREAT FROM MARRIAGE IN MIDDLE AMERICA 58 (W. Bradford Wilcox ed., The National Marriage Project, University of Virginia 2010), *available at* http://stateofourunions.org/2010/when-marriage-disappears.php.

21. SEAN F. REARDON & KENDRA BISCHOFF, GROWTH IN THE RESIDENTIAL SEGREGATION OF FAMILIES BY INCOME, 1970-2009 (US2010 Project, Russell Sage Foundation & Brown University 2011), *available at* http://graphics8.nytimes.com/packages/pdf/national/RussellSageIncomeSegregationreport.pdf.

22. *Id.* at 11.

23. *Id.*

24. Sabrina Tavernise, *Middle-Class Areas Shrink as Income Gap Grows, New Report Finds*, N.Y. TIMES, Nov. 15, 2011, *available at* http://www.nytimes.com/2011/11/16/us/middle-class-areas-shrink-as-income-gap-grows-report-finds.html.

25. WHEN MARRIAGE DISAPPEARS, *supra* note 20, at ix.

26. *Id.* at 26.

27. Pamela Paul, *How Divorce Lost Its Groove*, N.Y. TIMES, June 19, 2011.

28. WHEN MARRIAGE DISAPPEARS, *supra* note 20, at 19.

29. *Id.* at 22–24.

30. Sabrina Tavernise and Robert Gebeloff, *Once Rare in Rural America, Divorce Is Changing the Face of Its Families*, N.Y. TIMES, Mar 23, 2011, *available at* http://www.nytimes.com/2011/03/24/us/24divorce.html.

31. *Id.*

32. Paul, *supra* note 27.

33. *Id.*, quoting Stephanie Dolgoff.

34. *Id.* at 53.

35. WHEN MARRIAGE DISAPPEARS, *supra* note 20, at 26.

36. BEATRICE GOTTLIEB, THE FAMILY IN THE WESTERN WORLD 269 (1993).

37. COONTZ, *supra* note 13, at 111.

38. *Id.*

39. *Id.* at 112.

40. *Id.* at 147.

41. Steven Mintz, *The Social and Cultural Construction of American Childhood*, in HANDBOOK OF CONTEMPORARY FAMILIES 47 (Marilyn Coleman & Lawrence H. Ganong eds., 2004).

42. *Id.*

43. CHERLIN, *supra* note 12, at 67.

44. *Id.*

45. COONTZ, *supra* note 13, at 110–11.

46. *Id.* at 153.

47. *Id.*

48. GOTTLIEB, *supra* note 36, at 270.

49. *Id.*

50. CHERLIN, *supra* note 12, at 83.

51. COONTZ, *supra* note 13, at 202.

52. *Id.* at 203.

53. *See generally* ERNEST W. BURGESS ET AL., THE FAMILY: FROM INSTITUTION TO COMPANIONSHIP (1963). The term may have originated with Judge Ben Lindsey. *See* BEN B. LINDSEY & WAINWRIGHT EVANS, THE COMPANIONATE MARRIAGE (1927).

54. AMATO ET AL., *supra* note 4, at 14.

55. COONTZ, *supra* note 13, at 252 (emphasis in original).

56. CHERLIN, *supra* note 12, at 82.

57. *Id.* at 93.

58. COONTZ, *supra* note 13, at 268.

59. CHERLIN, *supra* note 12, at 4.

60. PEW RESEARCH CENTER, THE DECLINE OF MARRIAGE AND RISE OF NEW FAMILIES 21 (2010), *available at* http://pewresearch.org/pubs/1802/decline-marriage-rise-new-families. The survey results are from a poll conducted by Pew Research Center, in association with *Time* magazine, on October 1–21, 2010.

61. CHERLIN, *supra* note 12, at 188.

62. AMATO ET AL., *supra* note 4, at 16.

63. CHERLIN, *supra* note 12, at 188.
64. Betsey Stevenson & Justin Wolfers, *Marriage and the Market*, CATO UNBOUND (Jan. 18, 2008), http://www.cato-unbound.org/2008/01/18/betsey-stevenson-and-justin-wolfers/marriage-and-the-market/.
65. WHEN MARRIAGE DISAPPEARS, *supra* note 20, at 28, 38.
66. COONTZ, *supra* note 13, at 278.
67. *Id.* at 276.
68. LINDA WAITE & MAGGIE GALLAGHER, THE CASE FOR MARRIAGE (2000).
69. *Id.* at 113.
70. *Id.* at 74.
71. Ambrose Bierce, *The Devil's Dictionary*, in THE COLLECTED WRITINGS OF AMBROSE BIERCE (1946).
72. JAMES Q. WILSON, THE MARRIAGE QUESTION 38 (2002).
73. DAVID POPENOE, COHABITATION, MARRIAGE, AND CHILD WELLBEING 12 (National Marriage Project 2008), *available at* http://www.virginia.edu/marriageproject/specialreports.html.
74. COONTZ, *supra* note 13, at 309-10.
75. WAITE & GALLAGHER, *supra* note 68, at 183.
76. CHERLIN, *supra* note 12, at 162.
77. Quoted in COONTZ, *supra* note 13, at 289.
78. WAITE & GALLAGHER, *supra* note 68, at 46.
79. Quoted in WAITE & GALLAGHER, *supra* note 68, at 39.
80. CHERLIN, *supra* note 12, at 138.
81. WAITE & GALLAGHER, *supra* note 68, at 63.
82. Robin Fretwell Wilson, *Evaluating Marriage: Does Marriage Matter to the Nurturing of Children?*, 42 SAN DIEGO L. REV. 872 (2005).
83. Judith A. Seltzer, *Cohabitation and Family Change*, in HANDBOOK OF CONTEMPORARY FAMILIES, *supra* note 41, at 63.
84. Anne Reneflot, *A Gender Perspective on Preferences for Marriage among Cohabitating Couples* 15 DEMOGRAPHIC RESEARCH 315 (2006), *available at* http://www.demographic-research.org/volumes/vol15/10/.
85. *Id.*
86. *Id.*
87. Philip Cowan & Carolyn Pape Cowan, *New Families: Modern Couples as New Pioneers*, in ALL OUR FAMILIES, *supra* note 10, at 172. *See generally* ARLIE HOCHSCHILD, THE SECOND SHIFT (1989).
88. JERRY A. JACOBS & KATHLEEN GERSON, THE TIME DIVIDE 53 (2004).
89. AMATO ET AL., *supra* note 4, at 166.
90. WAITE & GALLAGHER, *supra* note 68, at 26.
91. CHERLIN, *supra* note 12, at 190.
92. AMATO ET AL., *supra* note 4, at 173.
93. *Id.*
94. POPENOE, *supra* note 73, at 13.

95. Sam Roberts, *Study Finds Cohabitation Doesn't Make a Union Last*, N.Y. TIMES, Mar. 2, 2010, quoting Professor Kelly A. Musick.
96. KATHRYN EDIN & MARIA KEFALAS, PROMISES I CAN KEEP 136 (2005).
97. *Id.*
98. *Id.*
99. CHERLIN, *supra* note 12, at 142.
100. *Id.* (emphasis in original).
101. Roberts, *supra* note 95.
102. POPENOE, *supra* note 73, at 14.
103. *Id.*
104. *Id.*
105. WAITE & GALLAGHER, *supra* note 68, at 183.
106. Roberts, *supra* note 95.
107. Meg Jay, *The Downside of Cohabiting before Marriage*, N.Y. TIMES, Apr. 15, 2012.
108. *Id.*
109. David Popenoe, *The Roots of Declining Social Virtue: Family, Community, and the Need for a "Natural Communities Policy," in* SEEDBEDS OF VIRTUE 76 (Mary Ann Glendon & David Blankenhorn eds., 1995)
110. Tamar Lewin, *Census Finds Single Mothers and Live-in Partners*, N.Y. TIMES, Nov. 5, 2010.
111. Manning et al., *supra* note 5, at 137.
112. Wilson, *supra* note 82, at 852–53.
113. Amato, *supra* note 1, at 78.
114. Teachman, *supra* note 7, at 54.
115. E. Mavis Hetherington & Margaret Stanley-Hagan, *Diversity among Stepfamilies, in* HANDBOOK OF FAMILY DIVERSITY, *supra* note 7, at 173.
116. Wilson, *supra* note 82, at 859.
117. Wendy D. Manning & Kathleen A. Lamb, *Adolescent Well-Being in Cohabiting, Married, and Single Parent Families*, 65 J. MARRIAGE & FAM. 886 (2003).
118. Paula Fomby & Andrew Cherlin, *Family Instability and Child Well-Being*, 77 AM. SOC. REV. 182 (Apr. 2007).
119. Raley & Wildsmith, *supra* note 6, at 211.
120. Fomby & Cherlin, *supra* note 118, at 183.
121. Judith Wallerstein, *Children of Divorce, in* ALL OUR FAMILIES, *supra* note 10, at 79.
122. *Id.* at 73.
123. *Id.* at 71.
124. *Id.* at 75.
125. Roni Caryn Rabin, *Sons of Divorce Fare Worse than Daughters*, N.Y. TIMES, Jan. 25, 2011.
126. Amato, *supra* note 1, at 80.
127. *Id.*
128. *Id.*

129. *Id.*
130. *Id.*
131. AMATO ET AL., *supra* note 4, at 23.
132. Amato, *supra* note 1, at 83–84.
133. *Id.* at 84.
134. *Id.*
135. POPENOE, *supra* note 73, at 15.
136. Manning et al., *supra* note 5, at 153.
137. Stephen D. Sugarman, *Single-Parent Families, in* ALL OUR FAMILIES, *supra* note 10, at 25.
138. Michele T. Martin et al., *Single-Parent Families, in* HANDBOOK OF CONTEMPORARY FAMILIES, *supra* note 41, at 289.
139. *Id.*
140. Raley and Wildsmith, *supra* note 6, at 211.
141. *Id.* at 291.
142. *Id.*
143. *Id.* at 212.
144. *Id.*
145. Martin et al., *supra* note 138, at 62.
146. Manning et al., *supra* note 5, at 140.
147. *Id.* at 141.
148. Martin et al., *supra* note 138, at 64.
149. Manning et al., *supra* note 5, at 141.
150. *Id.*
151. *Id.*
152. Wilson, *supra* note 82, at 873.
153. Manning et al., *supra* note 5, at 152.
154. *Id.*
155. Raley & Wildsmith, *supra* note 6, at 210.
156. Susan L. Brown, *Family Structure Transition and Adolescent Well-Being*, 43 DEMOGRAPHY 449 (2006).
157. WAITE & GALLAGHER, *supra* note 68, at 38.
158. *Id.*
159. MATTHEW D. BRAMLETT & WILLIAM D. MOSHER, COHABITATION, MARRIAGE, DIVORCE, AND REMARRIAGE IN THE UNITED STATES (National Center for Health Statistics, Vital Health Stat 23 (2002)), *available at* http://www.ezjustice.com/topical_material/new%20cdc%20divorce%20study.pdf.
160. Mary Ann Mason, *The Modern American Stepfamily: Problems and Possibilities, in* ALL OUR FAMILIES, *supra* note 10, at 99.
161. AMATO ET AL., *supra* note 4, at 23–24.
162. Raley & Wildsmith, *supra* note 6, at 211–12.
163. *Id.* at 214.
164. Amato, *supra* note 1, at 81.

165. *Id.*
166. *Id.*
167. Kay Pasley & Brad Moorefield, *Stepfamilies, in* HANDBOOK OF CONTEMPORARY FAMILIES, *supra* note 41, at 320.
168. WAITE & GALLAGHER, *supra* note 68, at 38.
169. Manning & Lamb, *supra* note 117, at 890.
170. Brown, *supra* note 156, at 458.
171. Raley & Wildsmith, *supra* note 6, at 218.
172. Manning & Lamb, *supra* note 117, at 890.
173. Mason, *supra* note 160, at 95.
174. *Id.*
175. *Id.*
176. Cynthia Grant Bowman, *The Legal Relationship between Cohabitants and Their Partners' Children*, 13 THEORETICAL INQUIRIES 127, 135 (2012).
177. *See, e.g.,* CAL. FAM. CODE § 3101 (granting reasonable visitation to stepparent if determined to be in child's best interests); KAN. STAT. ANN. § 60-1616(b) (providing visitation rights to grandparents and stepparents).
178. *See, e.g.,* OR. REV. STAT. §§ 107.105(1)(b), 109.119 (granting standing to third parties "who have established emotional ties creating a parent-like relationship" if visitation is in the child's best interests); VA. CODE. ANN. § 20-124.1 ("person with a legitimate interest" may petition for visitation.)
179. Bowman, *supra* note 176, at 140.
180. *Id.* at 144; Robinson v. Ford-Robinson, 208 S.W.3d 140, 143 (Ark. 2005).
181. *See, e.g.,* Multari v. Sorrell, 287 A.D.2d 764, 766 (N.Y. App. 2001) (equitable estoppel is not available to provide standing to seek visitation for live-in paramour who developed a six-year "fatherly" relationship with child, since petitioner was a biological stranger to the child and since the child already had an operative parental relationship); *In re* Marriage of Freel, 448 N.W.2d 26, 28 (Iowa 1989) (no visitation rights are available to a woman who lived with the child and his father for five years and established a de facto mother-child relationship; visitation rights are limited to noncustodial spouses and grandparents).
182. Margaret Mahoney, *Stepparents as Third Parties in Relation to Their Stepchildren*, 40 FAM. L.Q. 81, 86 (2006).
183. Wilson, *supra* note 82, at 875.
184. *Id.*
185. WAITE & GALLAGHER, *supra* note 68, at 139.
186. Martin et al., *supra* note 138, at 285.
187. Steven Mintz, *supra* note 41, at 49.
188. *Id.*
189. *Id.*
190. *Id.* at 50.
191. Stephanie Coontz & Donna Franklin, *When the Marriage Penalty Is Marriage*, N.Y. TIMES, Oct. 28, 1997.
192. PEW RESEARCH CENTER, *supra* note 60, at 11.

Chapter 4: The Children of Baby M

1. Elizabeth Scott, *Surrogacy and the Politics of Commodification*, 72 LAW & CONTEMP. PROBS. 113 (2009).
2. *In re* Baby M, 537 A.2d 1227 (N.J. 1988).
3. *Id.* at 1234.
4. *Id.* at 1250.
5. Scott, *supra* note 1, at 116.
6. *Id.* at 112.
7. *Id.*
8. *Id.* at 145.
9. A.G.R. v. D.R.H. & S.H., No. FD-09-1838-7 (N.J. Super. Ct. Ch. Div. Dec. 23, 2009), *available at* http://pub.bna.com/fl/09183807.pdf.
10. *Id.* at 5–6.
11. *Id.* at 5.
12. *See* Crystal Phend, *Rapid Increase Seen in Assisted Reproduction*, MedPage Today (May 28, 2009), http://www.medpagetoday.com/OBGYN/Infertility/14405 (reporting a 25.6 percent jump in the number of ART cycles performed worldwide from 2000 to 2002).
13. DAVID M. SMITH & GARY J. GATES, GAY AND LESBIAN FAMILIES IN THE UNITED STATES: SAME-SEX UNMARRIED PARTNER HOUSEHOLDS 1 (Human Rights Campaign, 2001), *available at* http://www.urban.org/UploadedPDF/1000491_gl_partner_households.pdf.
14. JOYCE A. MARTIN ET AL., BIRTHS: FINAL DATA FOR 2005, at 8 (Nat'l Vital Stat. Rep., Vol. 56, No. 5, 2007), *available at* http://www.cdc.gov/nchs/data/nvsr/nvsr56/nvsr56_06.pdf.
15. *Id.*
16. Bruce L. Wilder, *Assisted Reproduction Technology: Trends and Suggestions for the Developing Law*, 18 J. AM. ACAD. MATRIMONIAL LAW 177, 195 (2002).
17. Dena Moyal & Carolyn Shelley, *Future Child's Rights in New Reproductive Technology: Thinking Outside the Tube and Maintaining the Connections*, 48 FAM. CT. REV. 431, 433 (2010).
18. CHARLES P. KINDREGAN & MAUREEN MCBRIEN, ASSISTED REPRODUCTIVE TECHNOLOGY 93 (2006).
19. Blew v. Verta, 617 A.2d 31, 36 (Pa. Super. 1992).
20. *See* M. Celeste Schejbal-Vossmeyer, *What Money Cannot Buy: Commercial Surrogacy and the Doctrine of Illegal Contracts*, 32 ST. LOUIS U. L.J. 1171 (1988). The Michigan Court of Appeals has held that the right to privacy protects the decision to bear and beget a child but that it does not preclude the state from interfering in the contractual arrangement entailed in surrogacy. *Id.* at 1175. The Kentucky Supreme Court has similarly held surrogacy contracts voidable under the state's adoption consent statutes. *Id.* at 117.
21. *See* Stephanie Saul, *Building a Baby, with Few Ground Rules*, N.Y. TIMES, Dec. 13, 2009, at 1.

22. *Id.*

23. June Carbone & Naomi Cahn, *Which Ties Bind? Redefining the Parent-Child Relationship in an Age of Genetic Certainty,* 11 WM. & MARY BILL RTS. J. 1011, 1025 (2003).

24. Katherine Drabiak et al., *Ethics, Law, and Commercial Surrogacy: A Call for Uniformity,* 35 J.L. MED. & ETHICS 300, 301 (2007).

25. *In re* Baby M, 527 A.2d 1227, 1249 (N.J. 1987).

26. Susan Frelich Appleton, *Adoption in the Age of Reproductive Technology,* 2004 U. CHI. LEGAL FORUM 393, 425 (2004).

27. Martha M. Ertman, *What's Wrong with a Parenthood Market? A New and Improved Theory of Commodification,* 82 N.C. L. REV. 1, 10 (2003).

28. *Id.*

29. LIZA MUNDY, EVERYTHING CONCEIVABLE: HOW ASSISTED REPRODUCTION IS CHANGING MEN, WOMEN, AND THE WORLD 101 (2007).

30. Ertman, *supra* note 27, at 7.

31. J. Herbie DiFonzo & Ruth C. Stern, *The Winding Road from Form to Function: A Brief History of Contemporary Marriage,* 21 J. AM. ACAD. MATRIMONIAL L. 1, 3 (2008).

32. Appleton, *supra* note 26, at 403 (citing ELAINE TYLER MAY, BARREN IN THE PROMISED LAND 127 (1997)).

33. *Id.* at 405–6.

34. *Id.* at 406.

35. MUNDY, *supra* note 29, at 46.

36. Saul, *supra* note 21, at 47.

37. *See* MUNDY, *supra* note 29, at 47.

38. Appleton, *supra,* note 26 , at 428–29.

39. *Id.* at 401.

40. *Id.* at 432.

41. MUNDY, *supra* note 29 , at 10.

42. *Id.* at 11.

43. *Id.*

44. *See* Paula L. Ettelbrick, *Who Is a Parent? The Need to Develop a Lesbian Conscious Family Law,* 10 N.Y.L. SCH. J. HUM. RTS. 513, 516–17 (1993). This issue is extensively discussed in chapter 5.

45. S. Marina et al., *Sharing Motherhood: Biological Lesbian Co-Mothers, a New IVF Indication,* 25 HUM. REPROD. 938, 939 (2010), *available at* http://humrep.oxfordjournals.org/content/25/4/938.full.pdf.

46. *Id.*

47. *Id.* at 940.

48. Hal B. Levine, *Gestational Surrogacy; Nature and Culture in Kinship,* 42 ETHNOLOGY 173, 175 (2003).

49. Appleton, *supra* note 26, at 443.

50. MUNDY, *supra* note 29, at 13.

51. BRADY E. HAMILTON ET AL., BIRTHS: PRELIMINARY DATA FOR 2007, at 3,

13 tbl.7 (Nat'l Vital Stat. Rep., Vol. 57, No. 12, 2009), *available at* http://www.cdc.gov/nchs/data/nvsr/nvsr57/nvsr57_12.pdf.

52. MUNDY, *supra* note 29, at 157.

53. *Id.*

54. *Id.*

55. Lori Gottlieb, *The XY Files*, ATLANTIC MONTHLY, Sept. 2005, at 149–50, *available at* http://www.theatlantic.com/magazine/archive/2005/09/the-xy-files/4172/.

56. *Id.* at 144.

57. *Id.*

58. *Id.* at 141.

59. *Id.* at 143.

60. *Id.*

61. *Id.* at 150.

62. Katie Cottingham, *Fact or Fiction: Artificial Reproductive Technologies Make Sick Kids*, SCI. AM., Jul. 1, 2010, *available at* http://www.scientificamerican.com/article.cfm?id=artificial-reproductive-tech-kids.

63. Chitose Suzuki, *Researchers: Most "Test Tube" Kids Are Healthy*, USA TODAY, Feb. 22, 2010, *available at* http://www.usatoday.com/news/health/2010-2-22-test-tube-babies_N.htm (last visited Aug. 5, 2011).

64. Dina Kraft, *Where Families Are Prized, Help Is Free*, N.Y. TIMES, Jul. 17, 2011.

65. *Id.*

66. ELIZABETH MARQUARDT ET AL., MY DADDY'S NAME IS DONOR 5 (2010), *available at* http://www.familyscholars.org/assets/Donor_FINAL.pdf.

67. *Id.* at 15–16.

68. *Id.* at 16.

69. *Id.*

70. Scott, *supra* note 1, at 136.

71. *See* MARQUARDT ET AL., *supra* note 66, at 21–25.

72. Levine, *supra* note 48, at 183.

73. MUNDY, *supra* note 29, at 94.

74. Levine, *supra* note 48, at 177.

75. Scott, *supra* note 1, at 125.

76. *Id.* at 117.

77. *In re* Baby M, 537 A.2d 1227, 1264 (N.J. 1988).

78. A.G.R. v. D.R.H. & S.H., No. FD-09-1838-7, at *3 (N.J. Super. Ct. Ch. Div. Dec. 23, 2009), *available at* http://pub.bna.com/fl/09183807.pdf. Although it was unclear whether an exchange of money was contemplated or carried out in connection with the surrogacy, the court stated that this point was unnecessary to its resolution of the case. *Id.* at *2–3.

79. *Id.* at *4.

80. Karen Busby & Delaney Vun, Revisiting the Handmaid's Tale: Feminist Theory Meets Empirical Research on Surrogate Mothers 8 (2009) (unpublished manuscript), *available at* http://claradoc.gpa.free.fr/doc/329.pdf.

81. Lorraine Ali & Raina Kelley, *The Curious Lives of Surrogates*, NEWSWEEK, Apr. 7, 2008, at 47.

82. Compare *In re* Baby M, 537 A.2d 1227, 1254–55 (N.J. 1988) (dismissing an equal protection claim by a sperm donor against Whitehead, the surrogate mother who used her own eggs to fertilize the pregnancy), with A.G.R., No. FD-09-1838-7, at *2 (noting that the surrogate mother, Robinson (A.G.R.), carried the fetus created by eggs donated by an unknown woman).

83. A.G.R., No. FD-09-1838-7, at *2.

84. *Id.*

85. *Id.* In December 2011, at the conclusion of a protracted custody struggle, the trial court awarded sole legal and primary physical custody of the twins to their father, Sean Hollingsworth. Angelia Robinson was awarded specified parenting time. Consistent with the court's earlier decision invalidating the surrogacy agreement, Donald Hollingsworth, the other intended father, has no formal rights with regard to the children. Because of his marriage to Sean, Donald is the twins' stepfather. Since he is the brother of the gestational mother, he is also their uncle. A.G.R. v. D.R.H., No. FD-09-01838-7 (N.J. Super. Ct. Ch. Div. Dec. 13, 2011).

86. *See* Scott, *supra* note 1, at 120–21.

87. Ali & Kelley, *supra* note 81, at 49.

88. Busby & Vun, *supra* note 80, at 40.

89. *Id.* at 14.

90. Scott, *supra* note 1, at 121.

91. *Id.*

92. Drabiak et al., *supra* note 24 , at 301.

93. Ertman, *supra* note 27, at 24.

94. *Id.*

95. Janet L. Dolgin, *Status and Contract in Surrogate Motherhood: An Illumination of the Surrogacy Debate*, 38 BUFF. L. REV. 515, 549 (1990).

96. Busby & Vun, *supra* note 80, at 27 (quoting Hazel Basilington, *The Social Organization of Surrogacy: Relinquishing a Baby and the Role of Payment in the Psychological Detachment Process*, 7 J. HEALTH PSYCHOL. 57, 61 (2002)).

97. *See, e.g.*, Levine, *supra* note 48, at 179.

98. Busby & Vun, *supra* note 80 , at 28.

99. Ali & Kelley, *supra* note 81, at 45.

100. *See* Levine, *supra* note 48, at 181.

101. Busby & Vun, *supra* note 80, at 18–20.

102. *Id.* at 19.

103. *Id.* at 22; *see generally* Ali & Kelley, *supra* note 81 (describing the lives of surrogates).

104. Busby & Vun, *supra* note 80, at 26.

105. Ali & Kelley, *supra* note 81, at 48.

106. *Id.*

107. *Id.* (quoting "Melissa Brisman, of New Jersey, a lawyer who specializes in reproductive and family issues, and heads the largest surrogacy firm on the East Coast.").

108. Busby & Vun, *supra* note 80, at 21.

109. *Id.*

110. *Id.* at 28.

111. *Id.* (citing HELÉNA RAGONÉ, SURROGATE MOTHERHOOD: CONCEPTION AT THE HEART 55 (1994)).

112. MUNDY, *supra* note 29, at 136.

113. Busby & Vun, *supra* note 80, at 31.

114. MUNDY, *supra* note 29, at 136.

115. Busby & Vun, *supra* note 80, at 32.

116. *Id.* at 39. In her interviews with surrogates, Mundy found that many women preferred to work with gay male couples. MUNDY, *supra* note 29, at 130–31. As one surrogate explained, "Infertile couples—surrogacy is their last choice. To them, every single part of this is just another hurdle to overcome. With a gay couple, it's their first choice. It's the way they get to have biological children, and they're thrilled." *Id.* at 135 (quoting Ann Nelson, a 29-year-old surrogate). Infertile couples undergoing IVF treatment may be subject to depression and anxiety as well as lowered self-esteem, poor marital communication, sexual dysfunction, and social isolation. Chun-Shin Hahn, *Review: Psychosocial Well-Being of Parents and Their Children Born after Assisted Reproduction*, 26 J. PEDIATRIC PSYCHOL. 525, 526 (2001).

117. *In re Baby M*, 537 A.2d 1227, 1248 (N.J. 1988).

118. Levine, *supra* note 48, at 176.

119. *Id.*

120. *Id.* at 177–78.

121. *Id.* at 177.

122. *Id.* at 178. A 2000 study of gestational surrogacy found that nearly a third of surrogates and intended parents do not share the same cultural, ethnic, and racial backgrounds. Busby & Vun, *supra* note 80, at 20. Some participants prefer to be matched with people of another race and ethnicity "because they believe that it would be less likely that the surrogate mother will feel a strong connection to a child who is different from her." *Id.* at 20–21.

123. Levine, *supra* note 48, at 178 (citing Heléna Ragoné, *Chasing the Blood-Tie: Surrogate Mothers, Adoptive Mothers, and Fathers*, 23 AM. ETHNOLOGIST 352, 352–65 (1996)).

124. *Id.*

125. Busby & Vun, *supra* note 80, at 29.

126. *Id.* at 38.

127. Levine, *supra* note 48, at 178.

128. *See id.* at 180.

129. *Id.*

130. *Id.* at 179–80.

131. *Id.*
132. *Id.* at 180.
133. Ali and Kelley, *supra* note 81, at 49.
134. *Id.* (quoting John Weltman, the president of Circle Surrogacy in Boston).
135. *In re* Baby M, 537 A.2d 1227, 1235 (N.J. 1988) ("We find no offense to our present laws where a woman voluntarily and without payment agrees to act as a 'surrogate' mother, provided that she is not subject to a binding agreement to surrender her child.").
136. Ertman, *supra* note 27, at 12.
137. Levine, *supra* note 48, at 181.
138. *See id.*; Ali & Kelley, *supra* note 81, at 48.
139. Dolgin, *supra* note 95, at 524.
140. *Id.*
141. *Id.*
142. Drabiak et al., *supra* note 24, at 305.
143. Ertman, *supra* note 27, at 17.
144. Drabiak et al., *supra* note 24, at 305.
145. *Id.* at 307.
146. *Id.* at 306.
147. *Id.*
148. *Id.* at 307.
149. *Id.* at 302.
150. Busby & Vun, *supra* note 80, at 52.
151. *Id.*
152. *See* Scott, *supra* note 1, at 109.
153. Busby & Vun, *supra* note 80, at 45.
154. *ART Report Section 5—ART Trends 1998–2007*, Ctrs. for Disease Control and Prevention (Jan. 13, 2010), http://www.cdc.gov/art/ART2007/section5.htm.
155. Josephine Marcotty & Chen May Yee, *Miracles for Sale*, MINNEAPOLIS STAR TRIBUNE, Oct. 21, 2007, at A1.
156. Jennifer Schneider, *It's Time for an Egg Donor Registry and Long-Term Follow-Up: Testimony at Congressional Briefing*, Ctr. for Genetics & Soc'y (Nov. 14, 2007), *available at* http://www.geneticsandsociety.org/article.php?id=3820.
157. Alison Motluk, *The Human Egg Trade: How Canada's Fertility Laws Are Failing Donors, Doctors, and Parents*, WALRUS (Apr. 2010), http://www.walrusmagazine.com/articles/2010.04-health-the-human-egg-trade/. The mean age of a mother at first birth increased nearly four years from 1970 to 2003. *See* MARTIN ET AL., *supra* note 14, at 2.
158. W. Kramer et al., *U.S. Oocyte Donors: A Retrospective Study of Medical and Psychosocial Issues*, 24 HUM. REPROD. 3144, 3144 (2009).
159. *Id.*
160. Schneider, *supra* note 156.
161. *See* MUNDY, *supra* note 29, at 133.
162. Schneider, *supra* note 156, at 180.

163. Michael Leahy, *Family Vacation,* WASH. POST (Jun. 19, 2005), *available at* http://www.washingtonpost.com/wp-dyn/content/article/2005/06/15/AR2005061501885.html (last visited Aug. 6, 2011).

164. Marcotty & Yee, *supra* note 155, at A18 (quoting Caitlin Karolczak, "an artist and antique dealer in Minneapolis" who has "been an egg donor twice").

165. Schneider, *supra* note 156.

166. Kramer et al., *supra* note 158, at 3146. Severe OHSS results in severe pain or swelling of the abdomen, decreased urination, and shortness of breath, necessitating hospitalization to drain excess fluids from the body. *Ovarian Hyperstimulation Syndrome,* MedlinePlus (Nov. 15, 2010), http://www.nlm.nih.gov/medlineplus/ency/article/00729 4.htm.

167. Kramer et al., *supra* note 158, at 3146.

168. *Id.* at 3148.

169. *Id.*

170. William Heisel, *Registry May Track Egg, Sperm Donors,* L.A. TIMES, Jan. 3, 2008, at B1.

171. *Id.*

172. Kramer et al., *supra* note 158, at 3147.

173. *Id.* at 3148.

174. *Id.* at 3147.

175. *Id.* at 3145.

176. *Id.*

177. *Id.* at 3148.

178. MUNDY, *supra* note 29, at 181.

179. *See* Heisel, *supra* note 170, at B1, B9.

180. *Id.* at B9.

181. MUNDY, *supra* note 29, at 191.

182. Ethics Comm. of the Am. Soc'y for Reprod. Med., *Interests, Obligations, and Rights of the Donor in Gamete Donation,* 91 FERTILITY & STERILITY 22, 22–23 (2009), *available at* http://www.asrm.org/uploadedFiles/ASRM_Content/News_and_Publications/Ethics_Committee_Reports_and_Statements/interests_obligations_rights_of_donor.pdf (last visited Aug. 6, 2011).

183. *Id.* at 22, 24–25.

184. *Id.* at 22.

185. Jennifer Schneider & Wendy Kramer, *Egg Donors Need Long-Term Follow-Up: Recommendations from a Retrospective Study of Oocyte Donors in the US,* IVF.net (Jan. 19, 2009), http://www.ivf.net/ivf/egg_donors_need_long_term_follow_up_recommendations_from_a_retrospective_study_of_oocyte_donors_in_the_us-o3950.html.

186. *Id.*

187. *Id.*

188. *In re* Baby M, 537 A.2d 1227, 1259 (N.J. 1988).

189. *Id.*

190. Rachel Dvoskin, *Newborns Can Bond to a "Mother" from a Different Species,* SCI. AM., Nov. 15, 2007, *available at* http://www.scientificamerican.com/article.cfm?id=strange-but-true-newborns-can-bond-to-mother-from-different-species.

191. *Id.*

192. *Id.*

193. Susan Golombok et al., *Surrogacy Families: Parental Functioning, Parent-Child Relationships, and Children's Psychological Development at Age 2,* 47 J. CHILD PSYCHOL. & PSYCHIATRY 213, 220 (2006).

194. *Id.* at 219.

195. *Id.* at 220.

196. *Id.* at 219.

197. Susan Golombok et al., *Families Created by the New Reproductive Technologies: Quality of Parenting and Social and Emotional Development of the Children,* 66 CHILD DEV. 285, 293 (1995).

198. Golombok et al., *supra* note 193, at 214.

199. Golombok et al., *supra* note 197, at 296.

200. *Id.*

201. Golombok et al., *supra* note 193, at 220.

202. Golombok et al., *supra* note 197, at 295.

203. Lutz Goldbeck et al., *Cognitive Development of Singletons Conceived by Intracytoplasmic Sperm Injection or In Vitro Fertilization at Age 5 and 10 Years,* 34 J. PEDIATRIC PSYCHOL. 774, 779 (2009).

204. *Id.* at 778.

205. *Id.* at 774.

206. *Id.* at 778.

207. C. Carson et al., *Cognitive Development Following ART: Effect of Choice of Comparison Group, Confounding and Mediating Factors,* 25 HUM. REPROD. 244, 247-48 (2010).

208. Hahn, *supra* note 116, at 530.

209. *Id.*

210. Shu-Hsin Lee et al., *Child Growth from Birth to 18 Months Old Born after Assisted Reproductive Technology,* 47 INT. J. NURSING STUD. 1159, 1164 (2010).

211. *Id.* at 1165.

212. Raymond D. Lambert, *Safety Issues in Assisted Reproductive Technology: Aetiology of Health Problems in Singleton ART Babies,* 18 HUM. REPROD. 1987, 1987 (2003).

213. Carrie Williams & Alastair Sutcliffe, *Infant Outcomes of Assisted Reproduction,* 85 EARLY HUM. DEV. 673, 675-76 (2009).

214. Susan M. Reid et al., *Cerebral Palsy and Assisted Reproductive Technologies: A Case-Control Study,* 52 DEV. MED. & CHILD NEUROLOGY 161, 165 (2009).

215. M. Bondulelle et al., *A Multi-Centre Cohort Study of the Physical Health of 5-Year-Old Children Conceived after Intracytoplasmic Sperm Injection, In Vitro Fertilization, and Natural Conception,* 20 HUM. REPROD. 413, 417-18 (2004).

216. Williams & Sutcliffe, *supra* note 213, at 675.

217. Michele Hansen et al., *Assisted Reproductive Technologies and the Risk of Birth Defects—a Systematic Review*, 20 HUM. REPROD. 328, 336 (2004); J. Reefhuis et al., *Assisted Reproduction Technology and Major Structural Birth Defects in the United States*, 24 HUM. REPROD. 360, 362–63 (2008).

218. Lambert, *supra* note 212, at 1988. Angelman syndrome may be associated with epilepsy and poor balance, while Beckwith-Weidemann syndrome is an overgrowth disorder. ANGELMAN SYNDROME GUIDELINE DEV. GROUP, MANAGEMENT OF ANGELMAN SYNDROME: A CLINICAL GUIDELINE 3 (2009); Lambert, *supra* note 212, at 1988. Epigenetic disorders result from genetic anomalies that do not actually alter DNA. John Cloud, *Why Your DNA Isn't Your Destiny*, TIME, Jan. 6, 2010, *available at* http://www.time.com/time/magazine/article/0,9171,1952313,00.html (last visited Aug. 6, 2011); Ethan Watters, *DNA Is Not Destiny*, DISCOVER, Nov. 2006, at 34, 36, *available at* http://discovermagazine.com/2006/nov/cover.

219. Williams & Sutcliffe, *supra* note 213, at 675. One study included a group of surrogate mothers, not infertile themselves, who were treated by IVF to carry the children of other couples. Michael Ludwig & Klaus Diedrich, *Follow-Up of Children Born after Assisted Reproductive Technologies*, 5 REPROD. BIOMED. ONLINE 317, 318 (2002). The children born to the surrogates appeared to have no increased risk of low birth weight, suggesting that it is the infertility and not the IVF procedure that contributes to higher rates of prematurity. *Id.*

220. Jeremy G. Thompson et al., *Epigenetic Risks Related to Assisted Reproductive Technologies*, 17 HUM. REPROD. 2783, 2783 (2002).

221. Bonduelle et al., *supra* note 215, at 418.

222. Nanette Garterell & Henry Bos, *U.S. National Longitudinal Lesbian Family Study: Psychological Adjustment of 17-Year-Old Adolescents*, 126 PEDIATRICS 1, 28, 33–34 (2010), *available at* http://pediatrics.aappublications.org/cgi/content/full/126/3/617-a.

223. *Id.* at 6–7.

224. Alice Park, *Study: Children of Lesbians May Do Better than Their Peers*, TIME, June 7, 2010, *available at* http://www.time.com/time/health/article/0,8599,1994480,00.html.

225. *See* MARQUARDT ET AL., *supra* note 66, at 5–6 (showing a summary of the study's findings).

226. *Id.* at 21.

227. *Id.*

228. *Id.* at 22.

229. *Id.* at 33–35.

230. *Id.* at 55–56.

231. *Id.* at 56.

232. *Id.* at 58.

233. *Id.*

234. *Id.* at 13.

235. *Id.*

236. *Id.*

237. *See id.* at 12–13 (showing the findings without explanation of the inconsistencies between them).

238. *Id.* at 11–12.

239. Susan Golombok et al., *The European Study of Assisted Reproduction Families: Family Functioning and Child Development*, 11 HUM. REPROD. 2324, 2324, 2329 (1996).

240. *Id.* at 2329.

241. *Id.*

242. Moyal & Shelley, *supra* note 17, at 435.

243. *Id.* at 437.

244. Ethics Comm. of the Am. Soc'y for Reprod. Med., *Informing Offspring of Their Conception by Gamete Donation*, 81 FERTILITY & STERILITY 527, 527 (2004).

245. *Id.* at 528.

246. Kirstin Mac Dougall et al., *Strategies for Disclosure: How Parents Approach Telling Their Children That They Were Conceived with Donor Gametes*, 87 FERTILITY & STERILITY 524, 525 (2007).

247. *Id.* at 526.

248. *Id.* at 526–31.

249. J. E. Scheib et al., *Adolescents with Open-Identity Sperm Donors: Reports from 12-17 Year Olds*, 20 HUM. REPROD. 239, 239 (2004).

250. *Id.* at 248.

251. Donor Sibling Registry, Educating, Connecting, and Supporting Families, http://www.donorsiblingregistry.com/ (last visited February 27, 2013).

252. *Id.*

253. Scheib et al., *supra* note 249, at 249.

254. Leahy, *supra* note 163.

255. *Id.*

256. Scheib et al., *supra* note 249, at 244.

257. Leahy, *supra* note 163.

258. *Id.*

259. MUNDY, *supra* note 29, at 168.

260. *See* PRACTICE COMMITTEE OF THE AMERICAN SOCIETY FOR REPRODUCTIVE MEDICINE AND PRACTICE COMMITTEE OF THE SOCIETY FOR ASSISTED REPRODUCTIVE TECHNOLOGY, 2006 GUIDELINES FOR GAMETE AND EMBRYO DONATION (2006), *available at* http://www.fpnc.com/pdfs/2006_Guidelines_GameteEmbryo Donation.pdf (suggesting limiting a donor to 25 births in a population of 800,000).

261. *See* Donor Sibling Registry, Viewing Registry, Fairfax Cryobank, http://www.donorsiblingregistry.com/members/ListRegistry.php?dpIdentityNumber=1476 (listing contact information for offspring of Fairfax Donor 1476); Children of Donor #1476, http://groups.yahoo.com/group/Donor1476/ (internet group for the parents of the children from Fairfax Donor #1476).

262. *See* Jacqueline Mroz, *One Sperm Donor, 150 Offspring*, N.Y. TIMES, Sept. 5, 2011, *available at* http://www.nytimes.com/2011/09/06/health/06donor.html?_r=1.

263. MUNDY, *supra* note 29, at 172.

Chapter 5: Parenthood in the 21st Century

1. Margaret M. Mahoney, *Forces Shaping the Law of Cohabitation for Opposite Sex Couples*, 7 J. L. & FAM. STUD. 135, 164 (2005). *See* Troxel v. Granville, 530 U.S. 57, 63 (2000) (plurality opinion) (noting that "[t]he demographic changes of the past century make it difficult to speak of an average American family"); Hofstad v. Christie, 240 P.3d 816, 820 (Wyo. 2010) ("Even if [the parties] are not married, nor related by blood, that they lived together on and off for approximately ten years, all the while sharing an intimate relationship which resulted in the birth of their twins is evidence that a family relationship exists."); J. Herbie DiFonzo & Ruth C. Stern, *The Winding Road from Form to Function: A Brief History of Contemporary Marriage*, 21 J. AM. ACAD. MATRIMONIAL L. 1, 38 (2008) ("The citadel of the biological/adoptive family has for some years been besieged by the burgeoning segment of nontraditional families."); Nancy E. Dowd, *Law, Culture, and Family: The Transformative Power of Culture and the Limits of Law*, 78 CHI.-KENT L. REV. 785, 789 (2003) ("Although our dominant legal norm is that family is a heterosexual, marital, biological unit, our social and cultural patterns expose a culture that is largely at odds with that nuclear, marital family norm.").

2. *See generally* Catherine DeLair, *Ethical, Moral, Economic and Legal Barriers to Assisted Reproductive Technologies Employed by Gay Men and Lesbian Women*, 4 DEPAUL J. HEALTH CARE L. 147, 162–73 (2000) (describing the legal system's assumptions about families). A minority of scholars believes that the norms of the prototypical 1950s marriage could still adequately shape contemporary families. *See, e.g.,* Daniel D. Polsby, *Ozzie and Harriet Had It Right*, 18 HARV. J.L. & PUB. POL'Y 531, 533 (1995) (arguing for the "superiority of the Ozzie-and-Harriet family"); Elizabeth S. Scott, *Social Norms and the Legal Regulation of Marriage*, 86 VA. L. REV. 1901, 1964 (2000) (noting that "many modern religious and cultural conservatives would like to return to an earlier era of both stable marriage and patriarchal gender roles.").

3. N.A.H. v. S.L.S., 9 P.3d 354, 359 (Colo. 2000).

4. Katherine R. Allen et al., *An Overview of Family Diversity: Controversies, Questions, and Values, in* HANDBOOK OF FAMILY DIVERSITY 1 (David H. Demo et al. eds., 2000); *see also id.* ("The key elements are "socioemotional ties and enduring responsibilities, particularly in terms of one or more members' dependence on others for support and nurturance."); CAROL B. STACK, ALL OUR KIN: STRATEGIES FOR SURVIVAL IN A BLACK COMMUNITY 31 (1996) (viewing a family as "the smallest, organized, durable network of kin and non-kin who interact daily, providing domestic needs of children and assuring their survival"); Marjorie Maguire Shultz, *Legislative Regulation of Surrogacy and Reproductive Technology*, 28 U.S.F. L. REV. 613, 618 (1994) ("Intention and biology are often mutually reinforcing in family design. When they are not, I would have the law prioritize intention and deliberative commitment over genes and gendered reproductive function.").

5. V.C. v. M.J.B., 748 A.2d 539, 556–57 (N.J. 2000) (Long, J., concurring) (quoting Dunphy v. Gregor, 642 A.2d 372 (N.J. 1994)).

6. V.C. v. M.J.B., 748 A.2d at 556; *see id.* (asserting that these family attributes "may

be found in biological families, step-families, blended families, single parent families, foster families, families created by modern reproductive technology, and in families made up of unmarried persons").

7. *See* Kris Franklin, *The "Authoritative Moment": Exploring the Boundaries of Interpretation in the Recognition of Queer Families*, 32 WM. MITCHELL L. REV. 655, 656 (2006) ("[T]hese cases ask the courts to think about the growing elasticity in cultural understandings of families in the United States, and to make decisions about where to draw the line in defining the legitimacy (or illegitimacy) of different kinds of families."). In assessing these dilemmas of contemporary family life, one state's supreme court remarked on the growing legal receptivity to the parenting arrangements and family structure the parties themselves have made.

> The recognition of de facto parents is in accord with notions of the modern family.... It is to be expected that children of nontraditional families, like other children, form parent relationships with both parents, whether those parents are legal or de facto.... Thus, the best interests calculus must include an examination of the child's relationship with both his legal and de facto parent.

E.N.O. v. L.M.M., 711 N.E.2d 886, 891 (Mass. 1999) (internal citations omitted).

8. *See In re* Parentage of L.B., 122 P.3d 161, 165 (Wash. 2005) (referring to the "advancing technologies and evolving notions of what comprises a family unit"). Legislative dictates are supposed to guide the judiciary in adjudicating family law disputes, but legislatures are not revising the statutory schemes fast or thoroughly enough. *See* J.F. v. D.B., 848 N.E.2d 873, 881 (Ohio Ct. App. 2006) (Slaby, J., concurring). Consider the plaintive and not-infrequent note struck by this appellate judge.

> The Ohio legislators have acknowledged but failed to address the rapid technological advances of surrogacy. The majority and I want to again emphasize that we do not address custody issues in this case. The case is the foundation of many and various issues to be decided by the state legislators or courts of the future. Extrapolating from the facts of this case, one can only imagine what the future can bring, the issues that will be raised, and the variety of conclusions that can result without legislative regulation.
>
> The majority points out that there are only a few states that have even begun to address the issue of determining who the parents of a surrogate child may be. Even the few states that have begun to address the issues involved have approached the issues from four different directions. Unless the state legislators begin to address the multiple issues involved, it will be the children that will be caught in a continual tug of war between the egg donor or donors, the sperm donor or donors, the surrogate parent or parents, and those that simply want to adopt a child from what they perceive as the ideal parents.

Id.

9. Raftopol v. Ramey, 12 A.3d 783, 785 (Conn. 2011); *see also* Carla Spivack, *The Law of Surrogate Motherhood in the United States*, 58 AM. J. COMP. L. 97, 101 (2010) (commenting on the confused state of the law regarding surrogacy and categorizing different approaches taken by various state legislatures, including inaction); Darra L. Hofman, *"Mama's Baby, Daddy's Maybe": A State-by-State Survey of Surrogacy Laws and Their Disparate Gender Impact*, 35 WM. MITCHELL L. REV. 449, 454 (2009) (noting that the "vast majority of states are silent or near silent on the issues of whether, when, and how surrogacy agreements are enforceable, void, or voidable").

10. Adam P. Plant, *With a Little Help from My Friends: The Intersection of the Gestational Carrier Surrogacy Agreement, Legislative Inaction, and Medical Advancement*, 54 ALA. L. REV. 639, 639 (2003). That surrogacy agreements are garnering increased public acceptance—or at least insouciance—may be seen in the lack of adverse reaction to the announcement that two grandchildren of Mitt Romney, the 2012 Republican candidate for president, had been born via a gestational surrogate in May 2012. See Ashley Parker, *2 New Grandchildren for Romney, With Help of Surrogate*, N.Y. TIMES, May 4, 2012.

11. *In re* Parentage of L.B., 122 P.3d at 176.

12. Charles P. Kindregan Jr., *Family Law in the Twenty-First Century: Collaborative Reproduction and Rethinking Parentage*, 21 J. AM. ACAD. MATRIMONIAL L. 43, 45 (2008).

13. *In re* Parentage of L.B., 122 P.3d at 169 n.9. A small number of states furnish exceptions to the general legislative languor in this area. *See, e.g.*, KY. REV. STAT. ANN. §§ 403.800–880 (2004), adopting the Uniform Child Custody Jurisdiction and Enforcement Act, which confers standing in a child custody dispute to "a person acting as a parent." The Kentucky Supreme Court noted that the statute grants standing "to a nonparent who, acting as parent to the child, has physical custody of the child." Mullins v. Picklesimer, 317 S.W.3d 569, 575 (Ky. 2010). In a similar vein, an Oregon statute provides for the rights of an individual "who establishes emotional ties creating child-parent relationship." OR. REV. STAT. § 109.119 (2009). The statute defines such a relationship in psychological, physical, and temporal terms.

> "Child-parent relationship" means a relationship that exists or did exist, in whole or in part, within the six months preceding the filing of an action under this section, and in which relationship a person having physical custody of a child or residing in the same household as the child supplied, or otherwise made available to the child, food, clothing, shelter and incidental necessaries and provided the child with necessary care, education and discipline, and which relationship continued on a day-to-day basis, through interaction, companionship, interplay and mutuality, that fulfilled the child's psychological needs for a parent as well as the child's physical needs. However, a relationship between a child and a person who is the nonrelated foster parent of the child is not a child-parent relationship under this section unless the relationship continued over a period exceeding 12 months.

Id. § 109.119(10)(a). *See In re* Marriage of O'Donnell-Lamont, 91 P.3d 721, 731 (Or. 2004) (noting that the statute supplies the legal standard for "determining custody as between a legal parent . . . and other persons who have established a child-parent relationship with a child").

14. *See* Janice M. v. Margaret K., 948 A.2d 73, 94 (Md. 2008) (Raker, J., dissenting) ("One thing is clear: the Maryland Legislature is silent when it comes to the question of visitation with children when a non-traditional family is dissolved. In the face of this silence, I believe that a de facto parent is different from 'third parties' and should be treated as the equivalent of a legal parent, with the same rights and obligations.") *See also* Alison D. v. Virginia M., 572 N.E.2d 27, 31 (N.Y. 1991) (Kaye, J., dissenting) ("[New York's] Domestic Relations Law . . . does not define the term 'parent' at all. That remains for the courts to do, as often happens when statutory terms are undefined."); James Herbie DiFonzo, *Toward a Unified Field Theory of the Family: The American Law Institute's Principles of the Law of Family Dissolution*, 2001 BYU L. REV. 923, 933 (2001) ("In order to accommodate the best interests of the children of these nontraditional unions, courts have begun re-commissioning and adapting doctrines from equity practice in order to adjust the statutory definition.").

15. *See, e.g., In re* Roberto d.B., 923 A.2d 115, 132 (Md. 2007) (Cathell, J., dissenting) ("This case illustrates that the process of manufacturing children can lead to unusual situations that would have been virtually inconceivable decades ago when the relevant statutory scheme was enacted. I do not necessarily agree or disagree that the remedy for the present situation created by the majority is appropriate or otherwise. I think it is wrong for the majority to fashion, in the first instance, the public policy it is creating as a remedy. The issues present in this case, going as they do to the very heart of a society, are, in my view, a matter for the Legislative Branch of government and not initially for the courts.") *See also In re* Clifford K., 619 S.E.2d 138, 162 (W.Va. 2005) (Maynard, J., dissenting) ("Although families in our society today have taken on new forms, many have not yet been recognized by our Legislature. In my opinion, this Court should not impose its judgment where the Legislature has not spoken.").

16. *See, e.g.,* Moore v. City of E. Cleveland, 431 U.S. 494, 504–6 (1976) (reversing a criminal conviction under an ordinance that narrowly defined the term *family* in light of historical nonlineal composition of families).

17. *See In re* Clifford K., 619 S.E.2d at 153–54 (West Virginia Supreme Court addressed a statutory gap and recognized a same-sex partner's right to challenge the custody award of a deceased partner's biological child to the child's maternal grandfather).

18. *See* Robinson v. Ford-Robinson, 208 S.W.3d 140, 144 (Ark. 2005) (the Arkansas Supreme Court held that an ex-wife stood in loco parentis to her stepson and thus was entitled, as "in all practical respects, a non-custodial parent," to visitation with the stepson, over objection by the natural parent).

19. *See In re* the Paternity and Maternity of Infant R., 922 N.E.2d 59 (Ind. Ct. App. 2010) (the Indiana Court of Appeals held that the husband and wife were legally the child's parents).

20. *See* Raftopol v. Ramey, 12 A.3d 783 (Conn. 2011) (the Connecticut Supreme Court held that the biological father's same-sex domestic partner was an intended parent who, as a party to a valid gestational agreement, may become a parent without first adopting the children and that the surrogate mother, a gestational carrier, had no parental rights with respect to the children, to whom she bore no biological relationship).

21. Mullins v. Picklesimer, 317 S.W.3d 569 (Ky. 2010) (the Kentucky Supreme Court held that the mother waived her superior right as natural parent to custody of the child in favor of a joint custody arrangement with her same-sex partner and, thus, that her partner was entitled to share custody of the child following the dissolution of the adults' relationship).

22. Judicial accommodation to the family in situ is consonant "with notions of the modern family." E.N.O. v. L.M.M., 711 N.E.2d 886, 891 (Mass. 1999). The E.N.O. court did not view its recognizing de facto parents as a radical departure, since "[i]t is to be expected that children of nontraditional families, like other children, form parent relationships with both parents, whether those parents are legal or de facto." *Id.*

23. *Id.*

24. *Id.*

25. *Id. See also* C.E.W. v. D.E.W., 845 A.2d 1146, 1147, 1152 (Me. 2004) (A de facto parent must have "undertaken a permanent, unequivocal, committed, and responsible parental role in the child's life," and the individual must be "understood and acknowledged to be the child's parent both by the child and by the child's other parent"). Some courts rely on the common-law doctrine of in loco parentis to grant nonbiological parents equal rights to their children. *See, e.g.,* Latham v. Schwerdtfeger, 802 N.W.2d 66, 72 (Neb. 2011) (quoting Weinand v. Weinand, 616 N.W.2d 1, 6 (Neb. 2000)) ("[A] person standing in loco parentis to a child is one who has put himself or herself in the situation of a lawful parent by assuming the obligations incident to the parental relationship, without going through the formalities necessary to a legal adoption, and the rights, duties, and liabilities of such person are the same as those of the lawful parent.") The American Law Institute promulgated a similar definition for a de facto parent, grounded in the parent living with the legal parent and child in a parenting arrangement enabled by the legal parent. AMERICAN LAW INSTITUTE, PRINCIPLES OF THE LAW OF FAMILY DISSOLUTION: ANALYSIS AND RECOMMENDATIONS 118 (2002).

26. Blixt v. Blixt, 774 N.E.2d 1052, 1061 (Mass. 2002); *see also* Jennifer L. Rosato, *Children of Same-Sex Parents Deserve the Security Blanket of the Parentage Presumption,* 44 FAM. CT. REV. 74, 74 (2006) (arguing that the parentage presumption "should apply equally to children born of a same-sex marriage, domestic partnership, or civil union, as well as to children who live with a same-sex partner in a parent-child relationship"); Courtney G. Joslin, *Protecting Children(?): Marriage, Gender, and Assisted Reproductive Technology,* 83 S. CAL. L. REV. 1177, 1178 (2010) (footnote omitted) ("To protect children from the emotional harm of being abruptly cut off from one of the only two parents they have ever known, courts in a growing number of states have heeded the call of Nancy Polikoff and others, and have applied a variety of judge-made equitable and com-

mon law doctrines to fill in the gaps and to ensure that children are provided with at least a minimal level of protection for their emotional and caregiving relationships with their functional but nonlegal parents.")

27. E.N.O. v. L.M.M., 711 N.E.2d at 894 (Fried, J., dissenting).

28. *See, e.g.,* Debra H. v. Janice R., 930 N.E.2d 184, 204 (N.Y. 2010) (Smith, J., concurring) ("Each of these couples made a commitment to bring a child into a two-parent family, and it is unfair to the children to let the commitment go unenforced.").

29. *In re* Clifford K., *supra*, 619 S.E.2d 138, 161 (W.Va. 2005) (Maynard, J., dissenting) ("I am dismayed that this Court has written an opinion that is so anti-family."). *But see id.* at 154, 158–60 (majority opinion describing the comprehensive nature and extent of the parent-child relationship between the lesbian coparent and the child).

30. Kulstad v. Maniaci, 220 P.3d 595, 610 (Mont. 2009).

31. *Id.* at 606 (applying MONT. CODE ANN. § 40-4-228 (2009)).

32. *Id.* at 606–10. A dissenting justice insisted that the statute should be struck down as an unconstitutional infringement on a natural parent's fundamental rights. *Id.* at 613–15 (Rice, J., dissenting). Although the majority was interpreting a statute and not relying on equitable principles, the dissent objected to the "equitable, case-by-case inquiry" that would follow from the majority's gloss on the statutory framework. *Id.* at 611. The dissent elaborated on the dangers of wielding equitable principles in order to ascertain parentage.

> Today the Court retreats from its clear declaration of the fundamental constitutional rights of parents. In exchange, the Court adopts an equitable, case-by-case inquiry to determine if a third party should be granted a parental interest of a child that must be balanced against a natural parent's rights. The Court's decision will open a Pandora's Box of potential attacks upon the right of fit and capable parents to raise their own children. I dissent from this weakening of parental constitutional rights.

Id.

33. Cotton v. Wise, 977 S.W.2d 263, 265 (Mo. 1998) (en banc); *see also* Debra H. v. Janice R., 930 N.E.2d at 194 (refusing to "sidestep[] [New York law] as presently drafted and interpreted . . . to create an additional category of parent—a functional or de facto parent—through the exercise of [the court's] common-law and equitable powers" and explaining that such a task is better suited for the legislature).

34. Nancy E. Dowd, *Law, Culture, and Family: The Transformative Power of Culture and the Limits of Law,* 78 CHI.-KENT L. REV. 785, 789 (2003).

35. Jeffrey Evans Stake & Michael Grossberg, *Roundtable: Opportunities for and Limitation of Private Ordering in Family Law,* 73 IND. L.J. 535, 554 (1998) (remarks by Michael Grossberg).

36. *See, e.g.,* Levi R. Smylie, *Strengthening Our Families: An In-Depth Look at the Proclamation on the Family,* 6 J.L. & FAM. STUD. 375, 376 (2004) (noting that family is

a "central component[]" of our society" and discussing the "important and distinct roles" that parents occupy within a family).

37. See, e.g., Janet L. Dolgin, *Choice, Tradition, and the New Genetics: The Fragmentation of the Ideology of Family*, 32 CONN. L. REV. 523, 524–25 (2000) (noting that today's modern family comes in many forms—despite the traditional belief that family ties flow from biology—and expressing the hope that regardless of an individual's view of familial relationships, "families will resemble one another in placing love and loyalty before all else"); Katherine T. Bartlett, *Saving the Family from the Reformers*, 31 U.C. DAVIS L. REV. 809, 816 (1998) (advocating "respect or moral accommodation for a broad range of family forms that are capable of providing nurturing environments to its members").

38. V.C. v. M.J.B., 748 A.2d 539, 551 (N.J. 2000). Referring to one of the coparents as a "third party" has been criticized as a distorted way to approach basic issues in a family created by two lesbians who have shared parenting. See Melanie B. Jacobs, *Micah Has One Mommy and One Legal Stranger: Adjudicating Maternity for Nonbiological Lesbian Coparents*, 50 BUFF. L. REV. 341, 350 (2002) ("Lesbian coparents are anything but third parties—they are involved, nurturing, loving, and supportive parents. Lesbian coparents are different from traditional third parties because they intend and plan, with their partner's agreement and encouragement, to be a parent. Lesbian coparents thus actively participate in the decision to create a family and, indeed, function as parents. But, because under existing law and court practice lesbian coparents are not protected by state divorce or parentage statutes, they are denied legal recognition of their actual parental role.")

39. C.E.W. v. D.E.W., 845 A.2d 1146, 1147, 1152 (Me. 2004).

40. Van v. Zahorik, 597 N.W.2d 15, 27 (Mich. 1999) (Kelly, J., dissenting); see id. ("It has long been a foundational tenet of American jurisprudence that, when legal remedies prove inadequate to solve a problem, society looks to the doctrine of equity and the courts.").

41. See Simons ex rel. Simons v. Gisvold, 519 N.W.2d 585, 587 (N.D. 1994) (identifying the purpose of psychological parent analysis as "prevent[ing] serious harm or detriment to the welfare of the child"); see also In re Parentage of L.B., 122 P.3d 161, 166 (Wash. 2005).

42. See V.C. v. M.J.B., 748 A.2d at 552 (noting that a critical factor is whether the biological or adoptive parent fostered and consented to the "creation of the psychological parent's relationship with the child"); id. (insisting that the biological or adoptive parent "has the absolute ability to maintain a zone of autonomous privacy for herself and her child").

43. Id.

44. T.B. v. L.R.M., 768 A.2d 913, 919 (Pa. 2011) (quoting J.A.L. v. E.P.H., 682 A.2d 1314, 1322 (Pa. Super. 1996)).

45. See, e.g., Quinn v. Mouw-Quinn, 552 N.W.2d 843, 846–47 (S.D. 1996) (noting that courts "have the right and obligation to protect children from the sometimes selfish and destructive actions of divorcing parents"); see generally FLORENCE BIENENFELD,

CHILD CUSTODY MEDIATION: TECHNIQUES FOR COUNSELORS, ATTORNEYS, AND PARENTS 1 (1983).

46. V.C. v. M.J.B., 748 A.2d at 550.

47. Quinn v. Mouw-Quinn, 552 N.W.2d at 847.

48. Cleveland Bd. of Educ. v. LaFleur, 414 U.S. 632, 639–40 (1974).

49. V.C. v. M.J.B., 748 A.2d at 550; see also Smith v. Org. of Foster Families for Equal. & Reform, 431 U.S. 816, 843 (1977) (noting that "biological relationships are not [the] exclusive determination of the existence of a family").

50. See E. Mavis Hetherington & Margaret Stanley-Hagan, *Diversity among Stepfamilies, in* HANDBOOK OF FAMILY DIVERSITY 177 (David H. Demo et al. eds., 2000) (analyzing relevant demographics); Kay Pasley & Bruce S. Moorefield, *Stepfamilies: Change and Challenges, in* HANDBOOK OF CONTEMPORARY FAMILIES 318 (Marilyn Coleman & Lawrence H. Ganong eds., 2005) (providing the 30 percent estimate based on analysis of U.S. Census data).

51. See, e.g., Stamps v. Rawlins, 761 S.W.2d 933, 935 (Ark. 1988) (holding that while a stepparent may be awarded custody of a minor child, the law recognizes a preference for a fit natural parent).

52. Margaret M. Mahoney, *Stepparents as Third Parties in Relation to Their Stepchildren*, 40 FAM. L.Q. 81, 85 (2006).

53. See id. at 82 ("In spite of the long history of stepfamily issues in the legal arena, and the increased demand for regulation in recent decades, little progress has been made in establishing a clear or consistent legal definition of the stepparent status."); David L. Chambers, *Stepparents, Biologic Parents, and the Law's Perceptions of "Family" after Divorce, in* DIVORCE REFORM AT THE CROSSROADS 104–5 (Stephen D. Sugarman & Herma Hill Kay eds., 1990) ("The stepparent relationship, by contrast [to the biological parent role], lacks—and, I would argue, cannot possibly obtain—a single paradigm or model of appropriate responsibilities.").

54. Mahoney, *supra* note 52, at 104–5 (discussing statutes).

55. See, e.g., Robinson v. Ford-Robinson, 208 S.W.3d 140 (Ark. 2005) (affirming the award of visitation to a stepparent standing in loco parentis, over the natural parent's objection). In a case in which a stepfather's relationship with a seven-year-old girl was "that of a father and daughter in all respects except for that of biology," the South Dakota Supreme Court affirmed the stepfather's right to visitation, insisting that its ruling "strikes the proper balance between a natural parent's custodial rights to his or her child and the child's personal welfare. Children come first." Quinn v. Mouw-Quinn, 552 N.W.2d 843, 847 (S.D. 1996).

56. See, e.g., McAllister v. McAllister, 779 N.W.2d 652 (N.D. 2010) (a stepparent who has become the child's psychological parent may be awarded custody over the natural parent if it is "'in the child's best interests to award custody to the psychological parent to prevent serious harm or detriment to the welfare of the child'") (quoting In re D.P.O., 667 N.W.2d 590, 593 (N.D. 2003).

57. See, e.g., Latham v. Schwerdtfeger, 802 N.W.2d 66 (Neb. 2011) (holding that the doctrine of in loco parentis, which had previously applied to stepparents and grandpar-

ents, extends to lesbian coparents and affords them standing to seek custody and visitation rights).

58. Courts are capable of conducting inquiries of this type no less than of any other contested facts. *See, e.g.,* Smith v. Jones, 868 N.E.2d 629 (Mass. App. 2007). In this case, the court held that the adoptive mother's former same-sex partner failed to satisfy the criteria for being the de facto parent of the mother's adopted child. The adoptive mother's lack of intent to foster a coparenting arrangement was demonstrated by the fact that she did not cede significant responsibilities to her former partner, that she did not name her former partner as the child's guardian in the event of the mother's death, that she traveled alone to a foreign country to adopt the child and chose her without consulting her former partner, and that the parties did not coadopt or execute a coparenting agreement. The appellate court explained that ascertaining the adoptive parent's intent to create a coparenting relationship "requires analysis of objective, observable indicia of agreement or lack of agreement to allow caretaking, responsibility, and decisionmaking." *Id.* at 634 n.8.

59. *See* Troxel v. Granville, 530 U.S. 57, 65–66 (2000) (plurality opinion).

60. *Id.*, 530 U.S. at 67 (holding Washington State's grandparent visitation act unconstitutional as applied).

61. Smith v. Guest, 16 A.3d 920, 931 (Del. 2011). As Smith v. Guest demonstrates, the issues that occupied the Supreme Court in Troxel have little bearing on lesbian coparent cases. This case involved a claim filed by Carol Guest, lesbian partner of Lynne Smith, the adoptive mother of the child. The Delaware Supreme Court pointedly rejected Smith's argument that awarding parental rights to Guest would violate her fundamental rights as articulated in Troxel v. Granville.

> Guest is not "any third party." Rather, she is a (claimed) *de facto* parent who (if her claim is established, as the Family Court found it was) would also be a legal "parent" of [the child]. Because Guest, as a legal parent, would have a co-equal "fundamental parental interest" in raising [the child], allowing Guest to pursue that interest through a legally-recognized channel cannot unconstitutionally infringe Smith's due process rights. In short, Smith's due process claim fails for lack of a valid premise.

Id. (footnote omitted). *See also In re* Parentage of L.B., 122 P.3d 161, 178 (Wash. 2005) (holding that "de facto parents [are placed] in parity with biological and adoptive parents" and, thus, that *both* have a fundamental liberty interest in the care, custody, and control of their children).

62. A recent opinion of the United States Court of Appeals for the Second Circuit explains the word and its derivation.

> "Chutzpah" as a legal term of art is analytically similar to "unclean hands," though not necessarily coterminous with that concept as understood in Chancery. The "classic definition" of chutzpah has been described as "that quality enshrined in

a man who, having killed his mother and father, throws himself on the mercy of the court because he is an orphan."

Motorola Credit Corp. v. Uzan, 561 F.3d 123, 128 n.5 (2d Cir. 2009) (quoting LEO ROSTEN, THE JOYS OF YIDDISH 92 (1968)).

63. Simmons v. Comer, 438 S.E.2d 530, 540 n.15 (W.Va. 1993) (quoting JOSEPH GOLDSTEIN ET AL., BEYOND THE BEST INTERESTS OF THE CHILD 98 (1979)). This argument, lodged by biological or adoptive parents in an effort to *dis*lodge their former partners, is unfortunately common. One pristine example may be found in Bethany v. Jones, a 2010 Arkansas Supreme Court case in which the lesbian partner (Emily Jones) was seeking to establish her rights to parent E.B, the biological child of Alicia Bethany whom both women had raised.

> [Emily] cared for the child's every need every day for three and one-half years. [Emily] fed, bathed, clothed, nurtured, supervised, and supported E.B., and performed every other act a parent would do for their [sic] child. [Emily and Alicia] agreed to co-parent the child, and [Emily] stood *in loco parentis* to the minor child to the exclusion of all others besides [Alicia]. . . . [Emily] stood not only in the position of a parent to the child for three and one-half years, but the child saw [Emily] as her parent for those years.

Bethany v. Jones, 378 S.W.3d 731, 735–36 (Ark. 2010) (quoting the trial court findings). Despite this record, whose "facts are largely undisputed," Alicia Bethany argued that Emily Jones had no legal relationship with the child. The court held that Emily stood in loco parentis to the child and, thus, that her rights to direct and govern the care, custody, and control of her child warranted constitutional protection. *Id.* at 733.

64. Estoppel principles lead to the same conclusion. *See, e.g.,* Rubano v. DiCenzo, 759 A.2d 959, 968 (R.I. 2000) (estoppel doctrine bars a mother from asserting that a lesbian coparent is barred from recognition as a de facto parent because she was not a biological parent). In its PRINCIPLES OF THE LAW OF FAMILY DISSOLUTION: ANALYSIS AND RECOMMENDATIONS (2002), the American Law Institute defined a "parent by estoppel" to include a person who

> lived with the child since the child's birth, holding out and accepting full and permanent responsibilities as parent, as part of a prior co-parenting agreement with the child's legal parent (or, if there are two legal parents, both parents) to raise a child together each with full parental rights and responsibilities, when the court finds that recognition of the individual as a parent is in the child's best interests. . . .

Id. at § 2.03(1)(b)(iii). Determining that one partner is a "parent by estoppel" serves "to estop the legal parent from denying the individual's status as a parent." *Id.* at § 2.03 cmt. b. It should also estop the chutzpah argument.

65. *See generally Surrogacy Laws: State by State,* Human Rights Campaign (2009), http://preview.hrc.org/2486.htm; *Guide to State Surrogacy Laws,* Center for American Progress (2007), http://www.americanprogress.org/issues/women/news/2007/12/17/3758/guide-to-state-surrogacy-laws/.

66. Belsito v. Clark, 644 N.E.2d 760, 763 (Ohio Com. Pl. 1994).

67. *Id.; see* Kermit Roosevelt III, *The Newest Property: Reproductive Technologies and the Concept of Parenthood,* 39 SANTA CLARA L. REV. 79, 97 (1998) ("Historically, gestation proved genetic parentage beyond doubt, so it was unnecessary to distinguish between gestational and genetic mothers.")

68. Reproductive technology has injected entropy into this branch of family law. Charles P. Kindregan Jr. noted that by the mid-20th century, "issues of legal parenthood were well settled in American law; in the first decade of the twenty-first century, those issues are hardly settled at all." Kindregan, *supra* note 12, at 43.

69. *See* Amy M. Larkey, *Redefining Motherhood: Determining Legal Maternity in Gestational Surrogacy Arrangements,* 51 DRAKE L. REV. 605 (2003). Recent developments in reproductive technologies have obliged courts to confront issues in determining *maternity* for the first time in history. *See, e.g., In re* Roberto d.B., 923 A.2d 115, 122 (Md. 2007) (considering the novel question of "construing the parentage statutes in a way that affords women the same opportunity to deny parentage as men have"); UNIF. PARENTAGE ACT art. 8 introductory cmt. (amended 2002), 9B U.L.A. 75 (Supp. 2010) ("[B]y definition, a child born pursuant to a gestational agreement will need to have maternity as well as paternity clarified.").

70. Alison D. v. Virginia M., 572 N.E.2d 27, at 28 (N.Y. 1991).

71. *Id.*

72. *Id.* at 29. In 2010, the court of appeals reaffirmed the "core holding" of Alison D., that "parentage under New York law derives from biology or adoption." Debra H. v. Janice R., 930 N.E.2d 184, 191 (N.Y. 2010).

73. Troxel v. Granville, 530 U.S. 57 (2000) (upholding on due process grounds the parents' decision regarding the extent of visitation afforded to the child's grandparents).

74. Culliton v. Beth Israel Deaconess Med. Ctr., 756 N.E.2d 1133 (Mass. 2001).

75. *Id.* at 1137.

76. *Id.* The court concluded that the paternity statute "is simply an inadequate and inappropriate device to resolve parentage determinations of children born from this type of gestational surrogacy." *Id.*

77. *Id.* The court also elaborated on the importance of rapid and accurate determinations of parentage for minimizing adverse consequences to children born through alternative reproduction.

> Delays in establishing parentage may, among other consequences, interfere with a child's medical treatment in the event of medical complications arising during or shortly after birth; may hinder or deprive a child of inheriting from his legal parents should a legal parent die intestate before a postbirth action could determine parentage; may hinder or deprive a child from collecting Social Security

benefits... and may result in undesirable support obligations as well as custody disputes (potentially more likely in situations where the child is born with congenital malformations or anomalies, or medical disorders and diseases).

Id.

78. Other representative cases include *In re* the Paternity and Maternity of Infant R., 922 N.E.2d 59 (Ind. Ct. App. 2010); S.N. v. M.B., 935 N.E.2d 463, 468 (Ohio Ct. App. 2010); J.F. v. D.B. (*Surrogate Triplets*), 879 N.E.2d 740 (Ohio 2007); and Johnson v. Calvert, 851 P.2d 776 (Cal. 1993).

79. UNIF. PARENTAGE ACT art. 8 introductory cmt. (amended 2002), 9B U.L.A. 75 (Supp. 2010).

80. Joanna L. Grossman, *Time to Revisit Baby M? A New Jersey Court Refuses to Enforce a Surrogacy Agreement* (pt. 2), VERDICT (Jan. 20, 2010) http://writ.news.findlaw.com/grossman/20100120.html.

81. 750 ILL. COMP. STAT. ANN. 47/15 (West 2010).

82. *Id.* at 47/35 (setting forth requirements for determining how "a parent-child relationship shall be established prior to the birth of a child born through gestational surrogacy").

83. UNIF. PARENTAGE ACT § 801(a), 9B U.L.A. 76.

84. The American Bar Association's Section of Family Law has included an assisted reproduction provision that is neutral concerning gender and marital status in its Model Act Governing Assisted Reproductive Technology (ABA Model Act). AM. BAR ASSOC., MODEL ACT GOVERNING ASSISTED REPRODUCTIVE TECHNOLOGY § 603 (2008), http://www.abanet.org/family/committees/artmodelact.pdf ("An individual who provides gametes for, or consents to, assisted reproduction by a woman as provided in Section 604 with the intent to be a parent of her child is a parent of the resulting child.").

85. Johnson v. Calvert, 851 P.2d 776 (Cal. 1993).

86. *Id.* at 782.

87. *Id.* The court made the obvious point that the couple's goal "was to bring Mark's and Crispina's child into the world, not for Mark and Crispina to donate a zygote to Anna." *Id.*

88. *Id.*

89. *See id.* at 786–87. The court held that genetic consanguinity and giving birth are means of establishing a mother-child relationship but that "when the two means do not coincide in one woman, she who intended to procreate the child—that is, she who intended to bring about the birth of a child that she intended to raise as her own—is the natural mother under California law." *Id.* at 782.

90. Katharine K. Baker, *Bargaining or Biology? The History and Future of Paternity Law and Parental Status,* 14 CORNELL J. L. & PUB. POL'Y 1, 29, 11 (2004) ("Commentators and courts widely endorse the preconception intent standard as the appropriate one to decide disputed parental rights issues stemming from reproductive technologies that allow people to conceive without intercourse and separate genetic contributions from gestational ones."); *see also* Lori B. Andrews, *Legal and Ethical Aspects of New Re-*

productive Technologies, 29 CLINICAL OBSTETRICS & GYNECOLOGY 190, 199–200 (1986) (arguing that the preconception intent should govern in cases of artificial insemination); John Lawrence Hill, *What Does It Mean to Be a "Parent"? The Claims of Biology as the Basis for Parental Rights*, 66 N.Y.U. L. REV. 353, 418 (1991) ("[T]he intended parents should be considered the 'parents' of the child born of [reproductive technologies] . . . .").

91. *In re* Marriage of Buzzanca, 72 Cal. Rptr. 2d 280 (Cal. Ct. App. 1998).

92. *Id.* at 293 ("Even though neither Luanne nor John are biologically related to Jaycee, they are still her lawful parents given their initiating role as the intended parents in her conception and birth.")

93. *See* Joslin, *supra* note 26, at 1177.

94. The sources for this story include the pleadings and court orders culminating in Boseman v. Jarrell, 704 S.E.2d 494 (N.C. 2010); *Soles, Boseman End Historic Careers in Legislature*, WWAYTV3.com (July 9, 2010), http://www.wwaytv3.com/only_3_soles_boseman_end_historic_careers_legislature/07/2010; Gary D. Robertson, *Update: Justices Hear Arguments in Same-Sex Adoption Case*, Associated Press, Sept. 8, 2010, available at http://www.news-record.com/content/2010/09/08/article/nc_justices_hearing_arguments_in_same_sex_adoption; *Jarrell Resigns Softball Post with Seahawks*, UNC-WSports.com (June 6, 2008), http://www.scfun.net/ap-sb-jarrell-resigns.pdf (last visited July 24, 2011); Patrick Gannon, *Arguments Heard in Same-Sex Adoption Case of N.C. Sen. Julia Boseman*, StarNewsOnline.com (Sept. 8, 2010), http://www.starnewsonline.com/article/20100908/articles/100909706.

95. Boseman v. Jarrell, 704 S.E.2d at 497.

96. *Id.*

97. *Id.*

98. N.C.G.S.A. § 48-1-106 (c).

99. N.C.G.S.A. § 48-1-106 (d) (providing that an adoption by a stepparent does not have "any effect on the relationship between the child and the parent who is the stepparent's spouse.")

100. *See* N.C.G.S.A. § 48-1-101 (18) (defining a stepparent as "an individual who is the spouse of a parent of a child, but who is not a legal parent of the child"); N.C.G.S.A. § 51-1 (providing that a "valid and sufficient marriage" must have "the consent of a male and female person who may lawfully marry, presently to take each other as husband and wife").

101. N.C.G.S.A. § 51-1.2 ("Marriages, whether created by common law, contracted, or performed outside of North Carolina, between individuals of the same gender are not valid in North Carolina.").

102. Second-parent adoptions are permitted by statute in several states, such as Connecticut (*see* C.G.S.A. § 45a-724(3)) and New York (*see* 2010 Sess. Law News of N.Y., ch. 509 (S. 1523-A), § 1 (eff. Sept. 17, 2010)).

103. *See* Embry v. Ryan, 11 So.3d 408, 410 (Fla. App. 2009) (holding that Florida courts were required to give full faith and credit to a Washington adoption judgment involving a same-sex couple); Russell v. Bridgens, 647 N.W.2d 56 (Neb. 2002) (holding

that, under the full faith and credit clause, a Nebraska court must enforce a second-parent Pennsylvania adoption decree).

104. The scope of the full faith and credit clause's application to second-parent adoptions has recently been thrown into doubt. In Finstuen v. Crutcher, 496 F.3d 1139 (10th Cir. 2007), the U.S. Court of Appeals for the Tenth Circuit held that a California adoption decree obtained by a same-sex couple is entitled to recognition in Oklahoma under the full faith and credit clause. The court acknowledged that a recent state statute barring recognition of same-sex adoptions in Oklahoma clearly expressed that state's public policy. But the Tenth Circuit relied on U.S. Supreme Court precedent stating that there is "no roving 'public policy exception' to the full faith and credit due judgments" (Baker ex rel. Thomas v. Gen. Motors Corp. 522 U.S. 222, 233 (1998)). Accordingly, the court found the Oklahoma statute unconstitutional "in its refusal to recognize final adoption orders of other states that permit adoption by same-sex couples." Finstuen v. Crutcher, 496 F.3d at 1156. This ruling did not dispose of the case, however. The Oklahoma State Department of Health (OSDH) had refused to issue a supplementary birth certificate bearing the adoptive parents' names, contrary to the requirements of another state statute that provided for this procedure for adopted children. The court found that this refusal failed to accord full faith and credit to the adoption judgment, and it ordered the OSDH to issue the supplementary birth certificate.

In 2011, the U.S. Court of Appeals for the Fifth Circuit issued a decision considerably at odds with the Tenth Circuit opinion. In Adar v. Smith, 639 F.3d 146 (5th Cir. 2011) (en banc), unmarried same-sex adoptive parents of a child born in Louisiana but adopted in New York sued the State Registrar of Louisiana's Office of Vital Records and Statistics, seeking a judgment that the registrar's refusal to enforce the New York adoption decree and to issue an amended birth certificate violated the full faith and credit clause. The registrar had offered to issue an amended birth certificate with one but not both of the parent's names, relying on a Louisiana statute allowing only married parents to jointly adopt a child. In a severely divided en banc ruling, a majority of the Fifth Circuit noted that the full faith and credit clause imposes a duty on state courts to give an out-of-state judgment the same effect that the issuing court would give it. However, the court held that only the U.S. Supreme Court is authorized to review violations of full faith and credit by state courts. Because the couple sought enforcement initially in federal court, they were not entitled to relief. Alternatively, the Fifth Circuit held that the registrar's refusal to issue an amended birth certificate does not fail to give *recognition* to the out-of-state decree, because the full faith and credit clause does not extend to a state's *method of enforcement* of another state's judgment. In other words, the court upheld the registrar's determination that the New York adoption decree does not entitle the parents to the issuance of an amended Louisiana birth certificate with both their names. Finally, the Fifth Circuit majority opinion denied that the parents had been denied their rights under the equal protection clause, since unmarried adoptive parents were not a suspect class for constitutional analysis and since the registrar's actions were rationally related to Louisiana's policy of having parenthood focused on a married couple or a single individual, not an unmarried couple. *Id.* 639 F.3d at 149–62. Five judges dissented, arguing that the full faith and credit clause may properly be enforced in federal court, that it extends to accepting the out-of-state decree as a valid decree under Louisiana's enforcement regime, and that the registrar's actions did violate the equal protection clause. *Id.*, 639 F.3d at 165–86 (Wiener, J., dissenting). The Supreme Court denied certiorari (132 S.Ct. 400 (2011)), leaving the ultimate resolution of this important set of questions for another day.

105. Boseman v. Jarrell, 681 S.E.2d 374, 376 (N.C. App. 2009), *aff'd in part as modified, rev'd in part by* Boseman v. Jarrell, 704 S.E.2d 494 (N.C. 2010).

106. Julia requested that Melissa retain primary residential custody of Jacob, with Julia having secondary custody in the form of extensive visitation. *Id.*

107. *Id.* at 381–82.

108. Boseman v. Jarrell, 704 S.E.2d at 498–502. Two justices dissented from this ruling, arguing that the adoption in this case was not void but merely voidable and that Melissa had waited too long to challenge it. *Id.* at 505 (Timmons-Goodson, J., dissenting); *id.* at 505–10 (Hudson, J., dissenting).

109. *Id.* at 502.

110. *Id.* (quoting Price v. Howard, 484 S.E.2d 528, 531 (N.C. 1997)).

111. *Id.* at 503.

112. *Id.* (quoting David N. v. Jason N., 608 S.E.2d 751, 753 (N.C. 2005)).

113. *Id.* at 504.

114. *Id.*

115. *Id.* at 505.

116. That Julia has legal custody of Jacob does not mean that she is his legal parent. The custody statute provides that "[a]ny parent, relative, or *other person*, agency, organization or institution claiming the right to custody of a minor child may institute an action or proceeding for the custody of such child." N.C. GEN. STAT. § 50-13.1(a) (2007) (emphasis added).

117. Hall v. Hall, 655 S.E.2d 901, 906 (N.C. App. 2008), quoting Diehl v. Diehl, 630 S.E.2d 25, 27 (N.C. App. 2006); *see* N.C. GEN. STAT. § 50-13.2(b) (2007); 3 SUZANNE REYNOLDS, LEE'S NORTH CAROLINA FAMILY LAW, § 13.2b, at 13–16 (5th ed. 2002) (legal custody includes "the rights and obligations associated with making major decisions affecting the child's life").

118. Hall v. Hall, 655 S.E.2d at 906 (quoting Diehl v. Diehl, 630 S.E.2d at 28).

119. Despite these unresolved issues, some family lawyers see a clear direction emerging from the Boseman v. Jarrell decision: "There will now no longer be any legal question in North Carolina that if you were jointly raising a child with your partner who is the legal parent, then you will be entitled to pursue a claim for custody if you were to unfortunately break up." *NC Supreme Court Invalidates Second Parent Adoption*, EqualityNC. org, Dec. 22, 2010, http://equalitync.org/news1/nc-supreme-court-invalidates-second-parent-adoption (quoting family law attorneys Sharon Thompson and Corye Dunn).

120. GARY J. GATES & ABIGAIL M. COOKE, NORTH CAROLINA CENSUS SNAPSHOT: 2010 (2011), *available at* http://escholarship.org/uc/item/6rx7x7vg (last visited Mar. 10, 2013).

121. *Id.*

122. *Boseman Custody Case Could Set Same-Sex Adoption Precedent*, WWAYTV3.com, (Sept. 8, 2010), http://www.wwaytv3.com/boseman_custody_case_could_set_samesex_adoption_precedent/09/2010 ("So far the state has allowed more than 200 same-sex adoptions with the biological parent's consent.") Nationwide, lesbian or gay parents are raising approximately 65,500 adopted children, accounting to more than 4 percent of all adopted children. GARY J. GATES ET AL., ADOPTION AND FOSTER CARE BY GAY AND LESBIAN PARENTS IN THE UNITED STATES 7 (2007), available at http://escholarship.org/uc/item/2v4528cx.

123. *See* Campbell Robertson, *North Carolina Voters Pass Same-Sex Marriage Ban*, N.Y. TIMES, May 8, 2012, *available at* http://www.nytimes.com/2012/05/09/us/north-carolina-voters-pass-same-sex-marriage-ban.html.

124. Unless otherwise specified, the facts are drawn from the two published court opinions in this case, *In re* C.K.G., 2004 WL 1402560 (Tenn. App. 2004), *aff'd in part, vacated in part by In re* C.K.G., 173 S.W.3d 714 (Tenn. 2005).

125. *In re* C.K.G., 173 S.W.3d at 718.

126. Court records identify the children only by their initials: C.K.G., C.A.G., and C.L.G. *Id.*

127. *Id.* at 719 (quoting juvenile court).

128. *In re* C.K.G., 2004 WL 1402560 at *9. The court of appeals also held that given the conduct of the parties in planning and having these children, Charles was estopped from challenging Cindy's claim that she was their legal mother. *Id.* at *9–10.

129. *Id.* at *12.

130. *In re* C.K.G., 173 S.W.3d at 720. Consider the strikingly similar scenario presented in *McDonald v. McDonald*, 608 N.Y.S.2d 477 (N.Y. App. Div. 1994). In this case, the wife was unable to conceive naturally, and she and her husband agreed to an in vitro fertilization in which the husband's sperm was mixed with eggs from an anonymous donor. The fertilized eggs were then implanted in the wife's uterus, and she gave birth to twins. The parties later became engaged in a divorce action and bitterly contested child custody. The husband argued that the court should award him custody because the twins had no mother, since his wife was genetically unrelated to them. Deeming this case "a true 'egg donation' situation," the court ruled that when a woman gestates and delivers a child formed from the egg of another woman with the intent to raise the child as her own, the birth mother is the legal mother. *Id.* at 480.

131. *In re* C.K.G., 173 S.W.3d at 721.

132. *See id.* ("Parentage is an area of law governed primarily by statute. Unfortunately, Tennessee's parentage and related statutes do not contemplate many of the scenarios now made possible by recent developments in reproductive technology.") The court may have let a touch of exasperation show in remarking that the statutes "employ the term 'mother' in a way that assumes we already know who the 'mother' is. . . ." *Id.* at 723.

133. *Id.* at 726.

134. *Id.* at 730.

135. *Id.* at 728.

136. *Id.*

137. The court also noted that this maternity question did not involve "a controversy between a gestator and a female genetic progenitor where the genetic and gestative roles have been separated and distributed among two women." *Id.* at 730. Nor did the case require choosing between "a traditional or gestational surrogate and a genetically-unrelated intended mother." *Id.*

138. *Id.* at 729.

139. *Id.*

140. *Id.* at 736 (Birch, J., dissenting).

141. Rob Johnson, *Brentwood Triplets in Test-Tube Custody Fight*, TENNESSEAN, January 18, 2005, at A1, *available at* http://www.allaboutsurrogacy.com/forums/index.php?showtopic=4529 (last visited Aug. 23, 2011) (quoting Dr. Charles Galiwango).

142. *Id.*

143. *Id.*

144. *State's High Court Hears Arguments in Triplets Case*, SOUTHERN STANDARD, Apr. 17, 2005, at http://www.eclassifiedsnetwork.com/v2/content.aspx?module=ContentItem&ID=75318&MemberID=1259 (last visited Aug. 23, 2011) (quoting Cindy Culpepper).

145. Johnson, *supra* note 141 (quoting Larry Hayes Jr.).

146. *Id.* (quoting Pam Spicer).

147. *Id.* (quoting Kathy Hudson, director of the Genetics and Public Policy Center at Johns Hopkins University, commenting on Charles and Cindy's case).

148. *See* the preceding section of this chapter.

149. TENN. CODE ANN. § 36-1-102(48) (2010).

150. *In re* Baby, No. M2012-01040-COA-R3-JV, 2013 WL 245039 (Tenn. App. 2013) at *4.

Chapter 6: *Unsafe Havens, Unplanned Children, and Future Generations*

1. MICHEL DE MONTAIGNE, THE ESSAYS OF MICHEL DE MONTAIGNE 319 (William Carew Hazlitt ed., 1877).

2. *Id.*

3. *Id.*

4. WHEN MARRIAGE DISAPPEARS: THE NEW MIDDLE AMERICA xi (W. Bradford Wilcox ed., 2010), *available at* http://www.virginia.edu/marriageproject/pdfs/Union_11_12_10.pdf.

5. CHRISTOPHER LASCH, HAVEN IN A HEARTLESS WORLD 3 (1977).

6. Wilcox, *supra* note 4, at 16.

7. U.S. Dep't of Health and Human Services, Administration for Children and Families, Healthy Marriage Initiative, http://www.acf.hhs.gov/healthymarriage/index.html.

8. Pamela J. Smock & Wendy D. Manning, *Living Together Unmarried in the United States: Demographic Perspectives and Implications for Family Policy*, 26 LAW & POL'Y 101 (2004).

9. NAOMI CAHN & JUNE CARBONE, RED FAMILIES V. BLUE FAMILIES 163 (2010).

10. JAMES Q. WILSON, THE MARRIAGE PROBLEM 220 (2002).

11. *Id.* at 9 (emphasis added).

12. Smock & Manning, *supra* note 8, at 104–5; ROBERT LERMAN, MARRIAGE AND THE ECONOMIC WELL-BEING OF FAMILIES WITH CHILDREN: A REVIEW OF THE LITERATURE (2002), *available at* http://www.urban.org/UploadedPDF/410541 _LitReview.pdf.

13. Wilcox, *supra* note 4, at 79.

14. Smock & Manning, *supra* note 8, at 101.

15. PAMELA SMOCK ET AL., NONMARITAL COHABITATION: CURRENT KNOWLEDGE AND FUTURE DIRECTIONS FOR RESEARCH 11 (Population Studies Center, University of Michigan 2008), *available at* http://www.psc.isr.umich.edu/pubs/pdf/rr08-648.pdf.

16. Smock & Manning, *supra* note 8, at 96, 102–3.

17. Robert A. Hummer & Erin R. Hamilton, *Race and Ethnicity in Fragile Families*, 20 THE FUTURE OF CHILDREN 124 (2010), *available at* http://futureofchildren.org/futureofchildren/publications/docs/20_02_06.pdf.

18. Douglas S. Massey & Robert J. Sampson, *Moynihan Redux: Legacies and Lessons*, 621 ANNALS AM. ACAD. POL. & SOC. SCI. 6, 16 (2009).

19. *Id.*

20. Hummer & Hamilton, *supra* note 17, at 124.

21. Massey & Sampson, *supra* note 18, at 16.

22. *Id.*

23. Hummer & Hamilton, *supra* note 17, at 125.

24. ANDREA KANE & DONALD T. LICHTER, REDUCING UNWED CHILDBEARING: THE MISSING LINK IN EFFORTS TO PROMOTE MARRIAGE 1 (Brookings Institution, Center on Children and Families, CCF Brief No. 37, 2008).

25. Smock et al, *supra* note 15, at 10,

26. Wilcox, *supra* note 4, at 80.

27. Smock & Manning, *supra* note 8, at 104.

28. Kristin Turney & Marcia J. Carlson, *Multipartnered Fertility and Depression among Fragile Families*, 73 J. MARRIAGE & FAM. 570, 571 (2011), citing Marcia J. Carlson & Frank F. Furstenberg, *The Prevalence and Correlates of Multipartnered Fertility among Urban U.S. Parents*, 68 J. MARRIAGE & FAM. 718–32 (2006).

29. Marc Kaufman, *Unwanted Pregnancies Rise for Poor Women*, WASHINGTON POST, May 5, 2006, *available at* http://www.washingtonpost.com/wp-dyn/content/article/2006/05/04/AR2006050400820.html; *see generally* Katherine Suellentrop et al., *Monitoring Progress Toward Achieving Maternal and Infant Healthy People 2010 Objectives—19 States, Pregnancy Risk Assessment Monitoring System (PRAMS), 2000-2003*, Centers for Disease Control and Prevention (2006), *available at* http://www.cdc.gov/MMWR/preview/mmwrhtml/ss5509a1.htm.

30. Wilcox, *supra* note 4, at 23.

31. KANE & LICHTER, *supra* note 24, at 6.

32. JOYCE A. MARTIN ET AL., BIRTHS: FINAL DATA FOR 2008, at 8 (Nat'l Vital Stat. Rep., Vol. 59, No. 1, 2008), *available at* http://www.cdc.gov/nchs/data/nvsr/nvsr59/nvsr59_01.pdf.

33. Sharon Sassler & Anna Cunningham, *How Cohabitors View Childbearing*, 51 SOCIOLOGICAL PERSPECTIVES 4 (2008).

34. Sabrina Tavernise, *More Unwed Parents Live Together, Report Finds*, N.Y. TIMES, Aug. 16, 2011 (quoting Sheela Kennedy, research associate, Minnesota Population Center).

35. Kristin A. Moore, *Executive Summary: Nonmarital Childbearing in the United States*, *in* NATIONAL CENTER FOR HEALTH STATISTICS, REPORT TO CONGRESS ON OUT-OF-WEDLOCK CHILDBEARING, at viii (DHHS Pub. No. (PHS) 95-1257) (1995).

36. CENTERS FOR DISEASE CONTROL, NATIONAL VITAL STATISTICS REPORTS, 61, no. 1, at 8 (2012).

37. Barbara H. Dunn, *Unmarried Childbearing: Fragile Relationships, Costly Consequences*, Final Report to the Community Foundation, Richmond, Va., at 1 (2008), *available at* http://www.tcfrichmond.org/images/uploads/Unmarried_Childbearing_Final_Report.pdf.

38. CENTERS FOR DISEASE CONTROL, *Intended and Unintended Births in the United States: 1982-2010*, NATIONAL HEALTH STATISTICS REPORTS NO. 55 at 13 (2012).

39. Lawrence B. Finer & Stanley K. Henshaw, *Disparities in Rates of Unintended Pregnancy in the United States, 1994 and 2001*, 38 PERSPECTIVES ON SEXUAL AND REPRODUCTIVE HEALTH 93 (2006).

40. *Id.* at 92.

41. Penelope M. Huang & Koray Tanfer, *Young Adult Fertility and the Intendedness of Birth* 4 (Center for Studies in Demography and Ecology, University of Washington, Working Paper No. 02-4, 2002) *available at* http://csde.washington.edu/downloads/downloader/dl.pl?id=02-04.pdf.

42. *Id.;* Denise D'Angelo et al., *Preconception and Interconception Health Status of Women Who Recently Gave Birth to a Live Born Infant—Pregnancy Risk Assessment Monitoring System (PRAMS), United States, 26 Reporting Areas, 2004*, Centers for Disease Control and Prevention (2007), *available at* http://www.cdc.gov/mmwr/preview/mmwrhtml/ss5610a1.htm.

43. Emily Monea & Adam Thomas, *Unintended Pregnancy and Taxpayer Spending*, 43 PERSPECTIVES ON SEXUAL AND REPRODUCTIVE HEALTH 92 (2011).

44. DUNN, *supra* note 36, at 2.

45. Huang & Tanfer, *supra* note 41, at 16.

46. *Id.*

47. DUNN, *supra* note 36, at 7.

48. *Id.*

49. Quoted in Sassler & Cunningham, *supra* note 33, at 17.

50. KATHRYN EDIN & MARIA KEFALAS, PROMISES I CAN KEEP 204 (2005).

51. *Id.* at 205.

52. Joanna Reed et al., *Consistent and Inconsistent Contraception among Women 20-*

29: *Insights from Qualitative Interviews* (Stanford Center for the Study of Poverty and Inequality, Working Paper No. 11-1, 2011).

53. Sassler & Cunningham, *supra* note 33, at 5.

54. Sharon Sassler et al., *Planned Parenthood? Fertility Intentions and Experiences among Cohabiting Couples,* 30 JOURNAL OF FAMILY ISSUES 206, 213, 225 (2009).

55. *Id.* at 209; Sassler & Cunningham, *supra* note 33, at 6.

56. Sassler & Cunningham, *supra* note 33, at 6.

57. Child Trends, Births to Unmarried Women (2010), www.childtrendsdatabank.org/?q=node/196.

58. Sassler et al., *supra* note 54, at 209.

59. *See* Reed et al., *supra* note 52.

60. *Id.*

61. Pam Belluck, *Interest and Scientific Advances Lead to Progress on Contraceptive for Men,* N.Y. TIMES, Jul. 24, 2011.

62. Guttmacher Institute, Fact Sheet, Contraceptive Use in the United States (2012), *available at* http://www.guttmacher.org/pubs/fb_contr_use.pdf.

63. Adam Sonfield et al., *The Public Costs of Births Resulting from Unintended Pregnancies: National and State-Level Estimates,* 43 PERSPECTIVES ON SEXUAL AND REPRODUCTIVE HEALTH 98 (2011).

64. *Id.* at 97–98.

65. *Id.* at 99.

66. JENNIFER J. FROST ET AL., CONTRACEPTIVE NEEDS AND SERVICES: NATIONAL AND STATE DATA, 2008 UPDATE 5 (2010), *available at* http://www.guttmacher.org/pubs/win/contraceptive-needs-2008.pdf.

67. *Id.*

68. *See id.;* Monea & Thomas, *supra* note 43, at 89; FROST ET AL., *supra* note 66, at 3.

69. Sonfield et al., *supra* note 63, at 99.

70. Robert Pear, *Insurance Coverage for Contraception Is Required,* N.Y. TIMES, Aug. 1, 2011.

71. Sonfield et al., *supra* note 63, at 99.

72. DUNN, *supra* note 36, at 12.

73. *Id.* (emphasis in original).

74. GLADYS MARTINEZ ET AL., TEENAGERS IN THE UNITED STATES: SEXUAL ACTIVITY, CONTRACEPTIVE USE, AND CHILDBEARING, 2006–2010 NATIONAL SURVEY OF FAMILY GROWTH 2–3, 6 fig.1 (National Center for Health Statistics, Vital Health & Stat., Ser. 23, No. 31, (2011), *available at* http://www.cdc.gov/nchs/data/series/sr_23/sr23_031.pdf.

75. Crystal Tyler et al., *Sexual Experience and Contraceptive Use among Female Teens—United States, 1995, 2002, and 2006–2010,* Centers for Disease Control and Prevention (2012), *available at* http://www.cdc.gov/mmwr/pdf/wk/mm6117.pdf.

76. Associated Press, *Georgia: Study Finds Teenage Girls Are Using Better Birth Control,* N.Y. TIMES, May 3, 2012.

77. Sassler et al., *supra* note 54, at 226.

78. Reed et al., *supra,* note 52.

79. PEW RESEARCH CENTER, IN A DOWN ECONOMY, FEWER BIRTHS (2011), *available at* http://pewresearch.org/pubs/2115/births-fertility-rate-economy-recession.

80. GUTTMACHER INSTITUTE, A REAL-TIME LOOK AT THE IMPACT OF THE RECESSION ON WOMEN'S FAMILY PLANNING AND PREGNANCY DECISIONS 3–4 (2009), *available at* http://www.guttmacher.org/pubs/RecessionFP.pdf.

81. FROST ET AL., *supra* note 66, at 5.

82. Sassler et al., *supra* note 54, at 221.

83. Huang & Tanfer, *supra* note 41, at 13.

84. U. S. Census Bureau, Highlights, Current Population Survey, http://www.census.gov/hhes/www/poverty/about/overview/index.html; Sabrina Tavernise, *Soaring Poverty Casts Spotlight on "Lost Decade,"* N.Y. TIMES, Sept. 13, 2011.

85. Tavernise, *supra* note 34. In November 2011, the U.S. Census Bureau published a different rubric for calculating the percentage of Americans in poverty. According to this revised set of estimates, 18.2 percent of children live in poverty, a category that includes 13.6 million children. U.S. CENSUS BUREAU, THE RESEARCH SUPPLEMENTAL POVERTY MEASURE: 2010, 6 tbl.1 (2011), *available at* http://www.census.gov/hhes/povmeas/methodology/supplemental/research/Short_ResearchSPM2010.pdf.

86. Sassler & Cunningham, *supra* note 33, at 6.

87. Sassler et al., *supra note* 54, at 220.

88. Huang & Tanfer, *supra* note 41, at 17.

89. Sassler et al., *supra* note 54, at 223.

90. Hummer & Hamilton, *supra* note 17, at 118.

91. Kristen Harknett & Sara S. McLanahan, *Racial and Ethnic Differences in Marriage After the Birth of a Child,* 69 AM. SOC. REV. 790, 796 (2004).

92. Massey & Sampson, *supra* note 18, at 22.

93. Harknett & McLanahan, *supra* note 91, at 809.

94. Sassler & Cunningham, *supra* note 33, at 6, 21.

95. Harknett & McLanahan, *supra* note 91, at 796.

96. *Id.*

97. KANE & LICHTER, *supra* note 24, at 6.

98. Sassler et al., *supra* note 54, at 227.

99. *Id.* at 223.

100. *Id.* at 226.

101. *Id.*

102. Sassler & Cunningham, *supra* note 33, at 9.

103. Tamar Lewin, *College Graduation Rates Are Stagnant, Even as Enrollment Rises, a Study Finds,* N.Y. TIMES, Sept. 27, 2011, *available at* http://www.nytimes.com/2011/09/27/education/27remediation.html?emc=eta1.

104. *Id.*, quoting COMPLETE COLLEGE AMERICA, TIME IS THE ENEMY (2011), *available at* http://www.completecollege.org/docs/Time_Is_the_Enemy.pdf.

105. *Id.*

106. Tyler B. Jamison & Lawrence Ganong, *"'We're not living together': Stayover Rela-*

tionships among College-Educated Emerging Adults," 28 JOURNAL OF SOCIAL AND PERSONAL RELATIONSHIPS 537 (2011).

107. *Id.* at 553.
108. *Id.* at 538.
109. *Id.* at 551–52.
110. *Id.* at 538.
111. U. S. Census Bureau, *supra* note 84.
112. Tavernise, *supra* note 34, quoting Timothy Smeeding, director, Institute for Research and Poverty, University of Wisconsin–Madison.
113. *Id.*
114. WILSON, *supra* note 10, at 9.
115. Smock & Manning, *supra* note 8, at 106.
116. Sabrina Tavernise, *2010 Data Show Surge in Poor Young Families*, N.Y. TIMES, Sept. 19, 2011, *available at* http://www.nytimes.com/2011/09/20/us/poor-young-families-soared-in-10-data-show.html?_r=1&emc=eta1.
117. *Id.*
118. PAUL AMATO ET AL., ALONE TOGETHER 256 (2007).
119. CAHN & CARBONE, *supra* note 9, at 41.
120. *Id.*
121. Smock & Manning, *supra* note 8, at 105.
122. LASCH, *supra* note 5, at 139.
123. *Id.*
124. W. BRADFORD WILCOX, WHY MARRIAGE MATTERS: THIRTY CONCLUSIONS FROM THE SOCIAL SCIENCES, *Executive Summary* 1 (2011), *available at* http://www.americanvalues.org/pdfs/dl.php.
125. Stephanie Coontz, *The Future of Marriage*, CATO UNBOUND (Jan. 14, 2008), http://www.cato-unbound.org/2008/01/14/stephanie-coontz/the-future-of-marriage/.
126. *Id.*
127. *Id.*
128. DUNN, *supra* note 36, at 6.
129. Hope Yen, *Great Recession Yields a Lost Generation of Workers,* MSNBC.com (Sept. 22, 2011), http://www.msnbc.msn.com/id/44623502/ns/business-stocks_and_economy/t/great-recession-yields-lost-generation-workers/#.To-3wnO4Ki4.
130. Pew Research Center, *67% Optimistic about Future of Marriage* (January 6, 2011), http://pewresearch.org/databank/dailynumber/?NumberID=1163.
131. *Id.*

Chapter 7: The Uses of the Law for Contemporary Families

1. "Where There's Smoke," *ER*, Season 10, Episode 18, April 8, 2004 (NBC).
2. Niles Eldredge and S.J. Gould , *Punctuated Equilibria: An Alternative to Phyletic Gradualism, in* MODELS IN PALEOBIOLOGY 82–115 (T.J.M. Schopf ed., 1972).

3. 750 ILL. COMP. STAT. ANN. 75/1 (2011).
4. 750 ILL. COMP. STAT. ANN. 75/60.
5. 750 ILL. COMP. STAT. ANN. 45/2.
6. 705 ILL. COMP. STAT. ANN. 405/2-4(1)(a) (1992).
7. *In re* N.B., 730 N.E.2d 1086, 1088 (Ill. 2000).
8. *In re* C.B.L., 723 N.E.2d 316 (Ill. App. 1999).
9. *Id.* at 317.
10. The Illinois Parentage Act of 1984 defined a "parent and child relationship" as "the legal relationship existing between a child and his natural or adoptive parents" (750 ILL. COMP. STAT. ANN. 45/2). The statute prescribing who could petition for visitation, the Illinois Marriage and Dissolution of Marriage Act, specified that only a parent, stepparent, grandparent, great-grandparent, or sibling could do so. (750 ILL. COMP. STAT. ANN. 45/607).
11. *In re* C.B.L., 723 N.E.2d at 321.
12. *See In re* Marriage of Simmons, 825 N.E.2d 303 (Ill. App. 2005) (refusing to grant legal status to de facto parenthood).
13. *In re* Parentage of L.B., 122 P.3d 161, 176 (Wash. 2005).
14. *Id.* We discuss the jurisdictions adopting similar reasoning acknowledging de facto parenthood in chapter 5.
15. 755 ILL. COMP. STAT. ANN. 5/11-5.3 (1995).
16. 755 ILL. COMP. STAT. ANN. 5/11-5(b-1).
17. Petition of K.M., 653 N.E.2d 888 (Ill. App. 1995) (holding that unmarried same-sex cohabitants have standing to jointly petition for adoption).
18. 750 ILL. COMP. STAT. ANN. 50/0.01 *et seq.* (2008).
19. In the roughly two-thirds of the states whose appellate courts have considered second-parent adoption, most have allowed them (*see, e.g.,* Sharon S. v. Superior Court of San Diego County, 73 P.3d 554 (Ca. 2003)); while several have disallowed them (*see, e.g., In re* Adoption of Luke, 640 N.W.2d 374 (Neb. 2000)). *See generally* Jane S. Schacter, *Constructing Families in a Democracy: Courts, Legislatures and Second-Parent Adoption,* 75 CHI.-KENT L. REV. 933 (2000).
20. ABNER J. MIKVA & ERIC LANE, AN INTRODUCTION TO STATUTORY INTERPRETATION AND THE LEGISLATIVE PROCESS 4 (1997), quoting CASS R. SUNSTEIN, AFTER THE RIGHTS REVOLUTION 113 (1990). Former New York Court of Appeals judge Bernard S. Meyer cast doubt, however, on the view that legislation generally represents an intelligent and majoritarian resolution.

> The deference courts give to legislative action or inaction is predicated upon assumptions many of which are little more than fiction: that legislatures act in the interest of the majority, that most legislators who vote upon a given bill have studied it carefully and are knowledgeable concerning its provisions, and that legislators are aware of court decisions and have acted or have failed to act on the basis of that knowledge. In reality, what presently blocks the legislative origination of substantive laws or revision of ambiguous or obsolete statutes is usually

either inertia or the political pressures of one or more powerful groups rather than the considered decision of the majority.

Bernard S. Meyer, *Justice, Bureaucracy, Structure, and Simplification*, 42 MD. L. REV. 659, 677–78 (1983) (citations omitted).

21. David A. Strauss, *Common Law, Common Ground, and Jefferson's Principle*, 112 YALE L.J. 1717, 1731 (2003); *see id.* ("The common law approach does not treat past decisions as binding commands; it adheres to those decisions only because, and to the extent that, it makes good functional sense to do so."); Judith S. Kaye, *State Courts at the Dawn of a New Century: Common Law Courts Reading Statutes and Constitutions*, 70 N.Y.U. L. REV. 1, 5 (1995) ("While it is durable, certain, and predictable at its core, the common law is not static. It proceeds and grows incrementally, in restrained and principled fashion, to fit into a changing society.") (citation omitted).

22. *See* JOHN DEWITT GREGORY ET AL., UNDERSTANDING FAMILY LAW 2–3 (3d. ed. 2005).

23. *See, e.g.,* City of Lafayette Power & Light Co., 435 U.S. 389, 437 (1978) (Brennan, J., dissenting) ("[S]tate statutes often are enacted with little recorded legislative history, and the bare words of a statute will often be unilluminating in interpreting legislative intent."); Eric Lane, *Legislative Process and Its Judicial Renderings: A Study in Contrast*, 48 U. PITT. L. REV. 639, 651 (1987) (arguing that "legislative history is generally ignored because [state] legislators see no need for it").

24. Kaye, *supra* note 21, at 33–34.

25. *In re* C.B.L., 723 N.E.2d 316, at 318 (Ill. App. 1999).

26. *Id.*

27. 750 ILL. COMP. STAT. ANN. 45/607.

28. *See* AMERICAN LAW INSTITUTE, PRINCIPLES OF THE LAW OF FAMILY DISSOLUTION: ANALYSIS AND RECOMMENDATIONS (2002). The ALI principles support a determination of functional parenthood along the lines set out in the text. *See also* J. Herbie DiFonzo, *Toward a Unified Field Theory of the Family: The American Law Institute's Principles of the Law of Family Dissolution*, 2001 B.Y.U. L. REV. 923, 938 (describing the aim of the principles as resolving the tension between the allocation of full recognition to legal parents and the harm that results from disallowing the maintenance of bonds between children and functional parents); Barbara Bennett Woodhouse, *Horton Looks at the ALI Principles*, 4 J.L. & FAM. STUD. 151, 165 (2002) (affirming that the ALI Principles present a more flexible and functional definition of family).

29. *See* Suzanne B. Goldberg et al., *Family Law Scholarship Goes to Court: Functional Parenthood and the Case of Debra H. v. Janice R.*, 20 COLUM. J. GENDER & L. 348, 351–52 (2011).

30. *See id.* at 357 ("[T]he functional approach . . . endorsed by both scholars and numerous courts reflects the reality of family life today, and in doing so promotes the best interests of children. . . .").

31. 750 ILL. COMP. STAT. ANN. 75/5.

32. *See generally* JOANNA L. GROSSMAN & LAWRENCE M. FRIEDMAN, INSIDE THE CASTLE: LAW AND THE FAMILY IN TWENTIETH-CENTURY AMERICA 128–36 (2011).

33. Marvin v. Marvin, 557 P.2d 106 (Cal. 1976); *see* Mark K. Moller, *Almost Like Being Married*, LEGAL TIMES, Apr. 5, 2004, *available at* http://www.cato.org/research/articles/moller-040405.html (describing the notoriety of the Marvin case).

34. Lee Marvin had won the Oscar for Best Actor for *Cat Ballou* (1965). He also starred in *The Man Who Shot Liberty Valence* (1962), *The Dirty Dozen* (1967), and *Paint Your Wagon* (1969). Toward the end of this period, Marvin was earning a million dollars per movie. Even though he did not divorce his first wife until 1967, Michelle claimed palimony based on the six years she and Lee lived together, beginning in 1965.

35. *See* Trutalli v. Meravigila, 12 P.2d 430 (Cal. 1932); Vallera v. Vallera, 134 P.2d 761 (Cal. 1943).

36. Marvin v. Marvin, 557 P.2d at 116.

37. The California Court of Appeal summarized the trial court's findings of fact rejecting each of Michelle Marvin's contentions.

> [T]he parties to this lawsuit never agreed during their cohabitation that they would combine their efforts and earnings or would share equally in any property accumulated as a result of their efforts, whether individual or combined. They also never agreed during this period that plaintiff would relinquish her professional career as an entertainer and singer in order to devote her efforts full time to defendant as his companion and homemaker generally. Defendant did not agree during this period of cohabitation that he would provide all of plaintiff's financial needs and support for the rest of her life.

Marvin v. Marvin, 122 Cal. App. 3d 871, 873 (Cal. App. 1981).

38. *Id.* (citing the trial court's findings of fact).

39. Oddly, the trial court held that even though Lee Marvin had incurred no support obligations, he must pay Michelle "rehabilitation" payments of $104,000 to enable her to learn new employable skills. The appellate court reversed this holding, finding no basis for it in law or equity. *Id.* at 877.

40. Marvin v. Marvin, 557 P.2d at 118 n.16.

41. *Id.* at 118.

42. Kozlowski v. Kozlowski, 403 A.2d 902, 906 (N.J. 1979).

43. *See, e.g.*, Devaney v. L'Esperance, 949 A.2d 743, 754–58 (N.J. 2008) (Rivera-Soto, J., concurring) (discussing the range of state court rulings on the enforcement of nonmarital contracts).

44. Morone v. Morone, 413 N.E.2d 1154 (N.Y. 1980). Mississippi also refuses to recognize implied contracts for unmarried cohabitants. Cates v. Swain, __So.3d__, 2012 WL 1292639 (Miss. App.), cert. granted, 101 So.3d 1171 (2012).

45. Morone v. Morone, 413 N.E.2d at 1157. Even express contracts between cohabi-

tants present problems of proof, for quite similar reasons. *See* Soderholm v. Kosty, 676 N.Y.S.2d 850 (Chemung County Justice Ct. 1998).

46. Marvin v. Marvin, 557 P.2d at 122.

47. Soderholm v. Kosty, 676 N.Y.S. 2d at 853.

48. *See* NATIONAL CENTER FOR LESBIAN RIGHTS, MARRIAGE, DOMESTIC PARTNERSHIPS, AND CIVIL UNIONS: AN OVERVIEW OF RELATIONSHIP RECOGNITION FOR SAME-SEX COUPLES WITHIN THE UNITED STATES (2011), *available at* http://www.nclrights.org/site/DocServer/Relationship_Recognition_Update_-_09_03_08.pdf?docID=881.

49. National Conference of State Legislatures, Civil Unions & Domestic Partnership Statutes (Mar. 2013), http://www.ncsl.org/issues-research/human-services/civil-unions-and-domestic-partnership-statutes.aspx.

50. ORE. REV. STAT. ANN. §106.305(4) (2009).

51. ORE. REV. STAT. ANN. §106.340.

52. *See generally* J. Herbie DiFonzo, *Unbundling Marriage,* 32 HOFSTRA L. REV. 31, 58–60 (2003) (discussing various forms of publicly and privately sponsored domestic partnerships).

53. COLO. REV. STAT. ANN. §§ 15-22-101 to 112 (2009).

54. COLO. REV. STAT. ANN. § 15-22-105.

55. James Schaefer, *Domestic Partner Benefits in the United States,* GRAZIADIO BUSINESS REVIEW (Aug. 2010), http://gbr.pepperdine.edu/2010/08/domestic-partner-benefits-in-the-united-states/.

56. Cleveland Division of Assessments and Licenses, Domestic Partner Registry, http://www.cleveland-oh.gov/CityofCleveland/Home/Government/CityAgencies/Finance/AssessmentsandLicenses#domestic.

57. Damon Sims, *Cleveland Council Votes to Enact Domestic Partner Registry,* CLEVELAND PLAIN DEALER, Dec. 8, 2008, *available at* http://blog.cleveland.com/metro/2008/12/cleveland_council_votes_to_ena.html.

58. Thomas Ott, *Cleveland Approves Domestic-Partner Insurance Coverage,* CLEVELAND PLAIN DEALER, July 20, 2011, *available at* http://blog.cleveland.com/metro/2011/07/cleveland_considers_domestic-p.html.

59. *Id.*

60. In its *Principles of the Law of Family Dissolution* (2002), the American Law Institute proposed defining "domestic partners" in terms of behavior rather than contract or formal registration. *See* AMERICAN LAW INSTITUTE, *supra* n. 28, at § 6.03(1) (defining domestic partners as "two persons of the same or opposite sex, not married to one another, who for a significant period of time share a primary residence and a life together as a couple"). The ALI principles also provide that when two people have a common child and have "maintained a common household" for a specific length of time, called the "cohabitation parenting period," they are domestic partners. *Id.* at § 6.03(2). Several relevant factors are listed and elaborated. *Id.* at § 6.03(3)–(7). Further, in a critical shift from current legal

principles, the ALI principles provide that the property of a domestic partnership should be divided according to the principles set forth for the division of marital property. *Id.* at § 6.05. Similarly, a domestic partner is entitled to "compensatory payments," (the term for alimony in the ALI principles) on the same basis as a spouse. *Id.* at § 6.06.

On the one hand, these provisions have been criticized as attempts to reverse the long-term movement of the law from status to contract by defining domestic partnership as a status and imbuing it with attributes that these couples may not have intended. *See* David Westfall, *Forcing Incidents of Marriage on Unmarried Cohabitants: The American Law Institute's Principles of Family Dissolution*, 76 NOTRE DAME L. REV. 1467 (2001) (criticizing the ALI principles for attaching marital status to domestic partners for purposes of maintenance and property division). On the other hand, the provisions have been applauded as efforts to make "marriage matter less." *See* Nancy D. Polikoff, *Making Marriage Matter Less: The ALI Domestic Partner Principles are One Step in the Right Direction*, 2004 U. CHI. LEGAL F. 353. For more analysis of the domestic partnership provisions, see Margaret F. Brinig, *Domestic Partnership: Missing the Target?*, 4 J. L. & FAM. STUD. 19 (2002); and Martha M. Ertmann, *The ALI Principles' Approach to Domestic Partnership*, 8 DUKE J. GENDER L. & POL'Y 107 (2001). Clearly the ALI principles have not yet had the significant impact the drafters expected, in terms of broad acceptance by legislatures and courts. *See* Michael R. Clisham & Robin Fretwell Wilson, *American Law Institute's Principles of the Law of Family Dissolution, Eight Years after Adoption: Guiding Principles or Obligatory Footnote?* 42 FAM. L.Q. 573 (2008).

61. Ann Laquer Estin, *Family Law Federalism: Divorce and the Constitution*, 16 WILLIAM & MARY BILL RTS. J., 381, 382 (2007); *see* United States v. Morrison, 529 U.S. 598, 615–16 (2000) (identifying domestic relations jurisprudence as an "area of traditional state regulation").

62. *Id.* at 383; *see also* Kristin A. Collins, *Federalism's Fallacy: The Early Tradition of Federal Family Law and the Invention of States' Rights*, 26 CARDOZO L. REV. 1761, 1861 (2005) (citing historical sources to show that "there has never been a point in American history when the states exercised exclusive authority over family law and policy").

63. *See* William Baude, *Beyond DOMA: Choice of State Law in Federal Statutes*, 62 STAN. L. REV. 1371, 1374 (2012) ("Because of the large number of same-sex marriages and federal laws that refer to marital status, those choice-of-law cases will be numerous. And because of the wide divergence in state marriage laws, those conflicts will be difficult to dodge.").

64. *See* National Center for Lesbian Rights, Summary of Laws regarding Same-Sex Couples (2012), *available at* http://www.nclrights.org/site/DocServer/Relationship_Recognition_State_Laws_Summary.pdf.

65. *Id.*

66. *See* MARK STRASSER, SAME-SEX UNIONS ACROSS THE UNITED STATES 113 (2011) ("Congress or the courts must act to prevent states from imposing invidious burdens on same-sex parents and their children, which only result in harm to all con-

cerned. At a time when many decry the breakup of the family and the accompanying instability thereby imposed on innocent children, states' placing extra burdens on LGBT families is simply unconscionable.")

67. *See* U.S. Dep't of Justice, Statement of the Attorney General on Litigation Involving the Defense of Marriage Act (Feb. 23, 2011), http://www.justice.gov/opa/pr/2011/February/11-ag-222.html (describing President Obama's conclusion that DOMA is unconstitutional and that the Department of Justice should no longer defend the statute against court challenge); U.S. v. Windsor, No. 12-307, 570 U.S. __ (June 26, 2013).

68. *See* G. M. Filisko, *Patchwork Partnering: States Can't Agree on the Legal Status of Same-Sex Couples,* A.B.A. JOURNAL, Nov. 2011, at 18.

69. Vivian Hamilton, *Principles of U.S. Family Law,* 75 FORDHAM L. REV. 31, 33 (2006); *see id.* ("Same-sex couples and their families receive public benefits and protections in many cases, while proponents of the Defense of Marriage Act, state constitutional amendments, and the proposed Federal Marriage Amendment seek to withdraw or minimize those benefits and protections.").

70. Valarie King, *Nonresident Father Involvement and Child Well-Being: Can Dads Make a Difference?,* 158 J. FAM. ISSUES 78, 83 (1994).

71. *Id.* at 80, 87.

72. *Id.* at 87–88.

73. Joan B. Kelly, *Changing Perspectives on Children's Adjustment Following Divorce: A View from the United States,* 10 CHILDHOOD 237, 248 (2003).

74. Paul R. Amato & Joan G. Gilbreth, *Nonresident Fathers and Children's Well-Being: A Meta-Analysis,* 61 J. MARR. & FAM. 557, 558 (1999).

75. *Id.* at 569.

76. King, *supra* note 70, at 91.

77. Amato & Gilbreth, *supra* note 74, at 559.

78. Wendy D. Manning et al., *The Complexity of Fathers' Parenting Responsibilities and Involvement with Nonresident Children,* 24 J. FAM. ISSUES 645 (2003).

79. *Id.* at 663.

80. Elizabeth C. Cooksey & Patricia H. Craig, *Parenting from a Distance: The Effects of Paternal Characteristics on Contact between Nonresidential Fathers and Their Children,* 35 DEMOGRAPHY 187, 198 (1998).

81. Manning et al., *supra,* note 78, at 663–64.

82. *Id.* at 659.

83. Drew A. Swank, *The National Child Non-Support Epidemic,* 2 MICH. ST. DCL L. REV. 357, 358 (2003).

84. *Id.* at 368–78.

85. Leslie Joan Harris, *Questioning Child Support Enforcement Policy for Poor Families,* 45 FAM. L.Q. 157, 171 (2011).

86. *Id.* at 172.

87. Sandra L. Hofferth & Kermyt G. Anderson, *Are All Dads Equal? Biology versus Marriage as a Basis for Paternal Involvement,* 65 J. MARR. & FAM. 213, 231 (2003).

88. Cooksey and Craig, *supra* note 80, at 198.

89. Juliana Sobolewski and Valarie King, *The Importance of the Coparental Relationship for Nonresident Fathers' Ties to Children*, 67 J. MARR. & FAM. 1196, 1200 (2005).

90. Id.

91. Cooksey and Craig, *supra* note 80, at 199.

92. Manning et al., *supra,* note 78, at 665.

93. NANCY COTT, PUBLIC VOWS 224 (2000).

94. *Defense of Marriage Act: Update to Prior Report,* Letter from Dayna K. Shah, Associate General Counsel, General Accounting Office, to Bill Frist, Majority Leader, United States Senate, Jan. 23, 2004, *available at* http://www.gao.gov/new.items/d04353r.pdf.

95. Tara Siegel Bernard, *How Gay Marriage Will Change Couples' Financial Lives,* N.Y. TIMES, Jun. 27, 2011, quoting Susan Sommer, director of constitutional litigation, Lambda Legal.

96. James G. Palewski et al., *The Effects of Marriage, Civil Union, and Domestic Partnership Laws on the Health and Well-Being of Children,* 118 PEDIATRICS 349, 356 (2006): *see* Gregory M. Herek, *Legal Recognition of Same-Sex Relationships in the United States: A Social Science Perspective,* 61 AMER. PSYCH. 607–21 (2006) (concluding that "same-sex couples and their children are likely to benefit in numerous ways from legal recognition of their families, and providing such recognition through marriage will bestow greater benefit than civil unions or domestic partnerships").

97. LINDA J. WAITE & MAGGIE GALLAGHER, THE CASE FOR MARRIAGE 201 (2000).

98. COTT, *supra* note 93, at 224.

99. *See, e.g.,* Hamilton, *supra* note 69, at 71 (arguing that "Biblical traditionalism ultimately expresses an ideal that elevates family form over family function, unfairly excluding many families from the institutional benefits afforded marital families").

100. Palewski et al., *supra* note 96, at 351.

101. *Id.* at 361; *see* Herek, *supra* note 96 (reporting findings that "a parent's sexual orientation is unrelated to her or his ability to provide a healthy and nurturing family environment").

102. Deane v. Conaway, 2006 WL 148145 (Md. Cir. Ct. 2006), *rev'd sub nom.* Conaway v. Deane, 932 A.2d 571 (Md. 2007).

103. Palewski et al., *supra* note 96, at 352.

Conclusion

1. Andrew J. Cherlin, *The Deinstitutionalization of American Marriage,* 66 J. MARR. & FAM. 848, 857 (2004).

2. PAUL H. LANDIS, MAKING THE MOST OF MARRIAGE 8 (1955) (emphasis in original).

3. D'Vera Cohn et al., *Barely Half of U.S. Adults Are Married—a Record Low,* Pew Research Center (Dec.14, 2011), http://www.pewsocialtrends.org/2011/12/14/barely-half-of-u-s-adults-are-married-a-record-low/.

4. Cherlin, *supra* note 1, at 855.

5. *Id.* at 858.

6. *Id.*

7. Kelly Musick & Larry Bumpass, *Reexamining the Case for Marriage: Union Formation and Changes in Well-Being*, 74 J. MARR. & FAM. 1, 12 (2012).

8. *Id.* at 14.

9. *Id.* at 9.

10. *Id.* at 13.

11. *Id.* at 2.

12. *Id.* at 13.

13. Meg Jay, *The Downside of Cohabiting before Marriage*, N.Y. TIMES, Apr. 15, 2012.

14. Cherlin, *supra* note 1, at 858.

15. Jim Dwyer, *She Waited 40 Years to Marry, Then When Her Wife Died, the Tax Bill Came*, N.Y. TIMES, June 7, 2012.

16. U.S. v. Windsor, No. 12-307, 570 U.S. __ (June 26, 2013). Writing for the majority, Justice Kennedy stated that

> DOMA undermines both the public and private significance of state-sanctioned same-sex marriages; for it tells those couples, and all the world, that their otherwise valid marriages are unworthy of federal recognition. This places same-sex couples in an unstable position of being in a second-tier marriage. The differentiation demeans the couple, whose moral and sexual choices the Constitution protects . . . and whose relationship the State has sought to dignify. And it humiliates tens of thousands of children now being raised by same-sex couples. The law in question makes it even more difficult for the children to understand the integrity and closeness of their own family and its concord with other families in their community and in their daily lives.

Id., Slip Op. at 22–23.

17. Loving v. Virginia, 388 U.S. 1 (1967) (holding that the miscegenation statutes adopted by Virginia to prevent marriages between persons solely on basis of racial classification violated the equal protection and due process clauses of the 14th Amendment).

18. JEAN M. AUEL, THE LAND OF PAINTED CAVES (2011).

19. Jay, *supra* note 13.

20. Ken Fuchsman, *The Family Romance Transformed: American Domestic Arrangements since 1960*, 17 CLIO'S PSYCHE 275 (2011).

21. *Id.* at 285.

22. The baby boomers—prime movers of the divorce revolution—grew up in largely intact families. But their coming-of-age coincided with a cultural wave of free expression in romantic relationships. Today's commitment-averse young adults are reaping that whirlwind of instability.

INDEX

Note: Page numbers in italics indicate tables.

abuse. *See* domestic violence and physical abuse; drugs and substance abuse
acquired immunodeficiency syndrome (AIDS), 115
Administration for Children and Families, 111
adoption: about the stigma of childlessness, 68; *Baby M* case, 65–67; creating "family" through, 6, 85–86; fees and costs, 67–68; gay-lesbian issues, 80–81, 99–103, 131–35, 210n104; parental and legal rights, 36, 86–94, 146, 201n25; parent-child bonding, 79; same-sex households, 212n122; stepparent rights, 209n99; surrogacy issues, 94–99, 187n20; unmarried relationships and, 210n104
adultery, 19, 156n65, 161n130, 161n132, 169n34
A.G.R. v. D.R.H. and S.H., 66, 71–72
Alexander, Paul W., 19
alimony and spousal support, 15, 18, 37, 141, 157n84, 157n87, 161n123, 223n60
Amato, Paul, 54, 59, 125, 143
American Bar Association, 20, 96, 163n135, 208n84
American Community Survey (Census Bureau, 2012), 24

American family: about the changing picture of, 1–4; impact of reproductive technology on, 88–94; impact of single-mother-by choice on, 69–70; legal decisions impacting, 16; restoring stability and commitment, 150; 20th century views and legacy, 9–14, 154n28, 176n137; 21st century views and domestic arrangements, 25–26. *See also* nontraditional families; parent/rights and responsibilities
American Law Institute, 137, 201n25, 206n64, 222–23n60
American Society of Reproductive Medicine (ASRM), 78, 82
Angelman syndrome, 80
annulment. *See* divorce
Arizona, 157n73
artificial insemination (AI), 28, 65, 87–88, 170n46
Assisted Reproductive Technology (ART): about the issues of, 5–6; acceptance by society, 28; as solution to childlessness, 64–65; case of *A.G.R. v. D.R.H. and S.H.*, 66, 71–72; case of *Baby M*, 65–66, 74–75; changing nature of parental relationships, 86–87; defining "parent" in, 66–

228 INDEX

Assisted Reproductive Technology (*continued*)
70; definition of marriage and family, 6–7, 26–30; issues relating to donors, 76–78; issues relating to surrogacy, 71–76; issues relating to children of, 78–84; legal challenges to surrogacy, 94–99. *See also* egg and sperm donation; in vitro fertilization; surrogacy
Auel, Jean M., 150

Baber, Ray E., 24
Baby and Child Care (Spock), 13
baby boomer era, 4, 31, 43–44, 148, 152n10, 226n22
Baby M case, 5–6, 65–67, 74, 94–99
Baker, Katherine, 97
Beckwith-Wiedemann syndrome, 80
Bierce, Ambrose, 52
birth control, 12, 22, 50–51, 114–19
birth defects, 80–81
birth rates: cohabitation relationships and, 116–17; decline in marriage and, 28–29; economic stability and, 120; increase for unmarried women, 30, 69, 167n23, 170n48; increase in women over age 35, 66; increases from fertility treatment, 68, 70, 76, 187n12; married parents, 30; teens and unmarried women, 115, 120
blended families, 2, 25
bonding, issues relating to concept of: impact on children, 150; marital, 2, 48, 56, 169n35; maternal surrogate, 74–75; parent-child, 6, 62, 65–67, 74–75, 79; same-sex unions, 85, 89–93, 131–35
Boseman, Julia Catherine, 99–103
Boseman v. Jarrell (North Carolina, 2010), 99–103, 211n106, 211n108, 211n219, 212n122
Bumpass, Larry, 148–49
Burgess, Ernest, 49–50, 51
Buzzanca, John and Luanne, 98

Cahn, Naomi, 67
California, 15, 20, 66, 70, 73, 83, 96–98, 138–39, 157n76, 163n139, 164n146, 172n97, 208n89, 210n104, 221n37
Calvert, Johnson v. (California), 96–97
Carbone, June, 67
case studies: *Boseman v. Jarrell*, 99–103, 211n106, 211n108, 211n219, 212n122; Culpepper-Galiwango—in vitro fertilization, 103–8, 212n130; Kerry Weaver TV custody dispute, 128, 131–35; *Marvin v. Marvin*—palimony, 138–40, 221n34, 221n37, 221n39
census statistics. *See* U.S. Census Bureau
Cherlin, Andrew, 51, 55–56, 148
child support, 105–107, 130, 141, 143–45. *See also* custody
civil union and domestic partnership: about the recognition of, 2, 34; benefits and rights, 145, 172n95; children and parental rights, 131–37, 142, 201n26, 225n96; defined/described, 140; gender roles and division of labor, 42; legality among states, 142, 149, 168n26; registry, 140–41. *See also* same-sex unions
Clark, Homer H., Jr., 19
cognitive development, 80
cohabitation: about the growth and prevalence, 44; changing the definition of marriage, 1; comparison to marriage, 52–57; defined/described, 30–31; displacement of marriage, 29, 31–33; gender roles and division of labor, 41, 54–57; impact on children, 44–45, 60–63, 109; redefining parent-child relationships, 7; as substitute for marriage, 4–5. *See also* nontraditional families; same-sex unions; unmarried relationships
Cold War, marriage and family in the era of, 10–14
collaborative reproduction, 66–67. *See also* Assisted Reproductive Technology
Colorado, 86, 140, 164n152
commercial surrogacy, 67–70, 72–73, 76
commitment: about the changing nature of, 1–2, 27; cohabitation and, 5, 33, 56–57, 121–24, 145–46; cohabitation and economic factors, 124–27; impact on chil-

INDEX 229

dren, 60–61, 79; marriage as expression of, 51. *See also* love/romance, role in relationships
common-law doctrine/interpretations: adjudicating family law disputes, 87; assisted reproductive technology and, 89; de facto parenthood, 87, 131–35; illegitimate children (*filius nullis*), 166n12; *in loco parentis*, 201n25, 202n33; parent-child relationships, 135–37; surrogacy issues, 94
common-law marriage, 4, 14, 130, 138–39
companionate marriage, 22, 49–51, 63, 165n159, 182n53
compensatory payment. *See* alimony
conflict-of-law/choice of law, 141–42
Connecticut, 34, 86, 201n20
contemporary families. *See* American family; nontraditional families; nuclear family
contraception. *See* birth control
Cooksey, Elizabeth C., 144–45
Coontz, Stephanie, 45, 48–49, 50, 126
cooperative co-parental relationship, 59
Craig, Patricia H., 144–45
Culliton v. Beth Israel Deaconess Medical Center (Massachusetts), 95
Culpepper, Cindy Lee, 103–108
Cunningham, Anna, 122
custody: about the changing nature of, 2, 23; *Boseman v. Jarrell*, 99–103, 211n106, 211n108, 211n219, 212n122; cohabitation relationships and, 52; Culpepper-Galiwango - in vitro fertilization, 103–8, 212n130; de facto parents, 205n61; gender-based rulings, 37–38, 160n119; Kerry Weaver TV scenario, 128, 131–35; in loco parentis, 206n63; nontraditional family disputes, 88–93, 129, 199n13; paternity disputes, 143; same-sex unions, 201n21; stepparents, 62, 204n51, 204n56; surrogacy issues, 67, 78–79, 94–99, 190n85. *See also* child support; visitation rights

de facto parent: adjusting family law to address, 3, 87–88; defining rights and responsibilities, 200n14, 201n25, 205n58; legal decisions impacting, 198n7, 205n61; litigation and legal determinations, 88–94; needs within nontraditional families, 133–37, 146–47. *See also* parent/parenthood
Defense of Marriage Act of 1996 (DOMA), 34–35, 142, 149, 172–73n99, 223n63, 224n67, 226nn16
Deficit Reduction Act of 2005, 111
Delaware, 140, 205n61
District of Columbia, 34, 35
divorce: about the rise in rate, 11, 28–29, 162n135, 163n143; alimony and spousal support, 15, 18, 38, 141, 157n84, 157n87, 161n123, 223n60; annulment, 158n96, 161n132; establishing legal "guilt" and "innocence," 18–20; on grounds of adultery, 156n65; impact on children, 44–45, 59–60; marital cruelty and, 16, 19, 158n93, 161n130; marital rape and, 16, 158n89; marriage and American attitude toward, 14–15; post-WWI impact on, 49; post-WWII impact on, 9–11, 163n140. *See also* marriage; no-fault divorce
Dolgin, Janet, 75
domestic partnership. *See* civil unions and domestic partnership
domestic violence and physical abuse, 15–17, 113, 115
donor. *See* egg and sperm donation
donor insemination (DI), 78–83
donor registry, 77–78, 82–83
Donor Sibling Registry (DSR), 83–84
Drabiak, Katherine, 75–76
drugs and substance abuse, 81, 112, 113
Due Process Clause, U.S. 14th Amendment, 15, 92–93, 226n17

Earth's Children (Auel), 150
Edin, Kathryn, 116
education: ART and, 79–80; cohabitation relationships and, 55–57, 61–62, 122–23; economic stability and, 7, 32, 43–45, 53, 63, 112–13; gestational surrogacy and, 76–77; impact on children, 57–60; income

education (*continued*)
and earnings potential, 38, 125, 145; nuclear family parental roles, 12–15; social class and mobility, 46–47; unplanned pregnancy and, 114–24; women surpassing men, 47, 50–51

Eftimiou v. Eftimiou (1960), 16–17

egg and sperm donation: adjudicating family law disputes, 198n8; cognitive development issues, 79–80; defining "family" in light of, 2; defining the legal father in, 28; defining the natural mother, 74–75; disclosure of donor identity, 64–65; donor age, 78; donor health, 77–78; money and parental status, 67–70. *See also* Assisted Reproductive Technology; in vitro fertilization; surrogacy

employment: gender wage disparity, 38; low-income minorities, 113; opportunities for women, 12–13, 47; relationship to cohabitation and marriage, 112–13; same-sex benefits, 35. *See also* unemployment

epigenetic disorders, 80

equitable parent, 89–91, 96

Estin, Ann, 141

ethics, ART and, 78, 82, 87

ethnicity. *See* race and ethnicity

extended family, 12, 84, 154n29

Family in Transition (Skolnick and Skolnick), 151n2

family law: about the changing nature of, 128–30; case study—Kerry Weaver TV scenario, 128, 131–35; civil unions and domestic relationships, 140–41; palimony and enforceable contracts, 138–40, 221n34, 221n37, 221n39; parent-child relationships, 135–37; role of fathers, 142–45; state-federal "conflict-of-law," 141–42

family planning programs, 119–20

family therapy, 13

family/family structure: about the changing nature of, 151n1, 151n3; assessing the well-being of, 43–45; children in, 24–25, 57–63; decline in relevancy to marriage, 1–4, 22–23; defined/described, 27; litigation and legal determinations, 88–94; marriage as foundation, 110–11; marriage as option, 24; marriage promotion strategies, 111–14; member satisfaction, 27–28; role of economics, 109–10; unplanned births and pregnancy prevention, 114–19. *See also* bonding; cohabitation; nuclear family; parent/parenthood; stepfamilies/stepparents

Federal Defense of Marriage Act. *See* Defense of Marriage Act of 1996

Federal Marriage Amendment, 34–35, 224n69

The Feminine Mystique (Friedan), 12–13

fertility tourism, 70

Florida, 209n103

14th Amendment (U.S. Constitution), 15, 92–93, 226n17

Fretwell-Wilson, Robin, 54

Friedan, Betty, 12

Galiwango, Charles Kenneth, 103–8

Gallagher, Maggie, 52, 54–55, 145–46

Gallup polls, 14–15, 25–27

gay marriage. *See* same-sex unions

gender: changing the definition of marriage, 4–5; civil unions and domestic relationships, 42; cohabitation roles and division of labor, 41, 54–57; custody rulings, 37–38, 160n119; employment and wage disparity, 38–39; marriage roles and division of labor, 15, 37–42, 177–78n145; nuclear family parental roles, 48–49; poverty and, 175n126; roles in post–WWII marriage, 12–14

genetic engineering, 70

Gerould, Katharine Fullerton, 18

gestational surrogacy: increase due to ART, 28; legal contracts/adjudication, 87, 88, 95–96; race/ethnicity and, 191n122; second-parent disputes, 96–98, 105–106; societal acceptance, 199n10. *See also* surrogacy

Gilbreth, Joan G., 143

Glendon, Mary Ann, 27

Goldbeck, Lutz, 79

Golombok, Susan, 79
Gottlieb, Lori, 69–70
grandparents, 61, 93, 133, 136–37, 219n10
Granville, Troxel v. (U.S. Supreme Court, 2000), 95
Grossberg, Michael, 90
Grossman, Joanna, 95
Guttmacher Institute, 119

happiness, 18–20, 44, 47–48, 54, 127, 148, 152n8, 162n134, 169n36, 177–78n145. *See also* satisfaction and self-expression
Hartog, Hendrik, 40
Hawaii, 140
Healthy Marriage Initiative, 111–14
hedonic marriage, 51, 125
Hochschild, Arlie, 40
Hollingsworth, Donald and Sean, 66, 72
Hollingsworth v. Perry (U.S. Supreme Court, 2013), 172n97
hormonal ovarian stimulation, 77
Huang, Penelope M., 120–21
human immunodeficiency virus (HIV/AIDS), 115

illegitimacy, 25, 126, 159n96, 166n12, 198n7
Illinois, 26, 95–96, 131–35, 140, 161n132, 164n150
Illinois Marriage and Dissolution of Marriage Act of 1977, 136–37
Illinois Parentage Act of 1984, 131
Illinois Religious Freedom Protection and civil Union Act of 2011, 131, 168n26
infertility, 67–69, 77, 80, 195n219
infidelity. *See* adultery
Institute for Social Research (University of Michigan), 40
Institute of Women's Policy Research, 38
international adoption, 68. *See also* adoption
interracial marriage, 14–15
intracytoplasmic sperm injection (ICSI), 80
Iowa, 19, 34, 47, 161nn129–30, 186n181

Jarrell, Melissa Ann, 99–103
Jay, Meg, 56

Johnson v. Calvert (California), 96–97
judicial lawmaking, 89–91

Kaye, Judith S., 136
Kefalas, Maria, 116
Khrushchev, Nikita, 11
Kramer, Wendy, 77, 78, 83
Kulstad v. Maniaci (Montana, 2009), 90

Landis, Paul H., 9, 10, 148, 152n6
Lasch, Christopher, 126
lesbian families. *See* same-sex unions
Levine, Hal, 74
Long, Virginia A., 86
Love Story (movie, 1970), 22
love/romance, role in relationships: ART and, 64–65; birth control and, 50–51; family stability and, 44, 226n22; marriage and divorce, 18–22, 110–11, 121–23, 152n6; single parenthood and, 69–71. *See also* commitment
Loving v. Virginia (U.S. Supreme Court, 1967), 149

MacDougall, Kirstin, 83
Machung, Anne, 40
Maine, 34, 91
Making the Most of Marriage (Landis), 9
Manning, Wendy D., 33
marital cruelty, 16, 19, 158n93, 161n130, 161n132
marital fidelity, 53, 169n34
marital rape, 16, 158n89
Marquardt, Elizabeth, 81
marriage: about the changing nature of, 9–10, 47–48; benefits and rights of, 8; census statistics, 153n23; cohabitation as precursor, 30–33, 55–56; comparison to cohabitation, 52–57; decline in rates, 29–30, 50; defined/described, 52, 152n6; DOMA and, 34–36, 142, 149, 172–73n99, 223n63, 224n67, 226nn16; domestic violence and physical abuse, 15–17, 113, 115; gender roles and division of labor, 37–42, 48–49, 54–55, 155n43, 155n45–46, 156n53; idealization of, 4–5, 24, 26–27, 45, 153n22;

232   INDEX

marriage (continued)
    income inequality and, 46–47; love/romance role, 18, 51, 64, 110–11, 121–23, 150, 226n22; miscegenation statutes, 149, 226n17; "mythical golden age," 63; post-WWII impact on, 10–14; promotion strategies, 111–14; relevance in today's family and society, 1–3, 22–23; second marriages, 60–61. See also companionate marriage; divorce; unmarried relationships
marriage counseling, 13
Marriage of Buzzanca (California, 1998), 98
Marvin v. Marvin (California, 1976), 138–40, 221n34, 221n37, 221n39
Maryland, 34, 146, 160n111, 200n14
McGuire, Lydia and Charles, 16–17, 139–40
McGuire v. McGuire (Nebraska, 1953), 16–17
Michael, Robert T., 22
Minnesota, 34, 125, 157n81
Mintz, Steven, 63
miscegenation statutes, 149, 226n17
mixed race marriage, 14–15, 34, 157n75, 157n79
Model Act Governing Assisted Reproductive Technology (ABA), 96, 208n84
Montaigne, Michel de, 110–11, 126
Moynihan, Daniel Patrick, 45–46
Mundy, Liza, 69
Murdock, Brooke, 146
Musick, Kelly, 148–49

National Marriage Project, 46, 47, 112
nature vs. nurture, 2, 71, 86
Nebraska, 16, 209n103
New Hampshire, 34
New Jersey, 65–67, 86, 91–92, 139, 140
New York, 16, 34, 94–95, 136, 139, 145, 156n65, 158n96, 160n111, 161n132, 164n150, 200n14, 202n33, 207n72, 209n102, 210n104, 219n20
Nixon, Richard, 11
no-fault divorce: about the effects on marriage, 20–22; California family Law Act of 1969, 20, 163n139, 164n146; common-law rulings, 159n104; "marital breakdown" as cause for, 161n129, 163n135, 165n154; spread of, 164n150, 165n159. See also divorce
nonmarital births: cohabitation and the rate of, 44, 47; effects on the children, 1, 57; income inequality for women from, 113–14; trends and circumstances leading to, 114–15
nonmarital unions. See cohabitation
nontraditional families: about the changing nature of, 2, 109; de facto parenthood in, 133–35; economic stability and, 146–47; judicial and legislative response, 7–8, 62–63, 88–94, 129; parent-child relationships, 135–37, 198n7, 201n22; role of fathers, 143–45; use of ART, 66–70. See also American family; cohabitation; parent/rights and responsibilities
North Carolina, 7, 99–103, 209n101, 211n119
nuclear family: childrearing, 57–58; isolation from extended family, 49–50, 154n29; marriage and the idealization of, 10–12, 68, 152n10; parental gender roles, 12–15, 48–49; post-WWII stability, 156n62, 165n158. See also family/family structure

Obama administration, 119, 142, 224n67
Ogburn, Charlton, 20

palimony, 138–40, 221n37, 221n39
Panglossian paradigm, 9
parallel parenting, 59
parent by estoppel, 186n181, 206n64, 212n128
parent-child relationships. See bonding; family/family structure
parent/parenthood: about the changing nature of, 6–7, 85–87; at-home division of labor, 38–39; defined, in light of ART, 65–70; defined, natural mother, 74–75; equitable parent, 89–91, 96; issues of surrogacy, 71–76; litigation and legal determinations, 88–94; post-WWII impact on, 11–14; psychological parent, 89, 91–93, 135, 203n42, 204n56; surrogacy case law, 94–99; surrogacy case study—

Boseman v. Jarrell, 99–103; surrogacy case study—in vitro fertilization, 103–8. *See also* de facto parent; single parenthood
parent/rights and responsibilities: about changing family structures and, 1–2, 85–87; adoption and the preservation of, 134–35; cohabitation relationships, 103–108, 143; determination of preconception intent, 97–99, 208n90; gestational carriers and, 201n20; lesbian co-parenting issues, 99–103, 205n61; partner separation and apportionment of, 93–94; role of fathers, 142–45; same-sex unions and, 34–35, 173n101; stepparent status, 93; surrogacy and, 71–72. *See also* American family; nontraditional families
Parsons, Talcott, 12
paternity issues, 2, 95, 130, 143–44, 166n12, 207n69, 207n76, 208n90
Patient Protection and Affordable Care Act of 2010, 119
Peale, Norman Vincent, 13
Perry, Hollingsworth v. (U.S. Supreme Court, 2013), 172n97
Pew Research Center surveys, 27, 31
poverty/poverty rates: children in, 217n85; cohabitation and unintended pregnancy, 124–27; family stability and, 109–10; gender inequity, 175n126; marriage promotion strategies, 111–14; race and ethnicity, 32–33, 45–46; unplanned pregnancy and, 120–21
The Power of Positive Thinking (Peale), 13
pregnancy prevention, 114–19
Principles of the Law of family Dissolution (ALA, 2002), 136–37
psychological parent, 89, 91–93, 135, 203n42, 204n56

race and ethnicity: adoption issues, 68; birth rate, 167n23; education and economic stability, 32; income inequality and, 45–46, 112–13; marriage restrictions based on, 14–15, 34, 157n73, 157nn75–76, 157n79; miscegenation statutes, 149, 226n17; surrogacy and, 191n122
Ragoné, Heléna, 74

rape/marital rape, 16, 158n89
Reed, Joanna, 117–18
Rhode Island, 140
Robinson, Angelia, 66, 72
"Romantic divorce" (Gerould), 18
romantic involvement. *See* love/romance, role in relationships
ROPA (Reception of Oocytes from PArtner), 69
Rubino, Mike, 83–84

same-sex unions: about the legalization movement, 34–35; adoption issues/rates, 210n104, 212n122; changing the definition of marriage, 1, 4–5; conflict-of-law issues, 141–42; gender roles, 42; growth rate and visibility, 25–26; impact on children, 109; legal recognition by states, 34–36; termination of the relationship (divorce), 35–36; use of ART, 67, 80–81. *See also* civil union and domestic partnership; cohabitation
Sassler, Sharon, 116, 122
satisfaction and self-expression, 27, 50–52, 59–60, 68–69. *See also* happiness
Schneider, Jennifer, 78
Scott, Elizabeth, 66
second marriages, 60–61
sexual abuse. *See* rape/marital rape
sexual orientation, 25, 68, 146, 167n16, 225n101
sexually transmitted disease, 115
single parenthood: about ending the stigma, 25–28; impact on children, 44–45, 57–61, 109; income inequality/instability, 112–13, 124–25; social and economic impacts, 45–47. *See also* parent/parenthood
Skolnick, Arlene and Jerome, 151n2
Smock, Pamela J., 33
South Dakota, 92, 164n150, 204n55
Sperm Bank of California, 83
Spock, Benjamin, 13, 156n52
spousal abuse. *See* domestic violence and physical abuse
spousal support. *See* alimony and spousal support

stepfamilies/stepparents: adoption issues, 209n99; children in, 60–62, 109; cohabitation relationships and, 32–33; custody and visitation rights, 92–93, 200n18, 204n51, 204nn55–56
Stern, William and Elizabeth, 65, 78
Stevenson, Betsy, 51
surrogacy: acceptance by society, 28; altruism vs. financial motivation, 73–76, 78; *Baby M* case, 65–67, 74; case study - *Boseman v. Jarrell*, 99–103, 211n106, 211n108, 211n219, 212n122; case study—in vitro fertilization, 103–108; contracts, 67, 72–73, 78–84; parental legal status, 94–99. *See also* Assisted Reproductive Technology; egg and sperm donation; gestational surrogacy

Tanfer, Koray, 120–21
Troxel v. Granville (U.S. Supreme Court, 2000), 95

unemployment, 53, 113, 125, 127. *See also* employment
Uniform Parentage Act (2000), 96
University of California study (2010), 40–41
unmarried relationships: about the growth and prevelance, 4, 114; adoption and, 210n104; birth rates, 25–26, 69, 114–15, 167n23, 170n48; census statistics, 24, 29–30; clarifying legal rights, 8, 22–23, 166n13; common-law rulings, 166n12; creating "family" through ART, 7, 98; household income, 37, 52; idealization of marriage, 10, 26–27, 50, 153n22; palimony and enforceable contracts, 138–40; parental rights and child custody, 46–47, 103–108; pregnancy prevention, 115–19; promotion of marriage, 121–24; role of fathers, 142–45. *See also* cohabitation; marriage; single parenthood
U.S. Bureau of Labor Statistics, 38
U.S. Census Bureau: American Community Survey, 24; birth, marriage, and divorce rates, 29, 153n23, 170n48; children in poverty rates, 217n85; children-in-marriage rates, 30; diversity of domestic arrangements, 25–26; same-sex households, 25; unmarried women, childbearing rates, 30
U.S. Constitution: 14th Amendment, 15, 92–93, 226n17; Federal Marriage Amendment, 34–35, 224n69
U.S. Department of Health, Education, and Welfare, 151n1
U.S. Supreme Court: DOMA challenges, 149; *Hollingsworth v. Perry* (2013), 172n97; *Loving v. Virginia* (1967), 149; *Troxel v. Granville* (2000), 95; *U.S. v. Windsor* (2013), 172–73n99, 224n67

Vermont, 34, 131
Veroff, Joseph, 22
Virginia, Loving v. (U.S. Supreme Court, 1967), 149
Virtue, Maxine B., 20
visitation rights: about the changing nature of, 2, 88; adoption, 219n10; civil unions, 140; co-parenting arrangements, 94–95, 211n106; grandparents, 136–37, 207n73; joint legal custody, 102–3; nontraditional families, 186n178, 186n181, 200n14; paternity disputes, 143–44; same-sex unions, 128–33, 205n57; stepparents, 62, 92–93, 200n18, 204n55; surrogacy issues, 105–7. *See also* custody
in vitro fertilization (IVF), 68, 70, 76–82, 191n116, 195n219. *See also* Assisted Reproductive Technology

Waite, Linda, 52, 54–55, 145–46
Washington, 34, 87, 209n103
Weiss, Jessica, 13, 39
welfare reform, 125
Whitehead, Barbara, 44
Whitehead, Mary Beth, 65, 78–79
Wilentz, Robert, 67–68, 71, 75, 78–79
Wilson, James Q., 52, 53, 112, 125
Windsor, U.S. v. (U.S. Supreme Court, 2013), 172–73n99, 224n67, 226n16
Wolfers, Justin, 51
World War II: impact on divorce rate, 163n140; postwar impact on marriage and family, 9–14, 153n14, 153n16, 165n158